International Perspectives on Early Childhood Education and Development

Volume 37

Series Editors
Marilyn Fleer, Monash University, Frankston, Australia
Ingrid Pramling Samuelsson, Gothenburg University, Göteborg, Sweden

Editorial Board Members
Jane Bone, Monash University, Frankston, Australia
Anne Edwards, University of Oxford, Oxford, UK
Mariane Hedegaard, University of Copenhagen, Copenhagen, Denmark
Eva Johansson, University of Stavanger, Stavanger, Norway
Rebeca Mejía Arauz, ITESO, Jalisco, Mexico
Cecilia Wallerstedt, Gothenburg University, Göteborg, Sweden
Liang Li, Monash University, Frankston, Australia

Early childhood education in many countries has been built upon a strong tradition of a materially rich and active play-based pedagogy and environment. Yet what has become visible within the profession, is essentially a Western view of childhood preschool education and school education.

It is timely that a series of books be published which present a broader view of early childhood education. This series seeks to provide an international perspective on early childhood education. In particular, the books published in this series will:

- Examine how learning is organized across a range of cultures, particularly Indigenous communities
- Make visible a range of ways in which early childhood pedagogy is framed and enacted across countries, including the majority poor countries
- Critique how particular forms of knowledge are constructed in curriculum within and across countries
- Explore policy imperatives which shape and have shaped how early childhood education is enacted across countries
- Examine how early childhood education is researched locally and globally
- Examine the theoretical informants driving pedagogy and practice, and seek to find alternative perspectives from those that dominate many Western heritage countries
- Critique assessment practices and consider a broader set of ways of measuring children's learning
- Examine concept formation from within the context of country-specific pedagogy and learning outcomes

The series will cover theoretical works, evidence-based pedagogical research, and international research studies. The series will also cover a broad range of countries, including poor majority countries. Classical areas of interest, such as play, the images of childhood, and family studies will also be examined. However the focus will be critical and international (not Western-centric).

Please contact Astrid Noordermeer at Astrid.Noordermeer@springer.com to submit a book proposal for the series.

Angel Urbina-García • Bob Perry
Sue Dockett • Divya Jindal-Snape
Benilde García-Cabrero
Editors

Transitions to School: Perspectives and Experiences from Latin America

Research, Policy, and Practice

Editors
Angel Urbina-García
School of Education and Social Sciences
University of Hull
Hull, UK

Sue Dockett
School of Education
Charles Sturt University
Albury Wodonga, NSW, Australia

Bob Perry
School of Education
Charles Sturt University
Albury Wodonga, NSW, Australia

Divya Jindal-Snape
School of Education and Social Work
University of Dundee
Dundee, UK

Benilde García-Cabrero
Faculty of Psychology
National Autonomous University of Mexico
Mexico City, Mexico

ISSN 2468-8746   ISSN 2468-8754 (electronic)
International Perspectives on Early Childhood Education and Development
ISBN 978-3-030-98934-7   ISBN 978-3-030-98935-4 (eBook)
https://doi.org/10.1007/978-3-030-98935-4

© The Editor(s) (if applicable) and The Author(s), under exclusive license to Springer Nature Switzerland AG 2022
This work is subject to copyright. All rights are solely and exclusively licensed by the Publisher, whether the whole or part of the material is concerned, specifically the rights of translation, reprinting, reuse of illustrations, recitation, broadcasting, reproduction on microfilms or in any other physical way, and transmission or information storage and retrieval, electronic adaptation, computer software, or by similar or dissimilar methodology now known or hereafter developed.
The use of general descriptive names, registered names, trademarks, service marks, etc. in this publication does not imply, even in the absence of a specific statement, that such names are exempt from the relevant protective laws and regulations and therefore free for general use.
The publisher, the authors and the editors are safe to assume that the advice and information in this book are believed to be true and accurate at the date of publication. Neither the publisher nor the authors or the editors give a warranty, expressed or implied, with respect to the material contained herein or for any errors or omissions that may have been made. The publisher remains neutral with regard to jurisdictional claims in published maps and institutional affiliations.

This Springer imprint is published by the registered company Springer Nature Switzerland AG
The registered company address is: Gewerbestrasse 11, 6330 Cham, Switzerland

To Zyanya García – because you arrived in my life in the right moment at the right time to teach me how wonderful is to have you by my side, to see you grow, to educate you, raise you and guide you. Te Amo…

To Xiomani Urbina – because without you I would not be here. You started all this journey, and you keep being my motivation. You are my fan No. 1…and I am yours. Te Adoro…

Thank you both for being in my life…

Acknowledgments

We would like to thank all authors involved in the production of this book who despite the major challenges posed by the global health emergency triggered by COVID-19 decided to share their work and experiences with the world.

Contents

1 **Transition to School in Latin American Countries: Introducing some Perspectives and Experiences** 1
Angel Urbina-García, Divya Jindal-Snape, Bob Perry, Sue Dockett, and Benilde García-Cabrero

2 **Three Transitions in the Chilean Early Childhood Years** 23
Alejandra Cortazar, Ximena Poblete, and María Fernanda Ahumada

3 **Background on Continuities and Discontinuities in the Transition from Early Childhood Education to Primary: The Chilean Case** 41
Marigen Narea, Felipe Godoy, and Ernesto Treviño

4 **Lessons Learnt on the Transition from Preschool to Primary School in Mexico** 57
Benilde García-Cabrero, Angel Urbina-García, Robert G. Myers, Anisai Ledesma-Rodea, and Marla Andrea Rangel-Cantero

5 **Characteristics of Cuba's Early Childhood Educational and Scientific Experience** 79
Odet Noa Comans

6 **Play-Study Unit: The Pedagogical Conduct of Year One in Maringa, Brazil** 89
Ágatha Marine Pontes Marega and Marta Sueli de Faria Sforni

7 **The Transition from Early Childhood Education to Fundamental Education in São Paulo, Brazil: Formatives and Political (Dis)Agreements?** 103
Patrícia Dias Prado and Angélica de Almeida Merli

**8 Playing, Participating, and Learning
in Fundamental Education (Grades 1–9)
in São Paulo, Brazil: What Do the Children Say?**................ 117
Thais Monteiro Ciardella and Cláudia Valentina Assumpção Galian

**9 A Case Study. Transition in a Waldorf School
in São Paulo, Brazil: A Process Under Construction**.............. 133
Maria Florencia Guglielmo, Andrea Perosa Saigh Jurdi,
and Ana Paula da Silva Pereira

10 Experiences and Explorations of Transitions to School........... 147
Sue Dockett and Bob Perry

List of Tables

Table 1.1   Overview of educational systems 8
Table 2.1   Efforts to ease transition 31
Table 6.1   Didactic experiment: Content of the social role games 93

About the Editors

Angel Urbina-García is an international educational psychologist and an expert in child development with more than 15 years of experience in academia having worked in Asia, Europe, and America in the field of psychology and education working with students from more than 50 countries. He has held leadership positions in world-class universities and is an international researcher with significant experience in conducting research across continents using a mixed methodology and following a psycho-educational approach. Angel has led important international research projects with research grants from the prestigious British Academy, Leverhulme Trust, British Council, and the UK's Global Challenges Research Fund. He pioneered the research on preschool to school transition in Latin American contexts, and he has now created an important international network of researchers from South East Asia (e.g., Vietnam, Cambodia, Laos, Thailand, Singapore, Hong Kong, Australia, and New Zealand), North America (e.g., Mexico and United States), and Latin America (e.g., Chile, Honduras, Brazil, Cuba, Argentina, Ecuador, and Colombia) to conduct cross-cultural cutting-edge research. His research findings have been disseminated widely at international world-class conferences and have been published in international peer-reviewed journals. Angel sits on the editorial board of the *International Journal of Educational and Life Transitions* and is a reviewer for several international world-leading peer-reviewed journals. He also works closely with the Regional Bureau for Education in Latin America and the Caribbean: OREALC/UNESCO Santiago de Chile.

Bob Perry (Emeritus Professor) is an experienced researcher with over 45 years of work in mathematics education and educational transitions, with particular emphasis in both on early childhood, education of Indigenous children, social justice, and community capacity building. He is emeritus professor at Charles Sturt University, Australia, and director of Peridot Education Pty Ltd. In conjunction with Sue Dockett, he continues research, consultancy, and publication in early childhood mathematics education; educational transitions, with particular emphasis on transition to primary school; researching with children; and evaluation of educational. Currently, he is revising materials for a preschool mathematics intervention run by Australia's leading educational charity and, with Sue Dockett, has just published a book on the evaluation of educational transitions.

Sue Dockett is Emeritus Professor of Early Childhood Education and director of Peridot Education Pty Ltd., having recently retired from Charles Sturt University, Albury, Australia. Over more than 30 years, she has been actively involved in early childhood education as a teacher, academic, and researcher. Much of Sue's current research agenda is focused on educational transitions, in particular transitions to school and the expectations, experiences, and perceptions of all involved. This research has been published widely, and has had substantial impact on policy, practice, and research. Complementing her research around educational transitions is research that incorporates children's perspectives, engages with families in diverse contexts, reflects upon the practices of educators, and explores the importance of working with communities.

Divya Jindal-Snape is chair of education, inclusion, and life transitions in the School of Education and Social Work. She obtained her undergraduate and postgraduate qualifications in India. She taught in an all-through school and lectured in education for a few years before moving to Japan to do a PhD at the University of Tsukuba. After living in Japan for nearly 5.5 years, enjoying research and teaching, she moved to Dundee. Divya is now director of the Transformative Change: Educational and Life Transitions (TCELT) Research Centre at Dundee University, and her research interests lie in the field of inclusion, and educational and life transitions. A significant proportion of her work has been with children and young people with additional support needs, especially children and young people with visual impairment, autism, learning difficulties, emotional and behavioral needs, and complex life limiting conditions. Her research has led to creation of educational resources to enhance inclusion and facilitate transitions through drama (inspired by Boal's Theatre of the Oppressed), stories, games, and other creative art forms.

Benilde García-Cabrero is Professor of Educational Psychology in the Faculty of Psychology at UNAM. She holds an MA in educational psychology from the National Autonomous University of Mexico (UNAM) and a PhD from UNAM and McGill University in Canada. She participated as a member of a team of consultants, both for the National Institute of Educational Evaluation (INEE) and the "Construye T" Program, where she has designed, adapted, and validated instruments to measure socioemotional skills for teachers and elementary, secondary, and high school students. She has worked as a government advisor for the Mexican Ministry of Education and as a consultant and coordinator of a number of international projects for various organizations and institutions such as UNICEF, UNESCO, World Bank, OECD, and CONAFE. Her current research interests are related to teaching and learning in basic education (K-12), civic and citizenship education, and the affective dimensions of teaching and its relationship to students' socioemotional skills, situational interest, and academic engagement. She has published extensively in the form of scientific articles, national reports, international reports, and books, and is a member of a range of professional national and international bodies. She is currently a member of the editorial board of *the International Journal of Educational and Life Transitions* and of the scientific committee of *Revista Internacional de Educación Emocional y Bienestar* (International Journal of Emotional and Wellbeing Education, RIEEB).

Chapter 1
Transition to School in Latin American Countries: Introducing some Perspectives and Experiences

Angel Urbina-García ⓘ, Divya Jindal-Snape ⓘ, Bob Perry ⓘ, Sue Dockett ⓘ, and Benilde García-Cabrero ⓘ

Abstract In this chapter, we introduce a book on the transition to school in Latin American countries. This book showcases some of the quality work that researchers from Brazil, Chile, Cuba, and Mexico have done in this field, reflecting how the transition to primary school is experienced and how Latin American educational policies and cultural practices shape such an important process for stakeholders. The book offers the English-speaking world first-hand access to some Latin American transitions research, practices, and policies. The chapters in the book are also framed by the COVID-19 pandemic which placed the world in a global health emergency. The authors of the chapters themselves faced a number of challenges as a result of the pandemic when writing this material. It is our hope that this book will trigger future international collaborations between researchers, policy makers, and practitioners interested in transitions which could help produce a wealth of empirical evidence to inform educational policies and transitions practices across the world. This chapter introduces the reader to all the chapters in the book.

A. Urbina-García (✉)
University of Hull, Hull, UK
e-mail: m.urbana-garcia@hull.ac.uk

D. Jindal-Snape
University of Dundee, Dundee, UK
e-mail: d.jindalsnape@dundee.ac.uk

B. Perry · S. Dockett
Charles Sturt University, Bathurst, NSW, Australia
e-mail: bperry@csu.edu.au; sdockett@csu.edu.au

B. García-Cabrero
Universidad Nacional Autonoma de Mexico, Mexico City, Mexico

© The Author(s), under exclusive license to Springer Nature Switzerland AG 2022
A. Urbina-García et al. (eds.), *Transitions to School: Perspectives and Experiences from Latin America*, International Perspectives on Early Childhood Education and Development 37, https://doi.org/10.1007/978-3-030-98935-4_1

Rationale for This Book

The growing body of research on transition to school has led scholars to cover many aspects such as educational and transition policies; transition practices and tools to support the transition; perspectives and lived experiences of children and teachers, practitioners and assistants as well as parents; and teacher-child relationships. However, these studies are predominantly from Europe, USA, Hong Kong, and Australia (Dunlop, 2018). This trend might suggest that research regarding transitions to school has been undertaken mainly in these developed countries. However, this is likely due to research in other countries being written in the authors' mother tongue rather than in English; research undertaken in Latin American countries being a case in point. To date, there has been limited awareness and understanding of Latin American transitions research, policies, and practices amongst the non-Spanish/Portuguese speaking readers. To redress this balance, Latin American authors in this book have presented their work in English, with the aim of creating opportunities for cross-national learning, reflection and collaborations.

This book comprises ten chapters. This chapter (Chap. 1) introduces the book and provides a brief overview to set the context for the other chapters, such as the rationale for the book, conceptualisation of transitions, educational systems, and policies of the four Latin American countries included in the book (Chile, Mexico, Brazil, and Cuba) and the emerging context of COVID-19. Chapters 2, 3, 4, 5, 6, 7 and 8 present key information about transitions to schools in four Latin American countries, namely Chile (Chaps. 2 and 3), Mexico (Chap. 4), Cuba (Chap. 5) and Brazil (Chaps. 6, 7, and 8). Chapter 9, also from Brazil, differs from the other chapters by taking a particular focus on one independent system and the challenges presented by national policies for its philosophy and practice, It provides an in-depth example of the perhaps unforeseen challenges that can occur when government policies and early childhood education approaches clash. Chapter 10 concludes the book by synthesising the themes and directions presented in the previous chapters.

Brief Overview of COVID-19 and Related Challenges in Latin America

This section introduces some aspects of COVID-19 and its impact; however, these will be discussed in more detail in the final chapter (Chap. 10). On March 20th 2020, the World Health Organisation declared the COVID-19 pandemic, which has been one of the most difficult challenges faced by global contemporary societies in different areas of life. The education sector is not an exception. Formal schooling was massively disrupted across the world due to the measures taken by governments to tackle the spread of the SARS-CoV-2, which is the virus responsible for COVID-19 (Urbina-Garcia, 2021). The pandemic led global governments to close schools and promote the use of remote learning instead; however, these measures posed many challenges. Children from low-income families and rural areas were reported to have less access to electronic devices and internet (World Bank, 2021) exacerbating the existing inequities due to this digital divide. School closures meant that children could not physically attend the premises of their schools, affecting over 170 million pupils across the Latin American and Caribbean region (World Bank, 2021). This also led to highlighting structural inequalities in different societies across the world, and magnifying the social inequality that prevails in Latin America and the Caribbean region (United Nations Children's Fund (UNICEF) 2021; United Nations Educational, Scientific and Cultural Organisation (UNESCO), 2021). For example, only 43% of primary schools in the region, have access to internet for pedagogical purposes.

Specifically, the COVID-19 pandemic affected children's personal lives and schooling in very specific ways in Chile, Brazil, Cuba, and Mexico. For example, in **Chile**, all schools and preschools were closed for almost the entire 2020 academic year and in 2021 only few have re-opened, as localities enter and exit quarantines. In **Mexico**, many children could not access distance education due to different reasons: internet access gaps and lack of adequate technological devices; absence of safe spaces in their homes, especially in the case of girls who must, on many occasions, assume care roles or are victims of violence and sexual abuse; and existence of overcrowding, food insecurity, and poor hygiene conditions that hinder the continuity of learning. In **Brazil**, most schools were closed during the pandemic but the Leeman Foundation, with funding from the LEGO Foundation, developed an initiative called *Educação em Rede* (Online Education). This initiative for teacher education, has reached 500,000 teachers across different regions of Brazil aimed to upskill and train teachers in the use of digital devices and platforms to deliver remote learning (World Bank, 2021). In **Cuba**, schools were closed in March 2020 and re-opened in September 2020; however, they were again closed in early 2021. Televised programs were created to support children aged 0–5; however, there were children with limited access to these.

It is important to acknowledge that the chapter authors for this book were similarly experiencing professional and personal challenges during the writing of their chapters. We acknowledge their commitment to children's transitions to schools in their countries which made this book possible.

Importance of Transitions to School and Its Conceptualisation

The main purpose of early childhood education is to support a holistic social, emotional, physical, and educational development of a child which also sets the foundations for a love of learning, good health, wellbeing, and later personal development and life-long learning. Hence, offering a high-quality early childhood education is of utmost importance as it allows children to develop a range of social, motor, cognitive, and emotional skills which will form the basis of their personal development.

To this end, global governments ensure that early childhood education (UNESCO's International Standard Classification of Education; ISCED 0) is well-aligned with the demands and expectations related to transition to formal schooling which usually starts with primary school (ISCED 1) across the globe. Such alignment should aim to provide continuity between preschool and formal school provision as this could potentially impact children's personal, emotional, social, and academic development.

Therefore, transition to primary school has been internationally recognised as one of the most important, not only educational but also life transitions for young children. Some like, Mascareño et al. (2014), argue that the transition to primary school is a challenging process whereby children enter a new world of higher expectations where academic demands represent one of their main challenges comprising a more-structured learning environment, more teacher-directed activity, and academic assessments. Globally, this period of change has led governments to make efforts to facilitate this transition with a view to promoting children's wellbeing and optimum development given that some "research has found that some of the positive effects of participation in ECEC can fade in primary school when transitions between ECEC and school are ill-prepared" (Organisation for Economic Co-operation and Development (OECD), 2017, p. 41). The following chapters provide an understanding of the perspectives from four different countries (and at times multiple within the same country) of how governments have prioritised transition to primary school. This transition is regarded as a key period for children as they experience a number of significant changes including, but not limited to new environment, relationships, identities, roles, expectations, routines, and rules (Hirst et al., 2011; Perry et al., 2014).

Further, it is important to understand how different stakeholders have conceptualised transitions across the world. International organizations such as UNICEF (2012, p. 8) defines this transition as "children moving into and adjusting to new learning environments, families learning to work within a sociocultural system (i.e., education) and schools making provisions for admitting new children into the system". Fabian and Dunlop (2007, p. 3) define it as "…the process of change of environment and set of relationships that children make from one setting or phase of education to another over time". Pianta and Kraft-Sayre (1999) define it as a process of significant change from one environment to another quite different environment in which children will need knowledge, abilities, and skills to adapt to their new setting. Therefore, based on the literature published in English, which is primarily Western, it seems that a key element of this transition is a response to a *change or movement*. Bohan-Baker and Little (2002) define this as an *ongoing process* rather than *an isolated one-off event* in children's lives where members of the community (i.e., parents, teachers, policymakers) should be involved. Similarly, Jindal-Snape (2018) highlights the role of all stakeholders and defines "transition as an ongoing process of psychological, social and educational *adaptation* over time, due to changes in context, interpersonal relationships and identity, which can be both exciting and worrying, and requires ongoing support." (p. 283).

These studies have provided important and valuable cross-cultural information that has contributed to a better understanding of the concept of transition from different contexts. What we do not know is whether these are also common conceptualisations in Latin America. To this end, Chaps. 2, 3, 4, 5, 6, 7, 8 and 9 are crucial in providing us an understanding of this area. Here, we briefly highlight some conceptualisations that have been used by chapter authors, with details in the chapters themselves.

All chapters seem to have conceptualised transitions in the context of the relationship between early years education and compulsory schooling, and what their roles are in the process. In Chap. 6 for instance, the Brazilian authors' concept of transition seems to be about child's school readiness (focusing on preparing the child for school), with preschool teachers seen to have responsibility for preparing children for academic life in school, for instance by teaching scientific concepts using play as a vehicle. This emphasis on the child's readiness is proposed to enhance curriculum continuity. This view seems to be confirmed by the authors of Chap. 9 in their case study on transition in Brazilian Waldorf schools. Readiness in Waldorf is seen as the combination of a child's development of sensory, motor, cognitive, affective, and social skills and chronological age. However, it is not clear whether transition from a Waldorf preschool to a Waldorf primary school (which sometimes are in the same building) is smoother given the shared values, pedagogies, and aims, and potentially curricular continuity.

Chapter 7, also providing a Brazilian perspective, suggests that there is an emphasis on getting teachers ready with government's emphasis on educating teachers so that they can facilitate the transition framed by the rights of children to play. This seems to be underpinned by different expectations held by teachers from both levels, which seem to place a greater emphasis on the role of adults (i.e., teachers, managers, parents) to support children's transitions. Chapter 8 authors argue that there is the need to adapt the Brazilian curricula for both educational levels that would lead to more continuity. Further, Chap. 7 authors support the notion that the educational curricula should also be informed by children's voices. Whilst the transition seems to be conceptualised as a staged approach, there is a strong emphasis on children's rights to participate, play, and learn. According to these authors, there is the need to listen to children to ascertain how they understand and interpret the curriculum. A clear advantage of having at least two chapters about one particular country (the case for Brazil and Chile), is that it is possible to capture the notion of transition from different perspectives within the same context.

In Chap. 2, in a Chilean context, transition to school has been seen to be an *articulation*, and the term *articulation* is officially used to refer to transition. This notion places an important level of responsibility in adults' practices and agency to facilitate children's transitions. In fact, the transition is seen as a multidimensional process in this chapter with an important focus not only on school readiness, but also on having schools and stakeholders ready. Through their narrative, authors strongly emphasise the need to articulate the curriculum, support teacher education and improve policies to support the transition – rather than the focus being on having children ready. This chapter ends with the view that: *"Any change intended to ease transitions should follow the rule of thumb of redirecting all efforts towards all children's wellbeing"*. Certainly, the idea of promoting transitions to school with children's wellbeing as the main aim, is a welcome contribution to the scant literature in this area internationally. Other Chilean authors in Chap. 3, see the transition as the process whereby schools must be ready for children and propose that in doing so, we must avoid schoolification (structuring the preschool/kindergarten level in a more academic-led way, Shuey and Kankaraš 2018). Additionally, these authors seem to support the notion that this transition should emphasise supporting children's socioemotional development in light of the prioritisation of academic content in primary schools. Indeed, they go on to suggest that during this transition, the focus should be on children and not content coverage.

According to the Cuban author (Chap. 5), in Cuba the notion of school readiness is favoured. While the author argues that the transition occurs naturally and gradually, she also suggests that children must be prepared - by using play as a vehicle to prepare them for the *study activity*. Transition is seen as a staged approach which must prepare children to the *study activity* in primary school. Finally, in Chap. 4, the Mexican authors' conceptualisation of transition seems to mirror that of the other chapter authors. According to them, in Mexico, transition is viewed as getting the child ready for primary school; however, this notion is questioned by the authors and it is proposed that schools must also be ready, highlighting the interactionist approach (Mayer et al., 2010) to ascertain a good fit between each child and school. Children are seen as the agents who must develop skills to face the academic demands of primary school; however, the authors also argue that policies must be created to support this transition. These authors go on to propose that the curricula of both educational levels should be well-aligned, children must be prepared, and schools must be ready. Adults (teachers, parents, teaching assistants, and headteachers) are seen as active agents in this process who must help children get ready for primary school.

In conclusion, there does not seem to be a consensus as to what transition to school is and/or how it can be defined. However, there is a strong emphasis on readiness, of child and/or educational institutions. This notion seems to be strengthened by recognising the need to articulate curricula, educate teachers, and create policies to support this transition. There are lessons here about the importance of the voice of the child (that should also be considered in the context of their transitions) and children's wellbeing during transitions, given that some authors of chapters included in this book do recognise and emphasise the relationship with, and an active inclusion of, *the voices of children, school professionals, and parents* to inform school (and national) practices and policies. Further, given the enhanced focus on wellbeing due to the COVID-19 pandemic and ongoing global initiatives to support mental health and wellbeing in schools (United Nations (UN), 2014, 2020), the main focus of transitions practices and policies being on wellbeing outcomes rather than academic outcomes, might be gaining more traction internationally. However, it is important to be mindful that teachers will also be experiencing professional and personal transitions, some of which will be triggered due to children's transitions, and conversely, their transitions will trigger those of children and parents (see

Multiple and Multi-dimensional Transitions Theory, Jindal-Snape, 2016). Therefore, the focus of transitions practices and policies should not be limited to children's wellbeing but should also focus on the wellbeing and transition support of significant others in their environment (Jindal-Snape, 2018).

Education Systems in Chile, Brazil, Mexico, and Cuba

A great deal of transitions research has been undertaken in many parts of the world. Oftentimes comparisons are made and conclusions drawn about theoretical stances, conceptualisations, practices, and policies. While much can be gained from these explorations, the relevance and impact are limited if there is no consideration of context. One critical element of context relates to the content and structure of education systems. The following discussion considers the particular characteristics of the education systems that shape the transition in the countries included in this book: Chile; Mexico; Brazil; and Cuba. An overview is provided in Table 1.1.

Chile

In Chile, the establishment of early years education provision is recognised in the Chilean constitution under the law N° 19.634/1999 (Alarcón et al., 2015). The basic education system comprises initial education (Educación Parvularia) for children 0–2 years old; childcare centres (Jardines Infantiles) for children 2–4; first level of transition for children 4–5 and second level of transition for children aged 5–6 (OECD, 2017). The first cycle of primary education is provided for children aged 6–10 years old, albeit education in Chile is now compulsory from ages 5–18 as a result of a policy reform proposed on May 21st of 2013 by the Chilean president (Alarcón et al., 2015). Early childhood education is centre-based and aims to support children's development from a holistic perspective considering social, motor, emotional, and cognitive domains (OECD, 2016).

In terms of enrolment and coverage, Chile reports one of the lowest rates (55%) compared to other Latin American countries such as Brazil and Argentina (65% and 72% respectively). In Chile, the Ministry of Education is responsible for the design and implementation of educational policies as well as managing the funding provided at national level, whereas the National Council of Education is tasked with developing curriculum and assessment strategies (Consejo Nacional de Educación, 2021). The Quality of Education Agency, on the other hand, is in charge of assessing children's learning outcomes as well as monitoring and assessing of schools' performance. Finally, the Education Superintendent's Office, oversees the way in which resources are used, ensures that educational norms are followed and legal standards met, and addresses families' complaints (Consejo Nacional de Educación, 2021). Whilst the Ministry of Education sets the policy agenda and the national

Table 1.1 Overview of educational systems

Countries		Stages of preschool/school education	Age at each stage	Legal status of early years provision	Child: Teacher ratio in early years
Brazil	Right to free education, mandatory (6–14 years of age)	Preschool level	Creche 2–5 years	Brazilian constitution, article 6/1988	18:1 (in public ECEC 3–5 y.o.)
			Jardim 3–6 years		
		Fundamental education I	6–10 years		
		Fundamental education II	11–14 years		
		Upper secondary education (optional)	15–18 years		
Chile	Right to free education, mandatory (5–18 years of age)	Preschool (5 levels, starting at 85 days of age), 4–5 years is mandatory	0–5 years	Chilean constitution under the law N° 19.634/1999	20:1 in ECEC (3–6 y.o.)
		Primary school, grades 1–8	6–14 years		
		Secondary school, grades 9–12	15–18 years		
Cuba	Right to free education (including university education), mandatory (6–16 years of age)	Preschool level	0–5 years	Constitution of the Republic of Cuba (articles 39 and 51); the Child and Youth Code of 1978, whose article 17 specifically focuses on the care and education of children under six; and the Family Code	5:1 (aged 1–3 y.o.)
		Primary school education, grades 1–6	6–11 years		
		Secondary school education (basic and pre-university secondary education), grades 7–9	12–15 years		7:1 (aged 3–5 y.o.)
					13:1 (aged 5–6 y.o.)
Mexico	Right to free education, mandatory education (3 to 15 years of age)	Preschool	3–5 years	Constitution of the United Mexican States: Article No. 3	24:1
		Primary/elementary school, grades 1–6	6–12 years		27:1
		Junior high/middle school, grades 7–9	12–15 years		28:1
		Secondary education, grades 10–12	15–18 years		

framework in terms of education provision, municipalities are tasked with delivering education programs with certain degree of autonomy, including the increasing number of privately-owned educational institutions which are subsidized by the government (OECD, 2015). Chile is considered to have a good alignment between pre-primary and primary school education (OECD, 2017). In Chile, educational material related to the transition to school (guidelines, leaflets, flyers, websites, books) is prepared and shared between early childhood educators (Educadora de Párvulos) and primary school teachers. Chile has one of the highest child-teacher ratio in the first grade of primary school among OECD countries with 45 children per teacher – significantly higher than the ratio in the last year of preschool of 22.5 children for every adult. Expenditure per student in preschool and primary school education remains markedly lower in Chile compared to the OECD average (OECD, 2016).

Brazil

In Brazil, the 1988 Constitution (for an English translation, see Rosenn 2017) reflected the re-democratisation process in its description of education as a "fundamental social right" (Article 6) and through the establishment of the principles of education policy (Bucci & Gomes, 2018). Following Brazil's participation in the 1990 world conference that resulted in the *World Declaration on Education for All* (UNESCO, 1990), the Ministry of Education committed to including early childhood education as the first stage of basic education (Kramer & Nunes, 2013). The third edition of the Brazilian constitution (Câmara dos Deputados, 2010) continues to recognise education as "a right of all" (Article 205). Further, Article 208 determines that the government is responsible for guaranteeing "free compulsory elementary education from four to 17 years of age…" and "early education in nurseries and preschool for children up to 5 years of age". These articles reflect legislative changes in 2005 (Law 11.114/2005) and 2006 (Law 11.274/2006) which extended the period of basic (compulsory) education from 8 to 9 years by lowering the school starting age from 7 to 6 years. Extending the period of basic education was one of the targets of the National Education Plan outlined by the Ministry of Education (Brazil, 2001). Further constitutional changes established that municipalities held responsibility for early childhood education and the early years of elementary education (Bucci & Gomes, 2018). A further change related to financing basic education, with the establishment of Fund for the Development of Basic Education and for Enhancing the Value of the Teaching Profession (FUNDEB) in 2007 to redistribute resources to states and municipalities. Despite this fund, financial challenges have remained, with unequal distribution of funds (Mami, 2013).

Two levels of education are defined by Brazil's education law: basic education and higher education. Basic education consists of early childhood education (Educação Infantil, for children aged 4–5 years); elementary education (Ensino Fundamental, for children aged 6–14 years); and secondary education (Ensino Médio, for those aged 15–17 years). Early childhood education consists of 2 years of preschool for children aged 4–5 years. Prior to this, children can attend nursery schools (for children aged 0–3 years), although this is not compulsory. Elementary education is further divided into Fundamental education I (children aged 6–9 years) and Fundamental education II (children aged 10–14 years) (Monroy & Trines, 2019). The Organisation for Economic Cooperation and Development (2019, pp. 5–6) reports that:

In Brazil, enrolment of children under the age of three in early childhood education and care (ECEC) jumped from 10% in 2012 to 23% in 2017, although it remains below the OECD average of 36%. Enrolment among 3–5 year-olds also increased considerably, from 60% in 2012 to 84% in 2017, close to the OECD average of 87%. Among 5–6 year-olds, enrolment in either ECEC or primary education is largely universal.

According to the Constitution, compulsory education – since 2005 encompassing children aged 6–14, (9 years) and more recently encompassing children aged 6–17 (12 years) – is to be provided free of charge in public schools. However, it is noted that the public school system has "neither expanded enough to attend to this need nor improved its quality, a situation that opened a space for private institutions to expand and take an important role in ECE" (Mami, 2013, p. 3).

Recognising the significance of the change to school starting age, the Ministry of Education (Ministério da Educação, 2007) issued some guideless for the inclusion of six-year-olds in elementary school. While the legislation and guidance to support early childhood and elementary education sets out expectations, Campos (2018) emphasises the difference between what is written in official documents and what happens in practice. In addition to the great geographical diversity of Brazil, Campos notes vast economic and social diversity, all of which contribute to unequal access to education across the municipalities and educational levels. With 5, 570 municipalities across Brazil, encompassing major cities and remote areas, it is probably not surprising that considerable differences exist.

This diversity is reflected in the organisation of early childhood education. Many settings for younger children are offered by private organisations – including both for profit and not-for-profit organisations. Some municipalities prefer to support the services offered by not-for-profit organisations rather than establishing their own public services (Campos, 2018). In some municipalities, preschools are part of elementary schools; in others some preschools may be separate institutions. Differences in facilities and resources, as well as in pedagogy and teacher preparation have been noted (Bruns et al., 2012; Campos et al., 2011; Evans & Kosec, 2012). Promoting universal access to high-quality early childhood education across diverse contexts and for the diverse population remains an ongoing challenge (Oliveira, 2018).

National curriculum guidelines for early childhood education have been promulgated (Brazil, 2009) as have the most recent guidelines for basic education (Brazil, 2017). Both documents note the importance of transition between early childhood and elementary education. However, as these areas of education fall under the auspices of municipalities, guidance around transition mainly comes from municipal education authorities. The recent national curriculum (*Base Nacional Comum Curricular*; Brazil, 2017) covers all levels of education from early childhood to secondary, listing expected learning outcomes, skills, and competencies across each level. The rationale underpinning the national curriculum has been that "the alignment of all other education policies … will promote greater integration, synergies and exchanges among cities and states and lead to better outcomes for children" (Costin & Pontual, 2020, p. 48).

The second National Education Plan (2014–2024) (Brazil, 2014; Bucci & Gomes, 2018) sets ambitious goals for early childhood education, outlining plans for increased attendance for children, aiming at 100% preschool enrolment for children aged 4–5 years (Campos, 2018). However, the drastic impact of COVID-19 on early childhood education in Brazil is likely to dent these goals severely (Campos & Vieira, 2021).

Mexico

In México, Article No. 3 of the constitution establishes that every Mexican citizen has the right to free and secular education provided by the government (Aboites, 2012) including all levels comprised within the basic education scheme namely preschool, primary school and secondary school. The obligatory basic education scheme is run by the Ministry of Public Education (Secretaria de Educación Publica) and covers children aged 3–15 years old, although initial education – for children aged 0–3 – is not mandatory (OECD, 2013). The education system is divided into preschool (children 3–5 years of age), primary/elementary school (Grades 1–6; 6–12 years), Junior high/middle school (Grades 7–9; 12–15 years) and Secondary education (Grades 8–12; 15–18 years).

In 1992 a policy reform took place whereby the education sector was decentralised, meaning that each of the 32 states of México are in charge of the education provision; however, and despite the decentralisation, the federal government maintains control in matters of normative, evaluative, planning, and programming of the education provision. In 2002, the Mexican government approved an educational reform by which preschool education became mandatory for children aged three to six. This reform was gradually applied, starting in the 2004–2005 academic year for children aged five, in 2005–2006 for children aged four, and in 2008–2009 for children aged three (Alarcón et al., 2015; Rivera & Guerra, 2005). This policy reform required the Ministry of Public Education to place a greater focus on ensuring a high quality of education provided to all children. However, this reform also brought some important challenges. Firstly, Moreles (2011) suggests that this reform lacked empirical support and was mainly driven by political interests and a deep interest to fit the international agenda. The National Institute for the Evaluation of Education (Instituto Nacional para la Evaluación de la Educación, 2008) echoes López's (2016) views in that lawmakers should have considered the implications of a reform like this, such as infrastructure, physical spaces, classroom availability, teacher education, and so forth. Secondly, this reform created important challenges related to an increase demand, coverage, equity, and quality (López, 2016).

The National Plan of Development (2018–2024) clearly outlines the government's commitment to ensure employment, education, health, and wellbeing (Diario Oficial de la Federación, 2019a). From this document, the Regional Program of

Education (2020–2024) is derived, and which outlines the main activities to focus on for the 6 year period of the current's government tenure. There are six main aims described in this document which focus on the government's commitment to: (1) guarantee an egalitarian and inclusive education; (2) guarantee the right and access to an excellent pertinent and relevant education provision; (3) value teachers as agents of change; (4) generate favourable environments to facilitate the teaching-learning process; (5) guarantee the right and access to a physical education culture; and (6) ensure the hegemony and active national participation of the government to ensure the transformation of the education system (Diario Oficial de la Federación, 2019b).

Whilst the reform which made preschool education mandatory helped Mexico give an important step in terms of providing compulsory free education to all children, recent reports suggest that there are still challenges at national level regarding low quality of education, social inequality, poverty, high levels of crime, low quality of teacher education, and limited access to school for children from rural areas and from low income backgrounds (UNESCO, 2020). In fact, only 82% of children aged 3–5 are currently enrolled in early childhood and primary education programs which is below the OECD average of 88% (OECD, 2020) whereas only 15% of 3–5 years old are enrolled in private schools compared to a nearly 30% in average in other OECD countries. The child-teacher ratio in Mexico is 24 children per teacher at preschool level, which does not change significantly, with a ratio of 25:1 and 27:1 and 28:1 in primary school and junior high/middle school. Mexico's government invests on average USD 3320 per student on primary education which is lower compared to the average the average of USD 11,231 in other OECD countries.

Cuba

In Cuba according to Malott (2009), Cuban education provision is the sole responsibility of the revolutionary government led by the Ministry of Education. The Cuban National Education system aims to offer compulsory and free of charge education until the age of 16 (Malott, 2009) with the ultimate goal of "capital formulation through labour power" (Fox & Byker, 2015, p. 186). The education system supports the acquisition of Cuban values to counteract the values underpinning neoliberalism and capitalism ideologies (Fox & Byker, 2015) and heavily relies on the legacy of Paulo Freire related to using education to empower Cuban citizens to 'read the world' through critical lenses (Allman, 2001).

According to López (2011), the structure of the Cuban educational system comprises preschool level (children aged 0–5 years old), followed by 6 years of primary school education (6–11 years old), and 3 years of secondary school education (12–14 years old). Preschool education aims to support children's moral, aesthetic, physical, and intellectual development with a view to preparing them for further academic education. Preschool education is delivered by the *Educa a tu Hijo* program [Educate Your Child] which involves the wider community and parents. Primary education is regarded as 'General Education', is divided in two cycles (first to fourth grade and fifth to sixth grade), and aims to help children develop their personality, and to develop "...patriotic feelings and civic education, capable of identifying with the values and principles of our society, exalting the value of work as a source of wealth and acting as the protagonist in the leaning process" (López, 2011, p. 61).

López (2011) illustrates how Cuba has undergone deep internal changes due to changes in the global landscape of education which has also prompted the Cuban education system to evolve. The evolution of the Cuban system is argued to have gone through four specific phases. The first phase took place in 1961 when illiteracy was eradicated. In the second phase, the National System of Education was created in 1959 after the Cuban revolution and thus consolidated in 1970 which allowed the Cuban government to highlight the importance of ensuring access to education to all of its citizens (Abendroth, 2009). The third phase took place in 2000 which aimed to offer an ongoing and sustained process of education to ensure an efficient human development of young children, teenagers, and young people. Finally, the fourth phase is regarded as the current climate Cuba is living in the twenty-first century. The National System of Education is the government-led institution tasked with overseeing all levels of education in the country. While Cuba created the *Instituto Pedagógico*, aimed to train teachers to work in the national education system, Cuban teachers work in an undervalued profession – as it happens in other countries – and with one of the lowest pays for teachers ($25 USD per month) in the world (Fox & Byker, 2015). The child teacher ratio changes from 7:1 in the final year of preschool to 13:1 in primary school.

Overall, it can be observed that there are a number of educational and government policies and procedures which differ from country to country. These policies and procedures shape the direction of education provision in general, but they also shape the transition to school. In the following discussion, we consider more closely those policies which are specifically related to the transition to school.

Policies Supporting Transitions to School in the Four Latin American Countries

Within educational research, it is widely accepted that educational policies have a strong influence on different aspects of education provision namely, processes, environment, procedures, curriculum, teacher education, and leadership (Spring, 2014; Verger et al., 2012). Such influence also applies to the way in which school pupils experience the learning process. The chapters included in this book report on the policies that have been developed and which seem to influence the way in which the transition to school is experienced. Chapter 7 from **Brazil** highlights policies that the Brazilian government has in place around the transition to school, namely the National Curriculum Guidelines for Basic Education and the National

Curriculum Base (Brazil, 2017). These policies state the relevance of different transitions and indeed outline what schools should be doing to support transition from initial to formal education. In fact, the City Curriculum for Early Childhood Education (Sao Paulo, 2019) contains an entire chapter dedicated to transitions, emphasising the need for additional public policies to ensure curricular integration and relevant education of teachers. Additionally, in some municipalities there seem to be Municipal Education Networks which emphasise the importance of professional education of teachers to facilitate this transition. The impact of these policies is given particular focus in Chap. 9 with analysis pertinent to the particular Waldorf School system within Brazil.

Chile (Chap. 2) similarly recognises the relevance of transition to school by having important policies in place to support this process. Firstly, the National System of Quality Assurance established in 2011, has recognised the importance of early childhood education and thus included it in such a quality-related system to ensure a common infrastructure and structural quality among educational levels. Secondly, the relevance of the transition to school seems to be further strengthened with the recent publication of the *Transitions Decree* in 2017. This Decree requires all schools to plan transition activities involving teachers, children, and parents with a view to supporting the transition to first grade. This is further supported by the action of the Viceministry of Early Childhood Education which creates strategies to support the transition to primary school. While not focused specifically on preschool or first grade teachers, the *Teachers Career Law* established in 2016, aims to improve preservice training, foster professional development and enhance salaries which is expected to have a positive impact on the way in which teachers support this transition. However, Chap. 3 (**Chile**), reports interesting challenges regarding school funding and school competition which may impact this transition. This chapter makes the case of the pressure experienced by some Chilean primary schools whereby children seem to be pressured to perform well in national standardised tests, otherwise, the school may be at risk of being closed and pupils being sent to other schools. Interestingly, this chapter reports that the there is a direct correlation between high grades and funding for schools whereby the better grades obtained by children, would secure more government funding to schools. As a result of this, there seems to be an additional pressure on teachers in that they need to have children with high grades which could result in children feeling pressured to obtain high grades.

Although the **Cuban** chapter (Chap. 5), does not report in detail on the current policies that shape the transition to school, recent reports suggest that the Cuban education system has gone through a deep transformation to ensure a high-quality education provision for all Cuban children (Murray, 2017). The report documents that education policies support the involvement of families in their child's education, especially in day care centres (D'Emilio & Laire, 2016). The report and Chap. 5 highlight the Cuban government's community-based program *Educa a tu Hijo* [Educate your Child] which is formed of stakeholders from different sectors such as education, health, sports, and culture aimed to work with parents to support their child's development through home-based activities. The report goes on to describe that there are policies in place to identify at-risk families (low income families, history of violence and/or alcoholism) who need tailored attention at the start of each school year. On the other hand, the Preschool Education Program which was published in 1990, and is still in place, seems to favour development of early literacy skills (Hernández & Gómez, 2018) to prepare them for further academic education. While this may suggest that the Cuban education policies seem to place an emphasis on developing academic-related skills of preschool children, there seems the need to investigate further what specific policy-related mechanisms the Cuban government has, to specifically support this transition. Authors from **Mexico** on the other hand (Chap. 4), reflect on the fact that the Mexican Ministry of Education through the National Program of Education (2018–2024), acknowledges the need to articulate all basic education systems including preschool, primary, and secondary school curricula. However, no specific steps have been taken to produce specific guidelines or policies to support the transition to school nor are there guidelines or policies for teacher education in this respect. The authors highlight the need to conduct additional research to inform policy development around this transition.

Conclusions

The chapters in the book showcase some of the transitions research, practices, and policies underway in Brazil, Chile, Cuba, and México, making important contributions to knowledge and understandings of how the transition to school is perceived and experienced by different stakeholders. Each of the chapters outlines both advantages and challenges of current educational systems and approaches and the positions occupied by transition to school within these. Readers will no doubt identify similarities and differences with transitions research undertaken in various other parts of the world. However, our purpose in compiling these chapters is not to promote direct comparisons and the judgments that often accompany these. Rather, we recognise and value diverse perspectives and approaches and argue that there is limited value in aiming to seek or promote a universal definition or conceptualisaton of transition. Acknowledging that transition is contextually based, we propose that each of the chapters offers opportunities to reflect upon our own contexts and the ways in which transition is shaped by the actors involved, in line with their cultural practices, education systems, and policies. Indeed, the premise of this book is that we each have much to learn from others. One way we hope to achieve this is by sharing research that is sometimes not accessible to English-speaking audiences. However, this is not necessarily a simple task.

When the editors first mooted this volume and invited expressions of interest, potential contributors were identified from 14 Latin American countries. We – the editors – were delighted and thought that these contributions could provide broad perspectives of transition across a diverse range of countries and contexts. However, the COVID-19 pandemic has had a particularly devastating impact on Latin American countries (see Chap. 10 for discussion of the impact on early education and transition to school). At the time of writing, several Latin American countries continue to be severely affected by the pandemic. Reluctantly, several authors withdrew their participation to attend to their immediate concerns and contexts. Despite the challenges faced, other authors maintained their involvement and shared their research with us. We admire their resilience, perseverance, and commitment to writing their chapters. We also appreciate their assistance in responding to questions and clarifications throughout the process of compiling the book.

Our invitations to authors included options to submit chapters in English, Spanish, or Portuguese. We have appreciated the efforts of authors to write chapters in English, have their chapters translated into English, and for authors to translate other chapters into English. In particular, we wish to acknowledge the assistance of Thais Ciardella in translating Portuguese to English and clarifying the queries of the non-Portuguese speaking editors.

For many readers, this book may provide an initial opportunity to engage with transitions research, policy, and practice emanating from parts of Latin America. It also provides an opportunity for Latin American transition to school research to influence research beyond this region. However, the relatively limited attention to transitions research in Latin American countries within English chronicles to date should not be taken to indicate that nothing has been happening in this space. Indeed, the opposite is the case, with a great deal written about transitions and shared in both Spanish and Portuguese, accompanied by recent evidence from policy and practice that the focus on transitions has gained traction in several Latin American contexts. Our aim in preparing this volume has been to broaden the scope of international exchange around transitions research and to invite continued conversations, reflections, and shared commitments to the topic.

References

Abendroth, M. (2009). *Rebel literacy: Cuba's national literacy campaign and critical global citizenship*. Litwin Press.

Aboites, H. (2012). El derecho a la educación en México: del liberalismo decimonónico al neoliberalismo del siglo XXI [The right to education in Mexico]. *Revista Mexicana de Investigación Educativa* [Mexican Journal of Educational Research], *17*(53), 361–389.

Alarcón, J., Castro, M., Frites, C., & Gajardo, C. (2015). Desafíos de la educación preescolar en Chile: Ampliar la cobertura, mejorar la calidad y evitar el acoplamiento. [Challenges of preschool edcuaiton in Chile: Widening enrolment, improving quality and avoiding flattening]. *Estudios Pedagógicos (Valdivia), 41*(2), 287–303.

Allman, P. (2001). *Critical education against global capitalism: Karl Marx and revolutionary critical education*. Bergin & Garvey.

Bohan-Baker, M., & Little, P. M. D. (2002). *The transition to kindergarten: A review of current research and promising practices to involve families*. Harvard Family Research Project. http://www.hfrp.org/family-involvement/publications-resources/thetransition-to-kindergarten-a-review-of-current-research-and-promisingpractices-to-involve-families. Accessed 25 July 2021.

Brazil. (2001). *Plano Nacional de Educação* [National Education Plan]. http://www.planalto.gov.br/ccivil_03/leis/leis_2001/l10172.htm. Accessed 25 July 2021.

Brazil. (2009). *Diretrizes curriculares nacionais para a educação infantile* [National curriculum guidelines for early childhood education]. http://portal.mec.gov.br/dmdocuments/diretrizescurriculares_2012.pdf. Accessed 25 July 2021.

Brazil. (2014). *Plano Nacional de Educação, Bill 13005/2014* [National Education Plan]. www.planalto.gov.br/ccivil_03/_Ato2011-2014/2014/Lei/L13005.htm. Accessed 25 July 2021.

Brazil. (2017). *Base Nacional Comum Curricular (BNCC)* [National curriculum guidelines for basic education]. MEC. http://basenacionalcomum.mec.gov.br/. Accessed 25 July 2021.

Bruns, B., Evans, D., & Luque, J. (2012). *Achieving world-class education in Brazil*. The World Bank. https://openknowledge.worldbank.org/handle/10986/2383. Accessed 25 July 2021.

Bucci, M. P. D., & Gomes, F. A. D. (2018). A piece of legislation for the guidance of public education policies in Brazil: The National Education Plan 2014–2024. *The Theory and Practice of Legislation, 5*(3), 277–301. https://doi.org/10.1080/20508840.2018.1427526

Câmara dos Deputados [Chamber of Deputies]. (2010). *Constitution of the Federative Republic of Brazil 3rd edition 2010*. https://www.globalhealthrights.org/wp-content/uploads/2013/09/Brazil-constitution-English.pdf. Accessed 20 Aug 2021.

Campos, M. M. (2018). Curriculum and assessment in Brazilian early childhood education. In M. Fleer & B. van Oers (Eds.), *International handbook of early childhood education* (pp. 1147–1171). Springer.

Campos, M. M., & Vieira, L. F. (2021). COVID-19 and early childhood education in Brazil: Impacts on children's well-being, education and care. *European Early Childhood Education Research Journal, 29*(1), 125–140. https://doi.org/10.1080/1350293X.2021.1872671

Campos, M. M., Bhering, E. B., Espósito, Y., Gimenes, N., Abuchaim, B., Valle, R., & Unbehaum, S. (2011). The contribution of quality early childhood education and its impacts on the beginning of fundamental education. *Educação e Pesquisa, 37*(1), 15–33. https://www.scielo.br/pdf/ep/v37n1/en_v37n1a02.pdf. Accessed 20 Aug 2021.

Consejo Nacional de Educacion [National Council of Education]. (2021). https://www.cned.cl/sistema-nacional-de-aseguramiento-de-la-calidad-de-la-educacion-escolar-sac. Accessed 13 June 2021.

Costin, C., & Pontual, P. (2020). Curriculum reform in Brazil to develop skills for the twenty-first century. In F. M. Reimers (Ed.), *Audacious education purposes* (pp. 47–64). SpringerOpen. https://link.springer.com/chapter/10.1007/978-3-030-41882-3_2. Accessed 20 Aug 2021.

D'Emilio, A. L., & Laire, C. (2016). *Early childhood matters 2016. What we can learn from the Cuban early childhood development system*. Bernard Van Leer Foundation. https://bernardvanleer.org/app/uploads/2016/cuba7/Early-Childhood-Matters-2016_24.pdf. Accessed 13 June 2021.

Diario Oficial de la Federación. (2019a). *Programa Nacional de Desarrollo 2019–2024* [National plan of development 2019–2024]. http://www.dof.gob.mx/nota_detalle.php?codigo=5565599&fecha=12/07/2019. Accessed 13 June 2021.

Diario Oficial de la Federación. (2019b). *Programa Sectorial de Educacion 2020–2024* [Regional program of education 2020–2024]. https://www.dof.gob.mx/nota_detalle.php?codigo=5596202&fecha=06/07/2020. Accessed 13 June 2021.

Dunlop, A.-W. (2018). *Transitions in early childhood education*. Oxford Bibliographies. https://doi.org/10.1093/OBO/9780199756810-0204. https://www.oxfordbibliographies.com/view/document/obo-9780199756810/obo-9780199756810-0204.xml. Accessed 18 Aug 2021.

Evans, D., & Kosec, K. (2012). *Early childhood education: Making programs work for Brazil's most important generation*. The World Bank.

Fabian, H., & Dunlop, A. W. (2007). *Outcomes of good practice in transition processes for children entering primary school* (Working Papers in Early Childhood Development, No. 42). Bernard Van Leer Foundation.

Fox, B. L., & Byker, E. J. (2015). Searching for equity in education: A critical ethnographic exploration in Cuba. *Journal of Ethnographic & Qualitative Research, 9*(3), 183–196.

Hernández, C. B. M. C., & Gómez, C. R. B. A. (2018). Análisis histórico de la orientación a la familia en niños de la infancia preescolar, en Cuba [Historical analysis of work with families with preschool children in Cuba]. *Revista Conrado, 14*(62), 31–37.

Hirst, M., Jervis, N., Visagie, K., Sojo, V., & Cavanagh, S. (2011). *Transition to primary school: A review of the literature*. Australian Government Department of Health and Ageing.

Instituto Nacional para la Evaluacion de la Educacion (INEE). (2008). ¿Avance o retrocede la calidad educativa? Tendencias y perspectivas de la educación básica en México [Is quality education going forwards or backwards? *Tendencies and perspectives* of basic education in Mexico]. Instituto Nacional para la Evaluación de la Educación.

Jindal-Snape, D. (2016). *A–Z of transitions*. Macmillan International Higher Education.

Jindal-Snape, D. (2018). Transitions from early years to primary and primary to secondary schools in Scotland. In T. Bryce, W. Humes, D. Gillies, & A. Kennedy (Eds.), *Scottish education* (5th ed., pp. 281–291). Edinburgh University Press.

Kramer, S., & Nunes, M. F. R. (2013). Early childhood education and elementary school in Brazil: Public policy challenges in the time of expanding compulsory schooling. *Education, 3*(5), 255–261. https://doi.org/10.5923/j.edu.20130305.01

López, M. Q. (2011). Education in Cuba: Foundations and challenges. *Estudos Avançados, 25*(72), 55–71.

López, F. M. (2016). El INEE, la evaluación y la Reforma educativa en México. Avances, retos y perspectivas [The INEE, the evaluation and educational reform in Mexico. Progress, challenges and perspectives]. *Pluralidad y Consenso, 6*(28).

Malott, C. (2009). Education in Cuba: Socialism and the encroachment of capitalism. In D. Hill & R. Kumar (Eds.), *Global neoliberalism and education and its consequences* (pp. 227–244). Routledge.

Mami, Y. A. (2013). *Early childhood education in Brazil*. www.childresearch.net/projects/ecec/2013_10.html. Accessed 13 June 2021.

Mascareño, M., Doolaard, S., & Bosker, R. J. (2014). Profiles of child developmental dimensions in kindergarten and the prediction of achievement in the first and second grades of primary school. *Early Education and Development, 25*(5), 703–722.

Mayer, K., Amendum, S., & Vernon-Feagans, L. (2010). The transition to formal schooling and children's early literacy development in the context of the USA. In D. Jindal-Snape (Ed.), *Educational transitions: Moving stories from around the world* (pp. 85–103). Routledge.

Ministério da Educação (Ministry of Education, Brazil). (2007). *Ensino fundamental de nove anos: orientações para a incluso da criança de seis anos de idade* [Nine-year elementary school: Guidelines for the inclusion of the six-year-old child]. http://portal.mec.gov.br/seb/arquivos/pdf/Ensfund/ensifund9anobasefinal.pdf. Accessed 13 June 2021.

Monroy, C., & Trines, S. (2019). Education in Brazil. *World Education News + Reviews*. https://wenr.wes.org/2019/11/education-in-brazil. Accessed 13 June 2021.

Moreles, V. J. (2011). El Uso de la Investigacion en la Reforma de la Educacion Prescolar en Mexico. Un caso de evidencia basada en la politica [The use of educational research in the preschool education reform in Mexico]. *Revista Mexicana de Investigacion Educativa, 16*(50), 725–750.

Murray, J. (2017). Early years education as a global village. *International Journal of Early Years Education, 25*(1), 1–2. https://doi.org/10.1080/09669760.2017.1276878

Oliveira, Z. M. R. (2018). Early childhood education in Brazil. New challenges for a national curriculum definition. In J. L. Roopnarine, J. E. Johnson, S. F. Quinn, & M. M. Patte (Eds.), *Handbook of international perspectives on early childhood education* (pp. 31–40). Routledge.

Organisation for Economic Co-operation and Development (OECD). (2013). *Education policy outlook: Mexico*. OECD.

Organisation for Economic Co-operation and Development (OECD). (2015). *Education policy outlook: Making reforms happen*. OECD Publishing. https://www.oecd.org/education/highlightsChile.htm. Accessed 13 June 2021.

Organisation for Economic Co-operation and Development (OECD). (2016). *Starting strong IV: Early childhood education and care data country note: Chile*. https://www.oecd.org/publications/starting-strong-iv-9789264233515-en.htm. Accessed 13 June 2021.

Organisation for Economic Co-operation and Development (OECD). (2017). *Starting strong V: Transitions from early childhood education and care to primary education*. OECD Publishing. https://doi.org/10.1787/9789264276253-en

Organisation for Economic Co-operation and Development (OECD). (2020). *Early childhood education: Equity, quality and transitions*. OECD Publishing.
Perry, B., Dockett, S., & Petriwskyj, A. (Eds.). (2014). *Transitions to school – International research, policy and practice*. Springer.
Pianta, R. C., & Kraft-Sayre, M. (1999). Parents' observations about their children's transitions to kindergarten. *Young Children, 54*(3), 47–52.
Rivera, F. L., & Guerra, M. M. (2005). Retos de la educación preescolar obligatoria en México: la transformación del modelo de supervisión escolar [Challenges of mandatory preschool education in Mexico: The transformation of the school supervision system]. *REICE-Revista Electrónica Iberoamericana sobre Calidad, Eficacia y Cambio en Educación, 3*(1).
Rosenn, K. (2017). *Brazil's constitution of 1988 with amendments through 2017*. https://www.constituteproject.org/constitution/Brazil_2017.pdf?lang=en. Accessed 13 June 2021.
São Paulo. (2019). *Currículo da cidade: Ensino Fundamental: componente curricular: Língua Portuguesa* [City curriculum: Elementary School: Curricular component: Portuguese language]. SME, OPED. http://portal.sme.prefeitura.sp.gov.br/Portals/1/Files/50628.pdf. Accessed 6 June 2021.
Shuey, E., & Kankaraš, M. (2018). *The power and promise of early learning* (OECD Education Working Papers, No. 186). OECD Publishing. https://doi.org/10.1787/f9b2e53f-en
Spring, J. (2014). *Globalization of education: An introduction*. Routledge.
United Nations (UN). (2014). *Mental health matters: Social inclusion of youth mental health conditions*. https://www.un.org/esa/socdev/documents/youth/youth-mental-health.pdf. Accessed 13 May 2021.
United Nations (UN). (2020). *About the sustainable development goals*. https://www.un.org/sustainabledevelopment/sustainable-development-goals/. Accessed 13 May 2021.
United Nations Children's Fund (UNICEF). (2012). *School readiness: A conceptual framework*. Education Division UNICEF. https://resources.leicestershire.gov.uk/sites/resource/files/field/pdf/2020/1/7/School-readiness-a-conceptual-framework-UNICEF.pdf. Accessed 13 May 2021.
United Nations Children's Fund (UNICEF). (2021). *COVID-19 and school closures: One year of education disruption*. https://data.unicef.org/resources/one-year-of-covid-19-and-school-closures/. Accessed 20 Aug 2021.
United Nations Educational, Scientific and Cultural Organisation (UNESCO). (2020). *Latin American and the Caribbean. Inclusion and education: All means all. Key messages and recommendations*. UNESCO. https://unesdoc.unesco.org/ark:/48223/pf0000374614. Accessed 20 Aug 2021.
United Nations Educational, Scientific and Cultural Organisation (UNESCO). (2021). *National education responses to COVID-19: The situation of the Latin American and Caribbean*. UNESCO. https://unesdoc.unesco.org/ark:/48223/pf0000377074_eng. Accessed 20 August 2021.
United Nations Educational, Scientific and Cultural Organization (UNESCO). (1990). *World declaration on education for all and framework for action to meet basic learning needs*. https://www.humanium.org/en/world-declaration-on-education-for-all/. Accessed 26 June 2021.
Urbina-Garcia, A. (2021). Young children's well-being: Social isolation during the COVID-19 lockdown and effective strategies. *Diálogos Sobre Educación: Temas Actuales en Investigación Educativa* [Dialogue on Education issues: Current Topics and Debates in Educational Research], *22*(12), 1–16. http://dialogossobreeducacion.cucsh.udg.mx/index.php/DSE/article/view/781. Accessed 26 June 2021.
Verger, A., Novelli, M., & Altinyelken, H. K. (2012). Global education policy and international development: An introductory framework. In A. Verger, M. Novelli, & H. K. Altinyelken (Eds.), *Global education policy and international development: New agendas, issues and policies* (pp. 3–32). Continuum.
World Bank. (2021). *Acting now to protect the human capital of our children: The costs of and response to COVID-19 pandemic's impact on the education sector in Latin America and the Caribbean*. World Bank. https://openknowledge.worldbank.org/handle/10986/35276. Accessed 26 June 2021.

Angel Urbina-García is an Assistant Professor of Educational Psychology, an international educational psychologist and an expert in child development with more than 15 years of experience in academia having worked in Asia, Europe, and America in the field of psychology and education working with students from more than 50 countries. He has held leadership positions in world-class universities and is an international researcher with significant experience in conducting research across continents using a mixed methodology and following a psycho-educational approach. He has led important international research projects with research grants from the prestigious British Academy, Leverhulme Trust, British Council and the UK's Global Challenges Research Fund. He pioneered the research on the preschool to school transition in Latin American contexts, and he has now created an important international network of researchers from South East Asia (e.g., Vietnam, Cambodia, Laos, Thailand, Singapore, Hong Kong, Australia, New Zealand, etc.), North America (e.g., Mexico and United States), and Latin America (e.g., Chile, Honduras, Brazil, Cuba, Argentina, Ecuador, and Colombia) to conduct cross-cultural cutting-edge research. His research findings have been disseminated widely at international world-class conferences and have been published in international peer-reviewed journals. He sits on the Editorial Board of the International Journal of Educational and Life Transitions and is a reviewer for several international world-leading peer-reviewed journals in psychology and educational psychology. He also works closely with the Regional Bureau for Education in Latin America and the Caribbean: OREALC/UNESCO Santiago de Chile.

Divya Jindal-Snape is Professor of Education, Inclusion, and Life Transitions in the School of Education and Social Work, at the University of Dundee, Scotland. She is Director of the Transformative Change: Educational and Life Transitions (TCELT) Research Centre and leads on the International Network of Transitions Researchers. She is Editor-in-Chief for the *International Journal of Educational and Life Transitions*. Her research expertise is in the field of educational and life transitions (across the life span), inclusion, creativity, health education, voice, and comics. Her research has led to the creation of educational resources to facilitate transitions and inclusion through drama, stories, games, comics, and other creative art forms. She has developed a number of research-based transitions theories, including Educational and Life Transitions (ELT) Theory and Multiple and Multi-dimensional Transitions (MMT) Theory. She has acted as research consultant for national and international organizations. She has collaborated on research projects and publications internationally, for example in the USA, Canada, Brazil, Mexico, Nigeria, New Zealand, Australia, Finland, Romania, France, Spain, Republic of Ireland, the Netherlands, Germany, Poland, India, China, and Japan.

Bob Perry has recently retired after 45 years of university teaching and research. He is Emeritus Professor at Charles Sturt University, Australia, and Director, Peridot Education Pty Ltd. In conjunction with Sue Dockett, he continues research, consultancy, and publication in early childhood mathematics education; educational transitions, with particular emphasis on transition to primary school; research with children; and evaluation of educational programs. Bob continues to publish extensively both nationally and internationally in these areas. Currently, he is revising materials for a preschool mathematics intervention run by Australia's leading educational charity and, with Sue Dockett, has just published a book on the evaluation of educational transitions.

Sue Dockett is Emeritus Professor, Charles Sturt University, Australia, and Director, Peridot Education Pty Ltd. While recently retired from university life, Sue remains an active researcher in the field of early childhood education. Sue has been a long-time advocate for the importance of recognizing and responding to young children's perspectives. She maintains this position in her current work with children, families, and educators in explorations of transitions to school, children's play, and learning. Sue has published extensively both nationally and internationally in these areas. She is a co-chair of the Special Interest Group on Transitions at the European Early Childhood Education Research Association.

Benilde García-Cabrero is Professor of Educational Psychology at the Universidad Nacional Autónoma de México. She has worked as a consultant and coordinator of international educational/research projects in matters of educational assessment, curriculum development, civic education, socio-emotional skills, and technology-enhanced learning for several organizations, such as the Mexicab Ministry of Education, the Council for Educational Development (CONAFE), the former National Institute for Educational Evaluation (INEE, now MEJOREDU), UNICEF, UNESCO, and UNDP. Working with these organizations has led to the production of a vast body of empirical evidence regarding the improvement of quality education in Mexican urban and rural schools. She has published extensively in the form of scientific articles, national reports, international reports, books, and book chapters and is a member of a range of professional national and international bodies. She is currently a member of the Editorial Board of the International Journal of Educational and Life Transitions and of the Scientific Committee of the Revista Internacional de Educación Emocional y *Bienestar* (International Journal of Emotional and Wellbeing Education, RIEEB).

Chapter 2
Three Transitions in the Chilean Early Childhood Years

Alejandra Cortazar ⓘ, Ximena Poblete ⓘ, and María Fernanda Ahumada ⓘ

Abstract This chapter aims to understand how transitions affect children's experiences during their early childhood years. The authors discuss the three transitions that Chilean children experience during early childhood: from home to nursery (0–3 years old), from preschool to the transition levels of early years education (4–5 years old) and from transition levels to primary education (at age 6). Acknowledging the relevance of transitions in children's lives and the impact on their development and learning skills, the authors explore the characteristics of Chilean early childhood education (ECE) programmes, policies, and regulations to understand the ways these affect children's experiences. Furthermore, the efforts Chilean governments have made to ease these transitions are discussed as well as the challenges that are still present in the education system to ease transitions for children.

Introduction

Life is about changes, moving from what we know and are familiar with to the new and unknown. These changes require effort and energy. How much energy and effort is needed depends on personal skills, how prepared we are, as well as how the context facilitates or hinders the transition. The education system and the

---

A. Cortazar (✉)
Center for Early Childhood Studies, Santiago, Chile
e-mail: acortazar@cepinfancia.cl

X. Poblete
University Alberto Hurtado, Santiago, Chile
e-mail: xipoblete@uahurtado.cl

M. F. Ahumada
University College London, London, UK
e-mail: maria.medina.17@ucl.ac.uk

differences between education levels challenge children to transition to different contexts and conditions. The continuity at the structural level, programme characteristics, and pedagogical alignment will be critical influences on children's experiences (Kagan & Tarrant, 2010; Shuey et al., 2019).

The goal of this chapter is to problematise the ways in which Chilean children experience three transitions during their early childhood years: from home to preschool, from preschool to the transition levels and from the transition levels to primary education. By analysing programme characteristics, policies, and regulations, we aim to address the following question: What changes do children face during these three transitions? We present these three transitions, focusing on how children experience changes in these different settings and discuss the efforts the Chilean governments have made to ease these transitions. Finally, we discuss the challenges which the education system still presents for children to have a continuous educational experience.

Conceptual Framework

Transitions during the first years of life and between early childhood education (ECE) and primary education are complex and important events in children's lives. Promoting well-managed and smooth transitions may have important long-term effects on children's learning and development and could shape how children will face their future educational and social experiences (Fabian, 2013; Fabian & Dunlop, 2007; Kagan & Tarrant, 2010; Organisation for Economic Co-operation and Development (OECD), 2017). Even though change is usually exciting for children and they are enthusiastic about making new friends and learning new things, these events can also trigger high levels of anxiety and concern among children especially when there are multiple transitions in short periods of time and/or when they are sustained in time (Fabian & Dunlop, 2007). Research has shown the importance of addressing these difficulties as they could affect children's sense of identity and their status within their community. Changes might impact their motivation to learn, socialise, and adapt to the different environments and develop their learning and development potential (Corsaro & Molinari, 2000; Vogler et al., 2008).

In the educational field, transitions have been described in two dimensions. Vertical transitions refer to the change's children experience as they progress chronologically through their lives, for example from infancy to toddlerhood, or from nursery to school. These transitions are important in education as the different educational levels mark children's life milestones. Horizontal transitions comprise movements children experience among different spheres or domains in their lives, even in the same day, for instance from home to school or among different carers. Although horizontal transitions have been less studied in the education field, they also have an important impact on children's lives (Kagan & Tarrant, 2010; Vogler et al., 2008). These conceptualisations are important as they allow more complex understanding of children's experiences moving among the different settings and therefore highlight the ways in which different people and settings could develop connections to ease children's transitions (Kagan & Tarrant, 2010).

Considering the complexity involved in the two dimensions of transitions, this chapter draws on an ecological definition of educational transitions, that is a "process of change of environment and set of relationships that children make from one setting or phase of education to another over time" (Fabian & Dunlop, 2007, p. 3). This conceptualisation allows for a multidimensional perspective including not only children's experiences of a one-time event, but considers it as a "multiyear, multiperson, multiple resources process" that will directly impact children's success in the educational system as well as community wellbeing (Ramey & Ramey, 2010, p. 19). Conceptualisations of transitions imply a qualitative shift in children's lives and intensify the demands of adaptation to multiple areas of their daily life; such as new environment, activities, teaching styles, schedules, type of learning, interactions, and social expectations.

This adaptation is challenging as it demands children make sense of new cultural beliefs, discourses, and practices, constructing their new role and status (Vogler et al., 2008). It involves considering transitions as a central feature of early years development and therefore as providing opportunities to foster children's development (Kagan & Tarrant, 2010). In the educational field, this complex understanding also challenges a narrow focus on school readiness and the consequent schoolification of early childhood education institutions (Moss, 2012). Indeed, when transitions are considered as the passage from early years to primary education, often the emphasis is on children's level of development and to what extent their families and early years services have fostered the skills and knowledge required in primary school.

A comprehensive understanding of transition allows consideration of both the education and caring dimensions that are characteristics of early childhood education (ECE) services. These dimensions are often positioned in tension and as a dichotomy, in which services for children under 3 years old are more focused on the caring dimensions while the purposes of services for children between 3 and 6 years old are centred on the educational elements. In settings for older children, educational purposes tend to be prioritised over caring. However, both are considered indivisible dimensions of the service provided in early years and inherent to the quality of these services. It is then crucial that transitions processes consider these different and complementary purposes of ECE education and work to avoid schoolification.

It is important also to point out the diversity in the terminology regarding transitions. Terms such as *linkage, alignment, continuity,* and *articulation* are often found in the literature and educational policy documents in relation to transitions. These concepts are complementary to the transition process and refer to the ways transitions are fostered, and the need for a continuum, an alignment in the different components involved. In Chile the term *articulation* is officially used to refer to the transition process between early years and primary education and denotes the relation that should be promoted in the different levels of the educational system. In particular, it is used to emphasise the actions that adults must take to facilitate the transition processes experienced by children (Jadue, 2014).

Research has shown different elements that are involved in providing quality supportive and smooth transition processes for children such as curricula alignment, shared pedagogical practices and frameworks, provision for shared professional development, and opportunities of collaboration (Athola et al., 2011; Fabian & Dunlop, 2007; Kagan, 1991; OECD, 2015; Shuey et al., 2019). Kagan and Kauerz (2015, p. 5) refer to the structural approach to transitions involving three components that frame the transition process: "(i) the pedagogical component; (ii) the programmatic component; and (iii) the policy component". In addition, the structural approach stresses the importance of the contents, of what is changing in children's transitions. In line with this, the OECD (2015) also identifies the different elements that change during transitions and highlights the importance of these components to work towards an embedded alignment.

Within the pedagogical component it is possible to point out the relevance of curricula alignment and pedagogical continuity. The curriculum in early years and primary education tend to differ regarding their notion of children and learning, which affects the learning objectives, and pedagogical approaches for learning and therefore children's experiences in the educational system (Shuey et al., 2019). Research has shown that transitions between early years and primary education are often related to the notion of 'school readiness' which implies adapting early years education to the culture and pedagogical practices of primary education in ways such as higher teacher-child ratios, longer hours at school, teacher directed pedagogies, and less play time (OECD, 2017). Articulating the curriculum and assuring continuity and progression among different educational levels is an important challenge that requires accounting for children's developmental needs in order to promote children's wellbeing at each stage of education. This could promote the preparation of school for children rather than the preparation of children for school.

Professional continuity and the working conditions of the teaching workforce are other crucial factors affecting transitions. It is important that practitioners and teachers in different educational levels have opportunities to be prepared and receive enough support to help children's transitions. In this regard, it is important that the workforce has developed transition-related competencies and participates in professional development that includes both early years and primary school teachers (OECD, 2017; Shuey et al., 2019).

Furthermore, it is crucial to consider that the curriculum, pedagogic practice, and professional continuity are framed within broader policies. Transitions must be understood in relation to the organisation and governance system of early years and primary education. It is important to stress that while primary education often is organised and governed by a unique authority – usually the Ministry of Education – different countries have different approaches regarding the governance of the early years field. In this level it is possible to find a split system that differentiates between 'care' and 'early education', and where each type of service is regulated by different authorities. On the contrary, integrated early years systems are regulated under the same authority, and learning objectives consider the whole early childhood education period (Shuey et al., 2019).

Finally, regarding the programmatic component mentioned by Kagan and Tarrant (2010), it is important to understand how the different levels of education work with other community stakeholders that would support children's development and wellbeing.

The next sections of this chapter describe the Chilean educational system, the three transitions children experience in their early childhood years, and the efforts that the Chilean governments have made to ease these transitions.

Organisation of the Chilean Education System

The Chilean education system is organised in four levels: early childhood education (for children 0–6 years old); primary education (grades 1–8); secondary education (grades 9–12); and higher education. Compulsory education lasts 13 years starting at age 5 (Ministerio de Educación, 2003).

Early childhood education is divided into six levels: nursery 1, nursery 2, middle grade 1, middle grade 2, transition level 1 and transition level 2. Nursery and middle grades are offered in early childhood centres while transition levels are offered in schools. Early childhood centres are either publicly or privately funded. Publicly funded programs are provided by two national agencies (National Board of Kindergarten–JUNJI and Fundación Integra) or by non-profit organisations. Over one third of children aged 0–3 years attend early childhood centres and, from those, 70% participate in publicly funded programmes (Ministerio de Desarrollo Social, 2017).

Schools in Chile (transitions levels, primary, and secondary education) have three main types of providers: public, public subsidised (administered by private organisations), and private schools. Transition and primary levels have universal access and attendance rates are high: transition 1: 85%, transition 2: 91%, and primary levels: 100%. Most children (92%) attend publicly funded schools, 38% in schools administered by municipalities, and 53% in schools administered by the private sector (Ministerio de Desarrollo Social, 2017).

Given the structure of the educational system in Chile, children experience three important early transitions: from home to preschool; from preschool to transition level 1 and from transition level 2 to first grade of primary education. Although much attention is turned to the third transition – from transition level 2 to primary education – each one involves different challenges for children, their families, and institutions.

From Home to Preschool

In Chile around 70% of families with children under 3 years old prefer informal care instead of institutional early childhood education. The main reason is the lack of schedule flexibility offered by those programs (Educación 2020, 2019). Hence, during the first three years of life, infants and toddlers are usually raised in familiar environments having warm one-to-one interactions with the caregiver.

However, when young children enter the formal educational system, as opposed to informal arrangements described above, they start to experience drastic changes. The preschool setting is a new and huge space where individual interests and needs are met by adults who are responsible for five or more children, so one-to-one interactions are less frequent. Moreover, children enrolled in public preschool must attend full time five days a week, so the possibilities to interact with their main caregivers are considerably reduced. Therefore, we recognise this transition as the most challenging for young children since they should move from the warmth of a home to an unknown environment; from one-to-one interactions with adults to an adult responsible for 5–7 children; and from a flexible schedule to a rigid one.

How young children experience this transition depends on a wide variety of factors such as their parents' working conditions, the support network inside the family's community, and the characteristics of the ECE institution. Not all young children enrolled in ECE attend traditional programs. In order to expand ECE access, diversify the offerings, and strengthen the participation of families, the service providers JUNJI and Fundación Integra offer alternative ECE programs (Peralta, 2018). These programs vary in terms of modality, community engagement, and schedule. Thus, depending on the nature of the program, some children attend with their caregivers once a week, others participate three days a week without their caregivers, some of them participate in ECE in a classroom while others in the main square of their neighbourhood, and so on. These latter types of programs are more common in rural and small communities.

From Preschool to Transition Level 1

As a consequence of a governmental policy designed to increase ECE enrolment, the Ministry of Education incorporated transition level 1 and transition level 2 as educational levels at schools. Approximately 95.6% of children enrolled in transition level 1 attend ECE programs in public, private, or subsidized schools (Treviño et al., 2014). Consequently, children experience a second transition from preschool to transition level 1 at school, with children of similar age, entering a context with children across a wide variety of ages. We recognise three main dimensions impacting children during this transition: the physical setting where they will be taught; family participation; and the way children learn.

Usually, the school setting is huge in terms of construction, with standardised classrooms, new and strict rules for action and access, buildings with two or more floors, and a lot of older children and adults. Thus, children experience a transition from a cosy to an agitated environment; from a classroom with adaptable furniture and materials for free play, to one with textbooks, desks, and whiteboards; and from no clothing requirements to a mandatory uniform that might limit their play. Young children must know how to explore this new space to establish a safe attachment to it and be prepared to learn in a safe environment. Pilowsky (2016) discusses the concept of 'spatial attachment' which is understood as the emotional bond that connects one individual to a physical environment. Children perceive and live in places according to whether or not they feel emotionally supported by them, so the schools should be, infrastructurally, prepared to include and support preschoolers during this transition.

A second aspect in this transition is how families are included in children's learning process. Both public institutions JUNJI and Integra Foundation have an 'open doors' policy, in which caregivers have free access to the ECE building and the classroom anytime in the day. Families are included in children's learning experiences and invited to participate in important events and workshops. In this way, children have the opportunity to see how their family is engaged in this educational setting, which might increase their sense of security and appreciation in this new environment. However, once children enter transition level 1 at school, caregivers are not expected to enter the building (except the first day of class, parent conferences, and shows) and their participation becomes utilitarian. Hence, children not only will be sharing less with their caregiver but also might perceive a wider separation between the family and the school.

The third dimension corresponds to the schoolification of transition years, triggered by the inclusion of transition level 1 and transition level 2 in schools (Shuey et al., 2019). Instead of respecting the child-centred and play-based approach that is proper to this level, preschool is often conceived as a platform for fostering early literacy and numeracy skills that would allow children to succeed in primary levels, and prioritising stricter discipline and instructional methods to teach children. Consequently, socioemotional development and the wellbeing of young children are thought to have been undermined (Moss, 2012). Once children are immersed in this new system, free play is no longer conceived of as a source of development and learning; rather it is often restricted to recess periods outside the classroom. Although the preschool curriculum follows the same principles for children from 0 to 6 years old, now this curriculum is implemented through textbooks from the Ministry of Education (Subsecretaría de Educación Parvularia, 2016).

Hence, during the transition from preschool to transition level 1, children and their families start to face different structural challenges. Children are often in a state of uncertainty, schoolification has been anticipated and they are expected not to behave as preschoolers anymore. Also, there are many restrictions in how they and their families can participate in their learning process.

From Transition Level 1 to First Grade

Unlike the other two transitions, once children are promoted to first grade of primary school, they keep attending the same school building. Nevertheless, this transition is also remarkable because of the ambivalence in how children are perceived by the school community. For some agents, they are seen as independent grown-up children with new responsibilities and duties; for others they are conceived as naive and helpless little children. This lack of agreement is reflected in a wide variety of elements such as the curriculum (explicit and implicit), the schedule, the physical environment, the assessment process, and educational transition strategies.

Throughout all ECE levels, children's learning is based on one national curriculum, but for primary education, every grade has its own curriculum. Throughout their early childhood years, children have participated in holistic activities with the same educator. However, at primary school the curriculum is divided into five subjects and each one has a different teacher, textbook, and notebook. Hence, children are forced to separate their learning into different areas and get used to different teachers' pedagogical strategies.

There are other aspects in the curriculum that change during this transition at an implicit level. Now children are considered 'students' and they cannot call educators 'tías' (aunties) but must refer to them as teachers – evidence of a shift from a horizontal to a vertical relationship between these two educational agents. Secondly, although the national curriculum specifies children should fully develop literacy skills at the end of second grade, depending on the institutional project, they might be expected to do it in first grade. Indeed, there still are some schools demanding children learn to read and write at the end of transition level 2 to be promoted to first grade.

Once again, the children's schedule is modified. During the first transition, toddlers attended full-day preschool, and then shifted to a half-day schedule in transition level 1. In first grade, they have to go back to a full-day schedule. Thus, they must adapt to new schedules at least three times during their first 6 years of life. This change might impact children's executive functions (especially attention), the family time at home, as well as arrangements for children's commute from home to school and vice versa.

In terms of the physical setting in primary school, children are allowed to play in the 'grown-up' children's playground during recess. This is a new and huge space shared with older students, where first graders are still seen as the new little children. Unlike preschool playgrounds (often well-equipped), this new place usually is covered with cement and only equipped with some trees and benches. This might impact the movement of children, their sense of safety, and their possibilities to interact with others. Early childhood experts consider the environment as the third educator (along with the school and family). In this way, apparently the learning potential of the playground was only important during the early years but not for the upper educational grades.

Assessment is another milestone of this transition. During the ECE years educators implemented different instruments to assess children's learning and development (pedagogical documentation, rubrics, scales of assessment, portfolios, etc.) but, starting at first grade, children's learning is evaluated by tests and homework, resulting in grades. Thus, suddenly children start to receive a score (1–7 scale) that reflects how much teachers consider they have learned. This is often confusing for them since they, initially, do not know the meaning and the implication of a number applied to their learning. Children start to feel high levels of pressure to obtain good grades but also to obtain high scores in the national standardised test (SIMCE) they will take in fourth grade. Schools attach great importance to SIMCE since scores have accountability consequences. As a response, many teachers start to prepare children for this test in first grade, emphasising language and mathematics over the other subjects.

Efforts to Ease Transitions

During the last two decades it is possible to identify strategies and policies promoted by the Chilean government that have helped to ease at least one of children's early childhood transitions. This section presents the different policies and discusses how they have contributed to promoting alignment and easing children's transitions. The policies and other efforts are listed in Table 2.1.

Women Labour Laws

Since 2011, maternity leave in Chile is paid, mandatory, and can last up to 24 weeks after the date of birth (Biblioteca del Congreso Nacional de Chile (BCN), 2016). Once the mother is reinserted into her workplace, and if there are 20 or more hired women in that company, by law, her child can access ECE services paid by the

Table 2.1 Efforts to ease transition

	1st transition Home–preschool	2nd transition Preschool–transition levels	3rd transition Transition levels–first grade
Women labour laws	x		
Chile grows with you	x	x	
National system of quality assurance		x	x
Vice-ministry of early childhood education		x	x
Educators/teachers ladder		x	x
Transition decree			x

employee until the child is 24 months of age (BCN, 2016). Both policies might impact the transition of children in different ways, including later entry to ECE programs – instead of enrolling infants after their third month of life, they may be enrolled in the sixth month of age – and the creation of ECE programs inside workplaces, which promotes breastfeeding and safe attachment between the main caregiver and the child. Examples of these are the nursery programs in hospitals and universities.

Regardless of whether or not children under two years old are enrolled in an ECE program (traditional or alternative), their mothers have the labour right to take at least 1-h off the workday to breastfeed. In order to promote this practice, JUNJI and Integra Foundation have designated rooms exclusively for breastfeeding. The existence of those spaces might ease the transition from home to preschool assuring the continuity of breastfeeding, and offering mothers the opportunity to maintain emotional links to the infant. All these three initiatives help children face their first transition (from home to preschool) in a smoother way.

Chile Grows with You

Chile grows with you (Chile Crece Contigo) is an intersectoral policy that aims to provide families with integrated services starting in pregnancy and continuing during their children's early childhood years (Ministerio de planificación, 2009). It was first designed for children up to age five and only in 2017 was it extended for children up to age nine. *Chile grows with you,* through its educational programme, has universalised access to books, music, and other learning materials for all children from the first four income quintiles, allowing parents to stimulate their children with age-appropriate materials. This policy has empowered families in their parenting role and has prepared them to stimulate their children in their development, bridging children's first transition: the home-preschool transition. Parents are also provided with preschool information and encouraged to take their children to ECE. The role of the policy in helping children and families to transition from the transition levels to first grade is less clear.

National System of Quality Assurance

The national system of quality assurance was formally created by law in 2011, and it has been implemented in stages: first primary levels, followed by secondary (Ministerio de Educación, 2011). Presently the ministry is designing the system for the early childhood level, which should be implemented in the next few years. Including the early childhood level in this system was a way of formally recognising its importance and the need to develop strategies to warrant its quality. Early childhood levels will be required, as all other educational levels, to have official recognition by the Ministry of Education and therefore meet structural quality standards. Process quality standards for this educational level were recently developed, and assessment and orientation visits are in the process of being developed. This policy will ease transition, through regulations, between the different early childhood levels, as well as between ECE and primary education. As all ECE levels will need to meet the same standards, there will be increased homogeneity across children's learning experiences between settings. The same will be true between ECE and primary levels. All education levels will share common infrastructure and other structural quality requirements, providing children with a more continuous experience between educational institutions than what happens now, where there is great variability of the quality of ECE settings. Therefore, the national system of quality assurance helps to ease transitions two and three.

Creation of the Vice-Ministry of Early Childhood Education

The vice-ministry is in charge of designing, coordinating, and managing public policies, plans, and educational programs for children ages 0–6 (Ministerio de Educación, 2015). The creation and implementation of the vice-ministry has helped unify policies for the different ECE levels. Before its creation there were no clear national guidelines. Preschool providers made their own policies and transition levels depended on the school system. This new governance structure clearly contributes to providing children with a more homogeneous experience, in terms of structural conditions, during their early childhood years (second transition), through policies and programmes. The vice-ministry is also in charge of coordinating with schools and creating strategies to ease children's transitions into first grade (third transition).

Educators/Teachers Ladder

This law tries to generate one cohesive teacher and educator workforce by equating requirements, assessments, salaries, and training opportunities for all educators and teachers (Ministerio de Educación, 2016). Until this law the public system paid early childhood educators and primary school teachers differently, with early childhood educators earning less. Equating conditions and training opportunities will unite early childhood and teachers, facilitating alignment and continuity, therefore easing the third transition.

Also related to this law, until now schools have not recognised years of service of educators in early childhood centres and the same the other way around. This made mobility really difficult, generating two distinct groups of early childhood educators: the ones working in early childhood centres and the ones working in schools. This law allows educators to move from early childhood centres to schools or vice versa without losing the years of services recognition. Having a unified early childhood workforce will provide children with a smoother second transition (from preschool to the transition years).

Transitions Decree

This decree requires all schools to develop a transition plan for transition levels and first grade, with transition activities for teachers, children, and families (Ministerio de Educación, 2017). It recognises the role of play in children's learning and promotes the inclusion of play in the transition levels as well as in the first grades of primary education. This decree stipulated that the transition plan should be a participatory process involving all different community members. Plans should: be pertinent to children's contexts; flexible to children's needs and requirements; and have strategies to be implemented in different stages of the school year. The articulation between the transition levels and primary levels is critical for the success of the transition plan. School transition plans should help ease children third transition (between transition levels and first grade).

Discussion

There are multiple factors that are determinants in the continuity or discontinuity children experience in the educational system (OECD, 2017). These include how the system is organised, the different levels, and whether the levels share the same governance structure. How early childhood educators and teachers are trained is also critical, as is program and curricular alignment. Continuity in content and pedagogical practices is of great relevance when considering children's experiences in transitioning from one level to the next. Finally, there are all the structural characteristics of programs that can be more or less aligned, including infrastructure, adult child ratio, and teacher qualifications.

Chile has advanced in many of these factors. For example, all early childhood levels share the same governance structure, and both early childhood and primary levels depend on the same ministry: the Ministry of Education. Although early childhood educators and teachers have different training program requirements, the requirements for early childhood levels are increasing to meet those of schools. In the coming years, to lead a classroom for any education level in Chile will require a four-year university degree. Also, in the next few years educators and teachers will all be paid the same per hour and will share the same career ladder. This will facilitate educators' movement between levels as well as facilitate continuity of children's learning experiences.

Regarding content and pedagogical alignment, Chile has advanced in developing standards for both educational levels. Standards are developed with the same logic while keeping the particularities of each level. The transition decree states the need for schools to develop transition plans which align children's experiences between the transition and the primary levels.

Transitioning from home to preschool can be considered the most challenging transition for most caregivers and young children since it leads to drastic changes in one of the essential dimensions of development and learning: interactions. From one moment to the next, children must follow a new and rigid schedule through attending an ECE program, spending less time at home with their caregivers, and staying for around 8 h per day in a classroom where warm one-to-one interactions with educators are less frequent because of the adult-child ratio.

In order to foster appropriate childhood development and learning, this process should be accompanied by a transition programme which may include an orientation time to help caregivers and children to know and become familiar with the school environment (Dockett & Perry, 2001); provide schedule and attendance flexibility so children can adapt properly to the ECE system (Educación 2020, 2019); promote high-quality interactions between adults and children; and involve family more significantly in children's learning processes. Otherwise, infants and toddlers will keep being the most affected by this significant transition from home to preschool.

Chile Crece Contigo has taken an active role in supporting caregivers in their parenting, providing information about child development and learning, creating a supportive community, and facilitating access to early childhood programs. Nonetheless, there is a lack of articulation between education and the other areas involved (health system, social services) that could be related to the constant debate between the role of ECE: care vs. education (Adlerstein, 2012). This dilemma is reflected in the deficiency of this programme involvement in the educational sphere during transitions 2 and 3. This programme involvement in transitions has been mainly related to the first one, including some guidelines and recommendations to caregivers to support children during this process. For the following transitions it is important to orient families in their decisions about choosing a school through to the inclusion of essential aspects to be considered and to offer guidelines about how to make transitions gradual, rather than abrupt. Those strategies must be focused on fostering children's development and learning; adaptable to every sociocultural context; and strengthen the family and school alliance.

An important tension regarding transitions in the early years has been the one between the promotion of school readiness against a focus on preparing school for children. The former is linked to the notion of schoolification, which has been criticised in the literature. The latter appears to be a better way to ensure smoother transition experiences for children and involves putting the child development needs at the centre of the purposes and practice not only of early years education but also of primary school (Rebello Brito & Limlingan, 2012).

However, looking at this tension from an ecological understanding of transitions sheds light on the complexities involved. Indeed, considering a structural approach to transitions, it is important to include the multiple variables that must work to articulate and ease transition experiences for children. There is no fit-for-all answer regarding this multidimensional process, and research has shown how different countries have approached transitions within a spectrum of curricula alignment and with considerations to the broader policy context (Shuey et al., 2019).

Promoting quality and articulated transitions requires putting the children's developmental needs at the centre of the educational policies. This involves reconceptualising educational purposes at all levels of education with a focus on children's lived experiences, which importantly include considering children's families and communities.

Conclusion

This chapter has analysed the three transitions Chilean children experience during their early childhood years. Seeking to understand children's perspectives on these experiences, we have problematised the conditions of these three transitions looking at the policies, regulations, and programme characteristics of the different educational levels as well as the efforts made by Chilean governments to ease the transitions between them.

Fostering good transition experiences requires adopting an ecological understanding of transitions and the complexity these processes entail with the purpose of accompanying children in these multidimensional processes. The progress Chile has made regarding children's transitions reveals an important disarticulation of the different components involved in the processes and the lack of a comprehensive understanding of the early childhood education system, highlighting the segmented understanding of the purposes of the education system, particularly at the early childhood education level, in which different programmes target different areas of children's development with little to no coordination.

The Chilean educational system has made some major advances in recent years, offering a more developmentally appropriate education through the implementation of policies and new strategies at different levels (government, schools, teaching practices). However, those changes are not equitable for all ages: they are mostly addressed to those children who attend transition level 2 in a school while younger children have been left behind. Any change intended to ease transitions should follow the rule of thumb of redirecting all efforts towards all children's wellbeing.

References

Adlerstein, C. (2012). La política pública de la educación parvularia chilena: una mirada desde la historia y su actualidad [The public policy of Chilean preschool education: A look from history to the present]. *Revista Docencia, 48*, 30–45.

Athola, A., Silinskas, G., Poikonen, P. L., Kontoniemi, M., Niemi, P., & Nurmi, J. E. (2011). Transition to formal schooling: Do transition practices matter for academic performance? *Early Childhood Research Quarterly, 26*, 295–302. https://doi.org/10.1016/j.ecresq.2010.12.002

Biblioteca del Congreso Nacional de Chile (BCN). (2016). *Guía legal sobre Postnatal* [Legal guide on postnatal]. https://www.bcn.cl/leyfacil/recurso/postnatal. Accessed 9 July 2021.

Corsaro, W. A., & Molinari, L. (2000). Priming events and Italian children's transition from preschool to elementary school: Representations and action. *Social Psychology Quarterly, 63*(1), 16–33. https://doi.org/10.2307/2695878

Dockett, S., & Perry, B. (2001). Starting school: Effective transitions. *Early Childhood Research & Practice, 3*(2). https://ecrp.illinois.edu/v3n2/dockett.html. Accessed 9 July 2021.

Educación 2020. (2019). *1, 2, 3 por la infancia: Programa flexible para el aprendizaje familiar* [1, 2, 3 for children. Flexible program for family learning]. https://educacion2020.cl/documentos/1-2-3-por-la-infancia-programa-flexible-para-el-aprendizaje-familiar/. Accessed 9 July 2021.

Fabian, H. (2013). *Children starting school: A guide to successful transitions and transfers for teachers and assistants.* Routledge.

Fabian, H., & Dunlop, A.-W. (2007). *Outcomes of good practice in transition processes for children entering primary school, background paper prepared for the education for all global monitoring report 2007* (Strong foundations: Early childhood care and education). UNESCO. https://pure.strath.ac.uk/ws/portalfiles/portal/22677929/AlineDunlop1.pdf. Accessed 9 July 2021.

Jadue, D. (2014). *Transición y articulación entre la Educación Parvularia y la Educación General Básica en Chile: Características y evaluación* [Transition and articulation between early childhood education and basic general education in Chile: Characteristics and evaluation]. Ministerio de Educación-Centro de Estudios. https://centroestudios.mineduc.cl/wp-ontent/uploads/sites/100/2017/07/INFORME-FINAL-F911436.pdf. Accessed 9 July 2021.

Kagan, S. L. (1991). Moving from here to there: Rethinking continuity and transitions in early care and education. In B. Spodek & O. Saracho (Eds.), *Issues in early childhood education. Yearbook in early childhood education, volume 2* (pp. 132–151). Teachers College Press.

Kagan, S. L., & Kauerz, K. (2015). *Early childhood systems: Transforming early learning.* Teachers College Press.

Kagan, S. L., & Tarrant, K. (2010). *Transitions for young children: Creating connections across early childhood systems.* Brookes Publishing Company.

Ministerio de Desarrollo Social. (2017). *Informe de Diagnostico e Implementacion de la Agenda 2030 y los Objetivos de Desarrollo Sostenible en Chile* [Diagnosis and implementation report of the 2030 Agenda and the Sustainable Development Goals in Chile]. Ministerio de Desarrollo Social, Consejo Nacional para la implementacion de la Agenda 2030 para el Desarrollo Sostenible. https://biblioteca.digital.gob.cl/handle/123456789/2300. Accessed 9 July 2021.

Ministerio de Educación. (2003). *Ley n° 19.876. Reforma Constitucional que Establece la Obligatoriedad y Gratuidad de la Educación Media* [Law 19876. Constitutional reform establishing the obligatory and free of charge of middle education]. https://www.bcn.cl/leychile/navegar?idNorma=210495. Accessed 9 July 2021.

Ministerio de Educación. (2011). *Ley n° 20.529. Sistema Nacional de Aseguramiento de la Calidad de la Educación Parvularia, Básica y Media y su Fiscalización* [Law 20529. National system of quality assurance of kindergarten, basic, and middle education and its supervision]. https://www.bcn.cl/leychile/navegar?idNorma=1028635. Accessed 9 July 2021.

Ministerio de Educación. (2015). *Ley n° 20.835. Crea la Subsecretaría de Educación Parvularia, la Intendencia de Educación Parvularia y Modifica Diversos Cuerpos Legales* [Law 20835. It creates the Under Secretariat for Kindergarten Education, the Administration of kindergarten education and modifies several legal bodies]. https://www.bcn.cl/leychile/navegar?idNorma=1077041. Accessed 9 July 2021.

Ministerio de Educación. (2016). *Ley 20903. Crea el Sistema de Desarrollo Profesional Docente y Modifica otras Normas* [Law 20903. It creates the Teaching Professional Development system and modifies other rules]. https://www.rmm.cl/biblioteca-digital/ley-ndeg-20903-crea-el-sistema-de-desarrollo-profesional-docente-y-modifica-otras. Accessed 9 July 2021.

Ministerio de Educación. (2017). *Decreto 373. Establece Principios y Definiciones Técnicas para la Elaboración de una Estrategia de Transición Educativa para los Niveles de Educación*

Parvularia y Primer Año de Educación Básica [Decree 373. It establishes principles and technical definitions for the elaboration of an educational transition strategy for the levels of early childhood education and first year of basic education]. https://parvularia.mineduc.cl/wp-content/uploads/sites/34/2018/05/Decreto-Transici%C3%B3n-373.pdf. Accessed 9 July 2021.

Ministerio de planificación. (2009). *Ley núm. 20.379. Crea el Sistema Intersectorial de Protección Social e Institucionaliza el Subsistema de Protección Integral a la Infancia "Chile Crece Contigo"* [Law 20379. Creates the intersectoral system of social protection and institutionalises the subsystem of integral protection 'Chile grows with you']. https://www.bcn.cl/leychile/navegar?idNorma=1006044. Accessed 9 July 2021.

Moss, P. (Ed.). (2012). *Early childhood and compulsory education: Reconceptualising the relationship*. Routledge.

Organisation for Economic Co-operation and Development (OECD). (2015). *Early learning development: Common understanding*. https://www.oecd.org/education/school/ECEC-Network-Common-Understandings-on-Early-Learning-and-Development.pdf. Accessed 9 July 2021.

Organisation for Economic Co-operation and Development (OECD). (2017). *Starting Strong V – Transitions from early childhood education and care to primary education*. OECD. https://www.oecd.org/publications/starting-strong-v-9789264276253-en.htm. Accessed 9 July 2021.

Peralta, M. V. (2018). *Programas no-formales en la Educación Parvularia: aportes y proyecciones. Cuadernos de educación inicial 9* [Non-formal programs in early childhood education: Contributions and projections. Initial education notebooks 9]. Junta Nacional de Jardines Infantiles. https://www.junji.gob.cl/wp-content/uploads/2018/06/Cuaderno-educaci%C3%B3n-inicial-9.pdf. Accessed 9 July 2021.

Pilowsky, M. (2016). *Cuaderno 1: La "lugaridad" en el aprendizaje. Cuadernos de educación inicial 1* [Notebook 1: The 'place' of learning. Initial education notebooks 1]. Junta Nacional de Jardines Infantiles. https://www.junji.gob.cl/cuaderno-1-la-lugaridad-en-el-aprendizaje/. Accessed 9 July 2021.

Ramey, C. T., & Ramey, S. L. (2010). The transition to school: Concepts, practices, and needed research. In S. Kagan & K. Tarrant (Eds.), *Transitions for young children: Creating connections across early childhood systems* (pp. 19–32). Paul H. Brookes.

Rebello Brito, P., & Limlingan, M. C. (2012). *School readiness and transitions. A companion to the Child Friendly Schools Manual*. UNICEF. https://www.oxfordshire.gov.uk/sites/default/files/file/early-years-childcare/schoolreadinessandtransitionsunicef.pdf. Accessed 9 July 2021.

Shuey, E. A., Kim, N., Cortazar, A., Poblete, X., Rivera, L., Lagos, M. J., & Engel, A. (2019). *Curriculum alignment and progression between early childhood education and care and primary school: A brief review and case studies*. https://www.oecd-ilibrary.org/education/curriculum-alignment-and-progression-between-early-childhood-education-and-care-and-primary-school_d2821a65-en. Accessed 9 July 2021.

Subsecretaría de Educación Parvularia. (2016). *Hoja de ruta: Definiciones de Política para una Educación Parvularia de Calidad* [Roadmap: Policy definitions for quality early childhood education]. https://bibliotecadigital.mineduc.cl/handle/20.500.12365/543. Accessed 9 July 2021.

Treviño, E., Cortázar, A., & Vielma, C. (2014). *Informes para la Política Educativa N° 6* [Education policy reports no. 6]. Centro de Políticas Comparadas de Educación Universidad Diego Portales. https://cpce.udp.cl/wp-content/uploads/2016/08/IPE6.pdf. Accessed 9 July 2021.

Vogler, P., Crivello, G., & Woodhead, M. (2008). *Early childhood transitions research: A review of concepts, theory, and practice*. Bernard van Leer Foundation. https://files.eric.ed.gov/fulltext/ED522697.pdf. Accessed 9 July 2021.

Alejandra Cortazar, has worked for the last 15 years as researcher and consultant in the early childhood education field in Chile. She holds a degree in psychology from Pontificia Universidad Católica de Chile, and a doctoral degree in education from Teachers College, Columbia University. She is one of the founders, researchers and former executive director of CEPI (Center for Early Childhood Studies). She has worked as a consultant for UNICEF, RAND EUROPE, The Interamerican Dialogue and the World Bank. Currently she is part of the board of the Agency of Quality of Education in Chile.

Ximena Poblete is a Lecturer in the Department of Initial and Primary Education in the Faculty of Education at Universidad Alberto Hurtado. She is a doctoral researcher at UCL Institute of Education, holds a master's degree in International Education and Development from Sussex University and a psychology degree from Pontificia Universidad Católica de Chile. She is co-founder and researcher of CEPI and member of the Consultive board at World Vision Chile. Ximena academic interests focus on promoting a professional role of early childhood educators, and initial and continuous training in early years education.

María Fernanda Ahumada is an Early Childhood Educator. She has experience of teaching young children in the public Educational System in Chile and promoting high-quality interactions between caregivers and children in the United States. During her master's degree studies in Developmental Psychology at Columbia University, she has been involved in different research groups that investigate Early Mathematical Education and how caregivers interact with children while playing with them. Currently, Fernanda is a Ph.D. student at the University College London (Institute of Education) investigating the perceptions of childhood and parenting practices of migrant caregivers living in the UK. She is a permanent collaborator at the Development and Research in Early Math Education (DREME) from Stanford University and at the Early Childhood Board in the Explora Program from the Minister of Science in Chile.

Chapter 3
Background on Continuities and Discontinuities in the Transition from Early Childhood Education to Primary: The Chilean Case

Marigen Narea, Felipe Godoy, and Ernesto Treviño

Abstract This chapter analyses how early childhood and primary education are articulated to facilitate children's transition in Chile in terms of institutional arrangements, curricular differentiation, and pedagogical interactions of both levels. It considers to what extent this articulation fosters either a smooth and child-respectful transition or a greater schoolification of the early childhood education (ECE) system. There have been advances in favour of having a smoother transition. The 2 years of kindergarten (for children aged 5 and 6) were included in primary schools, with the aim of easing the transition. Undoubtedly, the transition can be done more organically, but this has also led to greater schoolification. Regarding the curriculum, there are essential differences between the two levels. Notably, while personal, social, and emotional development is highly foregrounded within the early childhood level, it is not in the primary school curriculum. Also, there are schoolification problems within the early years of the primary school level. The accountability pressures for this level could also jeopardise early childhood level objectives. Finally, in terms of pedagogical practices, ECE is focused on children's socioemotional development while this focus is gradually being lost as children are promoted through the school levels. We propose making the school ready for children, advocating for bringing into the primary school some features of the early childhood level's pedagogical practice, so that it is more flexible and focused on children's wellbeing.

M. Narea · E. Treviño
Pontificia Universidad Católica de Chile, Santiago, Chile
e-mail: ernesto.trevino@uc.cl

F. Godoy (✉)
Monash University, Melbourne, Australia

Center for Educational Justice, Pontificia Universidad Católica de Chile, Santiago, Chile
e-mail: felipe.godoyossa@monash.edu

Introduction

As a result of a massive expansion of early childhood education (ECE) coverage worldwide, children's transitions towards primary education have become an increasingly important area of research interest (Bingham & Whitebread, 2018; Moss, 2008; Organisation for Economic Co-operation and Development (OECD), 2017b). On the one hand, researchers have advocated implementing smoother transitions to facilitate children's adaptation to the school (Bingham & Whitebread, 2018; OECD, 2017b). On the other hand, scholars have claimed that facilitation of this transition may occur at the expense of schoolification of early childhood (Bingham & Whitebread, 2018; Bradbury, 2019; Brooks & Murray, 2018; Ring & O'Sullivan, 2018). When children enter school, they tend to face a whole new context where they experience a considerable change in adult-child ratios; an early introduction of a highly structured curriculum; an accountability agenda based in test regimes; teaching processes based on learning standards; and, generally, a fast transition towards teacher-centred pedagogical models (Bingham & Whitebread, 2018). All these features tend to be absent from, or not central to, ECE.

Chile is among the OECD countries with the largest increase in ECE coverage over the last 15 years (OECD, 2019). This rise has been accompanied by a series of reforms focused on enhancing institutional arrangements, structural quality indicators, and quality of teaching and pedagogical interactions in ECE, all of these through the design and adjustment of curricular and teaching practice guideline instruments (Subsecretaría de Educación Parvularia, 2018b). These features of the ECE system both concur and contrast with the school system arrangements, which have more established traditions of reforms, formalisation, standardisation, and high stakes accountability. Considering this massive access to ECE and the overstandardisation of the school system, there is growing concern among Chilean policymakers (Ministerio de Educación, 2017) and researchers about children's transition between ECE and the primary school system, beginning in Chile with two years of kindergarten (Jadue-Roa & Whitebread, 2012; Rupin et al., 2018).

This chapter provides an analytical overview of the degree to which the Chilean educational system facilitates children's educational transition from ECE to primary school. In particular, we examine the available information and research about institutional arrangements, curricular differentiation, and pedagogical interactions at both levels, analysing to what extent this articulation fosters either a child-respectful transition or a greater schoolification of the ECE system. The first section of the chapter briefly describes the recent literature on transitions and the schoolification risk of ECE. The following three sections describe and compare the early childhood and the primary education systems regarding their main institutional arrangements, curricular assemblages, and the available empirical evidence about pedagogical practices. To conclude, the fifth part sheds light on some critical points that public policy must consider for future reforms to respect children's learning processes during their transition from ECE to the school system.

Early Educational Transitions in Contexts of School Standardisation and Accountability: Understanding the Risks of Schoolification

Several studies have stressed how important it is that policymakers and educational centres design strategies for a smooth and children-centred transition process between ECE and the school system (Bingham & Whitebread, 2018; Cook & Coley, 2017; Fabian & Dunlop, 2007; Jadue-Roa & Whitebread, 2012; Lazzari et al., 2020; Moss, 2008; OECD, 2017b). According to the OECD in its last Starting Strong report (2017b), this transition is one of the first significant changes children experience during their lives. It is a critical period whose success would facilitate the children's ability to develop their capacities and to face future transitions with confidence.

In practice, several changes take place during this transition from one educational level to another. Children might experience changes regarding the professional profile of teachers, the probability of direct contact with teachers, the instructional and emotional priorities of these interactions, the number of classmates, the type of activities in which they participate, and the physical environments within classrooms and educational centres, among other aspects (OECD, 2017b). These changes imply a shift in children's identity, becoming 'pupils' who must learn new social rules and values, and understand that there are new demands when participating in a more formal institution (Bingham & Whitebread, 2018).

Various scholars agree that a closer relation between ECE and primary school may favour children's easier transition. However, this could be at the expense of increasing schoolification of ECE (Bingham & Whitebread, 2018; Bradbury, 2019; Brooks & Murray, 2018; Ring & O'Sullivan, 2018). Schoolification is a process in which the ECE level is required to adopt school features, such as a more prescriptive curriculum, a focus on 'core subjects' related to cognitive development, often to the detriment of social, emotional, or artistic skills; and more didactic and instructional approaches to teaching to prepare children to succeed in school (Bingham & Whitebread, 2018; Brooks & Murray, 2018; Ring & O'Sullivan, 2018).

As Bingham and Whitebread (2018, p. 368) have noted, "there is no serious evidence to support the 'earlier is better' position and a very significant body of evidence to support the alternative view that a later start at school might be advantageous in the long run". However, the trend towards ECE's schoolification has gained relevance for two reasons. First, Bingham and Whitebread (2018) have suggested that given scientific findings showing the importance of children's exposure to early learning experiences, it seems counterintuitive to delay the introduction of learning standards and curricula which grant an active role to teachers in children's learning processes. Second, Moss (2008) has noted that this schoolification risk can be understood when the school system has been historically identified as a cornerstone of the formation and cohesion of nation-states. Hence, it is natural that when there are measures to establish a relationship between ECE and primary education, it is the former which is permeated by the culture of the latter, probably because of the more recent consolidation of ECE as an educational level.

In this context, Moss (2008) suggests that this educational transition may take different paths depending on the relationship between ECE and the primary school levels. A first path is what he calls *Preparing the child for school*, where the primary school level is the evident dominant agent. Therefore, the ECE level's main objective is to pursue children's preparation for a competent performance during the school years. A second option is the *Standoff* mode of relationship, which assumes that the cultures of both levels are significantly different and, consequently, the interaction "may be marked by suspicion and some degree of antagonism" (Moss, 2008, p. 227). This fractured relationship may be sharper in contexts where ECE has a robust pedagogical tradition. A third path is called *Making the school ready for children*, which is the opposite of the school readiness paradigm seen in the *Preparing the child for school*. Being more critical of the traditional school, this stance advocates bringing into primary schools some early childhood-level pedagogical practice features, which are more flexible, and child-focused than traditional school practices. Finally, the fourth relationship mode defined by Moss is the *Vision of a meeting place* path which recognises the very different pedagogical traditions and cultures of both levels, advocating for an "appreciation of difference and a collaborative search for new and shared understandings, values and practices" (Moss, 2008, p. 229).

In the following sections, we analyse the Chilean educational system elements that facilitate or hinder transitions. We describe continuities and discontinuities in the transition from early childhood education to primary education system into three dimensions: institutional arrangements, curricular assemblages, and pedagogical practices. In each of these dimensions, we suggest to which of the four Moss modes of relationship the articulation responds.

Continuities and Discontinuities in the Institutional Arrangements: Policies and Regulations

Chile has been making systematic efforts in the last 30 years to improve access and quality of ECE. Public investment in ECE is above the OECD average, making Chile the second OECD country with higher rates of increase in coverage between 2005 and 2015 for children aged 4 (OECD, 2017a), reaching in 2019 an enrolment rate of 80% for children from age 3 to 5 (OECD, 2021). This has increased the number of children transitioning from ECE to primary school. Today there are more children than ever in ECE who will require smooth transitions to primary school that take their wellbeing into account. It is important to understand the institutional arrangements for these transitions, in the light of these developments.

Institutions

Efforts have been made to harmonise the institutional framework of ECE with that of the school system. A new ECE institutional structure has accompanied the efforts to extend coverage. In 2015, the Undersecretariat of Early Childhood Education was created, a specialised agency for early childhood education. It aims to design, coordinate, and manage education policies for children aged 0–6 years (Biblioteca del Congreso Nacional, 2016). This was an essential step since there had been no entity in charge of Early Childhood Education within the Ministry of Education. Today the Ministry of Education has three undersecretaries, the Undersecretariat of Early Childhood Education, the recently created Undersecretariat of Higher Education, and the Undersecretariat of Education. The Division of General Education, part of the Undersecretariat of Education, is in charge of the primary level.

As well, the Agency for Quality Education assesses compliance with quality standards established by the Quality Assurance System for ECE (Subsecretaría de Educación Parvularia, 2018a). The ECE evaluation and monitoring system is currently being designed and piloted. It will mark a significant advance in alignment between the ECE quality standards with the rest of the educational system quality standards. Finally, together with the above, the Early Childhood Education Intendency has been created, aiming to guide the Education Superintendent in its role overseeing compliance with the normative frameworks that regulate early childhood education (Ministerio de Educación, 2015).

Providers

The Chilean ECE system has different education providers. Children aged 0–4 years may attend any of four types of providers: (a) National Board of Kindergartens (JUNJI in Spanish), which is the leading public provider; (b) Fundación Integra, a private foundation within the government depending on the President's Office, which offers ECE to low SES children; (c) *Vía Transferencia de Fondos* (VTF) centres, which are publicly funded via voucher by JUNJI or Integra and privately managed. Private centres are also part of the supply.

Most children aged 4–6 years attend prekindergarten and kindergarten in primary schools as part of the national system. The educational system includes three types of providers, both in prekinder and kindergarten and primary school. There are public schools, private-subsidised schools, and private schools financed directly by the families.

It is important to note that, until 2015, there were no clear regulations for providers of centres serving children from 0 to 4. From 2015, the Ministry of Education set regulations for opening and operating an education centre offering ECE for these students. The requirements for ECE centres have been equated, to some extent, to the regulations for running a school.

All the structural changes in the institutional framework and regulation of ECE have been in equating early childhood education with the general educational system. This became urgent because of the significant step from early childhood education to the school education system which occurs at the transition levels when 4-year-old children move towards prekindergarten, which is offered in primary schools.

Staff

ECE pedagogical teams in Chile must be composed of ECE teachers – with a higher education degree – and classroom assistants with non-professional technical qualifications or upper secondary education. Prekindergarten must have at least one teacher and one assistant per 35 children. In contrast, in kindergarten, there is one teacher and one assistant per 45 children in the classroom, the same as in the primary level.

The recently approved Teacher Professional Development System (Teachers Career Law) seeks to attract better candidates to teaching programs than was previously the case (Ministerio de Educación, 2016). This system aims to improve pre-service training and establish a strategy to enhance salaries, along with encouraging better performance and fostering professional development. To date, while teachers trained in undergraduate university programs of at least eight semesters receive average monthly wages of USD 970, early childhood teachers' average monthly salaries are USD 670 (Mi Futuro, 2019). With the Teacher Professional Development System, this amount will be increased by 30% under the new law. While this increase is welcome, it will take some time as, from 2020 until 2025, only 20% of early childhood education teachers per year, will be able to make application to join the Teacher Professional Development System.

In this context of institutional arrangements, the educational transition path for the relationship between ECE and primary school levels is more *Preparing the child for school* (Moss, 2008) than any other. ECE's institutional structure and teacher regulations seek to have the same organisation as the school education level, where the school level is the evident dominant agent.

The Curricular Assemblages of the Early Childhood and Primary School Levels

This section describes and compares the curricular assemblages of the ECE and primary school level to understand how these tools offer continuity for teaching practice and children's educational experience between kindergarten and grade 1. For each level, we describe their curricular framework structure, the instruments that compose their curricular assemblage, the importance given to pedagogy, the characteristics of the learning objectives, and the relative emphasis given to the personal, social, and emotional development components.

The Curricular Structure

The early childhood education curricular framework and its learning objectives are organised within eight curricular cores, which are also structured into three learning experiences areas (Subsecretaría de Educación Parvularia, 2018a): (1) Integral communication; (2) Environment understanding and interaction; and (3) Personal and social development. Also, this curricular framework structures the educational trajectory of children into three levels: Nursery (0–2 years old children); middle level (2–4 years old); and transition level (4–6 years old). The transition level includes prekindergarten and kindergarten as the two years immediately prior to primary school.

The primary education curricular framework systematises the learning objectives for children from 6 to 11 years old (Ministerio de Educación, 2012). Its learning objectives are organised into 28 learning axes, which are structured into nine subjects: (1) Visual Arts; (2) Natural sciences; (3) Physical Education and Health; (4) History, geography, and social sciences; (5) Technology; (6) Mathematics; (7) Language and communication; (8) Music; and (9) Orientation. Also, this curriculum contains a set of cross-curricular learning objectives, which will be discussed later. Finally, it organises the educational trajectory into six Grades, from Grade 1 – for six-year-old children-, to Grade 6 – for 11-year-olds.

The Curricular Assemblage

The curricular assemblage for kindergarten level comprises two elements: the curricular framework; and the pedagogical programs. The curricular framework sets the expected learning objectives for all children during their early educational trajectory. The pedagogical programs offer pedagogical teams work guidelines, suggesting educational trajectories, breaking down the learning objectives into achievement indicators, and suggesting pedagogical activities (Ministerio de Educación, 2019).

At the primary school level, along with the curricular framework and the pedagogical programs, the curricular assemblage includes pedagogical plans (Ministerio de Educación, 2012). The curricular framework indicates the expected learning objectives for all children during their educational trajectory, similar to the early childhood level. The pedagogical programs provide a chronological and sequenced organisation of learning objectives, an estimation of the required school time, achievement indicators, and suggested pedagogical activities. Finally, the pedagogical plans organise the school time, defining minimum times for each subject to enable organisation within the pedagogical programs.

The Importance of Pedagogy

It is possible to note differences between ECE and primary education curricular assemblages relating to their pedagogical aspects. Notably, while in the ECE curriculum the pedagogical approaches and principles are explained in detail, in the case of primary education they are barely mentioned. In the ECE curriculum, a socio-constructivist approach is taken, putting the educator in the foreground as a "mediator of significant learnings through particularly relevant experiences in which each child plays, makes decisions, participates, identify themselves, constructs, gets involved, dialogues, works with others, explores his/her world, trusts, perceives and moves, self-regulates, knows him/herself, gives meaning, opines, expresses his/her feelings, amazes him/herself, develops his/her talents, organizes him/herself, enjoys, makes questions, listens and seeks answers" (Subsecretaría de Educación Parvularia, 2018a, p. 28).

Furthermore, the ECE curriculum explicitly includes certain pedagogical principles connected with the pedagogical identity of this level. These principles are: (1) wellbeing; (2) unity; (3) singularity; (4) activity; (5) play; (6) relation; (7) meaning; and (8) empowerment (Subsecretaría de Educación Parvularia, 2018a). Finally, in the ECE curricular framework, some specific pedagogical guidelines are offered within each of the cores of the curricular organisation. Conversely, in the pedagogical programs for primary education, only some examples of teaching practices are provided, but none of the other pedagogical features of the ECE level are described.

The Learning Objectives

The lack of pedagogical specifications within the primary school curriculum is compensated by a detailed emphasis on the learning objectives. In this regard, the pedagogical programs meticulously describe the learning goals of each subject, breaking them down into very specific indicators. It is relevant to highlight two features of these objectives. Firstly, the curricular framework explicitly links the objectives with the needs of standardisation and measurement required by the new Educational Quality Assurance System, which: "establishes that is necessary to define learning standards which allow ranking the educational centres according to the students' learning attainments and to the degree of compliance with these standards, referred to the general objectives indicated in the law and the curricular framework" (Ministerio de Educación, 2012, p. 12).

Secondly, some learning objectives are more important than others within the curriculum. As it is explicitly stated, this curricular framework "strongly emphasizes the development of students' written and spoken language abilities, and mathematical reasoning" (Ministerio de Educación, 2012, p. 5). Language and mathematics are the only subjects prescribed several compulsory hours per week (six and five, respectively).

Likewise, the learning objectives of the early childhood curricular framework are well detailed and broken into highly specific indicators in the pedagogical program document. However, in this case, the objectives are not explicitly linked to assessment or monitoring instruments, and all the curricular areas and cores are equally important. Thus, language and mathematics are not prescribed as more critical areas of knowledge than others.

Personal, Social, and Emotional Development

An important feature to analyse how ECE and primary level curricular assemblages are articulated is the priority given to personal, social, and emotional development. The ECE curriculum confers a prominent role on these types of learning. The social and personal development area is one of the three central learning experiences of the framework. This area is composed of the following curricular cores: (1) autonomy and identity; (2) citizenship and coexistence; and (3) movement and corporality (Subsecretaría de Educación Parvularia, 2018a). It is important to note that while this curricular area is set across the other areas, it has equal importance within the document, it has a chronological progression, and its objectives are included in the pedagogical program.

In the case of the primary level, the cross-curricular learning objectives, which include dimensions such as: (1) physical; (2) moral; (3) spiritual; (4) affective; (5) sociocultural; (6) cognitive; (7) proactivity and work; and (8) ICTs, are goals of a different nature than the 'regular' learning objectives. While these learning aims are transversally disposed as in ECE, they do not have the same priority compared to the learning objectives located into subjects, as revealed by their exclusion from the pedagogical programs and the lack of curricular progressions. However, the primary curriculum contains an orientation subject, which aims to contribute to the students' integral education, promoting their personal, affective, and social development. This subject does not share the same level of importance in the curriculum as other subjects.

Pedagogical Practices in ECEC Versus Primary Education

Using Moss' (2008) proposal as an umbrella, it is possible to state that ECE and primary education practices seem mainly aimed at preparing children but with some features from other types of relationships in the transition. The following analysis starts from the assumption that teacher-student interactions in the classroom entail emotional support, classroom organisation, and instructional support, following the Classroom Assessment Scoring System (CLASS) (Pianta et al., 2008). In this way, teaching practices in educational centres serving children aged 0–4 years seem to be more attentive to supporting children's integral development, as suggested by the curricular framework. For example, an assessment conducted in a northern region of Chile showed that these classrooms had medium to high levels of emotional support and a high level of classroom organisation, although the average for instructional support was low. Nearly 30% of teachers in these centres reached medium to medium-high instructional support (Treviño et al., 2020). Conversely, classrooms serving children aged 5 and 6, which offer preschool grades within the school system, are characterised by high levels of emotional support and classroom organisation, as well as low levels of pedagogical support (Treviño et al., 2018a). In general, this evidence suggests that educational centres that offer only ECE show a higher quality of interactions, perhaps in part, due to their focus on children's development instead of focusing on the curriculum coverage and teacher-centred approaches present in schools (Treviño et al., 2019).

The evidence shows that teacher-student interactions in primary schools are more teacher-centred, with medium levels of emotional support, high classroom organisation levels, and very low instructional support levels. Furthermore, classroom interactions show emotional neutrality in interactions in primary schools (Treviño et al., 2019). This emotional distance seems to be mediated through a change of approach from focusing on the children in ECE to concentrating on content in primary education. As well as this evidence from observational studies of classrooms, parallel analyses of both teacher-student interactions and drawing representations of the classrooms produced by children show that students portray their classrooms as places to be quiet, listening, and taking notes from the teacher who is seen as the main actor in the class (Godoy et al., 2016; Treviño et al., 2016). It is important to note that at least part of this transition may be due to the high-stakes accountability system and the school system's market organisation in Chile, which exerts enormous pressures on schools to achieve in a national standardised test for students. In the case of failing to meet the standards, schools may be closed, and students sent to other schools (Treviño et al., 2018a, b). ECE, on the contrary, is not subject to high stakes accountability, although the *Vía Transferencia de Fondos* (VTF) ECE centres are funded via vouchers based on attendance, as is the case with the school system.

In terms of teacher-student interactions in the classroom, the scant evidence produced in Chile suggests inequalities in the attention teachers provide to girls and boys both in ECE and primary education. For example, in ECE, teachers give boys more opportunities and engagement than girls (Cortázar et al., 2016). Meanwhile, in the school system, teachers systematically interact more frequently with male than female students. Only female students who are at the top of achievement within the classroom receive the average number of interactions of males (Ortega et al., 2021).

In sum, in the transition from ECE to the school system, children experience a change in classroom interactions, which move away from focusing on the children to focus on content coverage.

Conclusions

This chapter analysed institutional arrangements, curricular differentiation, and pedagogical interactions of both ECE and primary levels of education, exploring the extent to which this articulation fosters either a smooth and child-respectful transition or a greater schoolification of the ECE system in Chile.

Regarding the institutional arrangements, in the last five years, an attempt has been made to equate the new ECE institutions and regulations to the school system's institutional arrangements. Now, ECE seeks to have the similar institutions as school education levels, such as the Undersecretariat of Early Childhood Education, Early Childhood Education Superintendency, and the Agency for Quality Education. The structural changes in the institutional framework and regulation of ECE have been in the direction of equating the institutional framework of early childhood education with that of the primary educational system.

About curriculum, our analysis shows some similarities and differences between ECE and primary school level curricular assemblages. On the one hand, it is observed that both curricular structures contain very specific learning objectives, both are broken into indicators by pedagogical programs, and a chronological progression is set for most of their objectives. An essential feature of the ECE pedagogical programs is the specification within each curricular core of how they can be linked with learning aims at the primary school level.

However, some relevant differences can be explicitly identified between the two curricula. Notably, while personal, social, and emotional development is foregrounded within ECE, this is not the case in the primary school curriculum. This type of learning tends to be postponed, giving way to the subjects valued by the Quality Assurance System, with a strong focus on language and mathematics. This is not surprising at all, considering all the scholarship that has warned about the schoolification of the early years due to the educational standardisation and accountability processes that are taking place globally (Bingham & Whitebread, 2018; Bradbury, 2019; Brooks & Murray, 2018; Ring & O'Sullivan, 2018). Additionally, these results shed light on less explicit risks. While the comparison of both curricula allowed the sharp identification of the schoolification problems within the early years of primary school level, it also warns us about how the accountability pressures towards this level could also jeopardise ECE objectives and identity. As Moss

(2008) explains, due to the compulsory school level's dominant position in the relationship between early childhood and primary school, it is possible that the explicit pressures on grade 1 might implicitly trespass to kindergarten.

Finally, in terms of pedagogical practices, it has been shown that early childhood education is focused on children's socioemotional development, but this focus is gradually lost as the school levels are promoted. This could be related to the discussion of the curricula, where social-emotional development loses priority when moving from the ECE to the primary school.

The transition between ECE and the school system may take different forms according to contextual, historical, and regulatory features (Moss, 2008). The literature has proposed four types of relationships in this transition: (a) preparing for school; (b) standoff in opposition to primary education; (c) making school ready for children; and (d) making transition a meeting place (Moss, 2008). In light of these findings, we suggest that while some of the components of the Chilean early childhood and primary school systems tend to standoff in opposition to each other, others show a trend towards progressive schoolification.

On the one hand, for instance, we observe that the ECE system has resisted the schoolification trend, preserving some pedagogical principles, maintaining an integral approach in terms of its contents, and promoting high levels of emotional support in its classrooms. On the other hand, some ECE aspects have tended to emulate and adapt pre-existing primary school system features, such as developing specific indicators –which can be easily translated into standardised evaluation tools, adopting similar institutional arrangements committed to evaluate practices and child outcomes, and overseeing the compliance of minimum requirements. Hence, despite the schoolification risk, the Chilean ECE system also has demonstrated its capacity of preserving some of its pedagogical principles, including a child-centred and integral pedagogy. Furthermore, it is important to acknowledge the contributions of some primary school system features which the ECE system has emulated, such as the case of institutional arrangements aimed at designing pertinent policies, monitoring the system and regulating compliance with minimum functioning requirements. Conversely, it seems desirable that the primary school system starts adopting some ECE features, upgrading the teaching strategies that take place in the primary education, generating conditions in the system to develop a child-centred pedagogy and including socioemotional support practices.

Both ECE and primary education promote children's overall development for life, understanding children as future citizens who require support for socialisation in complex contemporary societal and scientific environments. Suppose an education system aims at preparing future generations for life. In that case, it seems that primary education in Chile needs to learn more from ECE to generate classroom interactions that promote students' overall development as persons and future citizens. Moving from teacher-centred to student-centred pedagogies and designing learning activities would allow students to explore, advance their hypotheses even in play situations, contrast with evidence, learn from that contrast, and re-start the cycle of learning. Such an approach, more generally found in ECE, is rare in primary education because the analysis of practices that transmit content is deemed more effective in terms of time use and learning for students.

Deep understanding of what happens in classrooms with a high pedagogical quality level may be an opportunity to provide valuable information on how prioritising the social-emotional support of children can, in turn, give pedagogical quality support. This may provide an opportunity to consider the social-emotional development of students in primary school, an aspect of their development which has been sent to the background. We know that students' wellbeing is the basis for their learning and helps them become citizens who seek the common good. Perhaps it is necessary to learn from early childhood education, as Moss (2008) says, *Making the school ready for children*. In other words, perhaps we should be advocating for bringing into the primary school some features of the early childhood level pedagogical practice, making it more flexible and focused on children's wellbeing.

The research for this article was funded by ANID-PIA-CIE160007 and the National Agency for Research and Development (ANID)/Scholarship program/ DOCTORADO BECAS CHILE 2019 -72200084.

References

Biblioteca del Congreso Nacional. (2016). *Ley 20.835 crea la Subsecretaría de Educación Parvularia, la Intendencia de Educación Parvularia y modifica diversos cuerpos legales* [Law 20,835 it creates the Undersecretariat of Early Childhood Education, the Administration of Early Childhood Education and modifies various legal bodies]. BCN. https://www.bcn.cl/leychile/navegar?idNorma=1077041. Accessed 19 July 2021.

Bingham, S., & Whitebread, D. (2018). School readiness in Europe: Issues and evidence. In M. Fleer & B. van Oers (Eds.), *International handbook of early childhood education* (pp. 363–391). Springer. https://doi.org/10.1007/978-94-024-0927-7_15

Bradbury, A. (2019). Datafied at four: The role of data in the 'schoolification' of early childhood education in England. *Learning, Media and Technology, 44*(1), 7–21. https://doi.org/10.1080/17439884.2018.1511577

Brooks, E., & Murray, J. (2018). Ready, steady, learn: School readiness and children's voices in English early childhood settings. *Education 3–13, 46*(2), 143–156. https://doi.org/10.1080/03004279.2016.1204335

Cook, K. D., & Coley, R. L. (2017). School transition practices and children's social and academic adjustment in kindergarten. *Journal of Educational Psychology, 109*(2), 166–177. https://doi.org/10.1037/edu0000139

Cortázar, A., Romo, F., & Vielma, C. (2016). Informes para la política educativa [Reports for educational policy]. *Centro de Políticas Comparadas en Educación, 11*. https://cpce.udp.cl/wp-content/uploads/2016/08/IPE11.pdf. Accessed 19 July 2021.

Fabian, H., & Dunlop, A.-W. (2007). *Outcomes of good practice in transition processes for children entering primary school* (Working papers in early childhood development, no. 42) (pp. 1–40). Bernard van Leer Foundation. https://pure.strath.ac.uk/ws/portalfiles/portal/22677929/AlineDunlop1.pdf. Accessed 9 July 2021.

Godoy, F., Varas, L., Martínez, M., Treviño, E., & Meyer, A. (2016). Interacciones pedagógicas y percepción de los estudiantes en escuelas chilenas que mejoran: una aproximación exploratoria [Pedagogical interactions and students' perception in Chilean schools that improve:

An exploratory approach]. *Estudios pedagógicos, 42*(3), 149–169. https://doi.org/10.4067/S0718-07052016000400008

Jadue-Roa, D. S., & Whitebread, D. (2012). Young children's experiences through transition between kindergarten and first grade in Chile and its relation with their developing learning agency. *Educational and Child Psychology, 29*(1), 29–43.

Lazzari, A., Balduzzi, L., Van Laere, K., Boudry, C., Rezek, M., & Prodger, A. (2020). Sustaining warm and inclusive transitions across the early years: Insights from the START project. *European Early Childhood Education Research Journal, 28*(1), 43–57. https://doi.org/10.1080/1350293X.2020.1707361

Mi Futuro. (2019). *Estadísticas por carrera* [Statistics by career] http://www.mifuturo.cl/buscador-de-estadisticas-por-carrera/. Accessed 19 July 2021.

Ministerio de Educación. (2012). *Bases curriculares primero a sexto básico* [Curricular bases first to sixth grade]. Unidad de Currículum y Evaluación, Ministerio de Educación, Gobierno de Chile. https://bibliotecadigital.mineduc.cl/handle/20.500.12365/2342?show=full. Accessed 19 July 2021.

Ministerio de Educación. (2015). *Ley n° 20.835. Crea la subsecretaría de educación parvularia, la intendencia de educación parvularia y modifica diversos cuerpos legales* [Law 20835. It creates the Under Secretariat for kindergarten education, the Administration of kindergarten education and modifies several legal bodies]. https://www.bcn.cl/leychile/navegar?idNorma=1077041. Accessed 9 July 2021.

Ministerio de Educación. (2016). *Ley 20903. Crea el sistema de desarrollo profesional docente y modifica otras normas* [Law 20903. It creates the teaching professional development system and modifies other rules]. https://www.rmm.cl/biblioteca-digital/ley-ndeg-20903-crea-el-sistema-de-desarrollo-profesional-docente-y-modifica-otras. Accessed 9 July 2021.

Ministerio de Educación. (2017). *Decreto 373. Establece principios y definiciones técnicas para la elaboración de una estrategia de transición educativa para los niveles de educación parvularia y primer año de educación básica* [Decree 373. It establishes principles and technical definitions for the development of an educational transition strategy for the levels of early childhood education and the first year of primary education]. https://parvularia.mineduc.cl/wp-content/uploads/sites/34/2018/05/Decreto-Transici%C3%B3n-373.pdf. Accessed 19 July 2021.

Ministerio de Educación. (2019). *Programa pedagógico para primer y segundo nivel de transición* [Pedagogical program for first and second level of transition]. Unidad de currículum y evaluación, Ministerio de Educación, Gobierno de Chile. https://parvularia.mineduc.cl/wp-content/uploads/sites/34/2020/09/Programa-Pedag%C3%B3gico-NT1-y-NT2.pdf. Accessed 19 July 2021.

Moss, P. (2008). What future for the relationship between early childhood education and care and compulsory schooling? *Research in Comparative and International Education, 3*(3), 224–234. https://doi.org/10.2304/rcie.2008.3.3.224

Organisation for Economic Co-operation and Development (OECD). (2017a). *Education at a glance 2017: OECD indicators*. OECD Publishing. https://doi.org/10.1787/eag-2017-en

Organisation for Economic Co-operation and Development (OECD). (2017b). *Starting strong V: Transitions from early childhood education and care to primary education*. OECD Publishing. https://doi.org/10.1787/9789264276253-en

Organisation for Economic Co-operation and Development (OECD). (2019). *Education at a glance 2019: OECD indicators*. OECD Publishing. https://doi.org/10.1787/f8d7880d-en

OECD. (2021). *Education at a Glance 2021: OECD Indicators*. OECD Publishing, Paris. https://doi.org/10.1787/b35a14e5-en

Ortega, L., Treviño, E., & Gelber, D. (2021). The inclusion of girls in Chilean mathematics classrooms: Gender bias in teacher-student interaction networks [La inclusión de las niñas en las aulas de matemáticas chilenas: sesgo de género en las redes de interacción profesor-estudiante]. *Journal for the Study of Education and Development, 4*(3), 623–674. https://doi.org/10.1080/02103702.2020.1773064

Pianta, R., La Paro, K., & Hamre, B. (2008). *CLASS classroom assessment scoring system, manual pre-K. Spanish version*. Paul H. Brookes Publishing.

Ring, E., & O'Sullivan, L. (2018). Dewey: A panacea for the 'schoolification' epidemic. *Education 3–13, 46*(4), 402–410. https://doi.org/10.1080/03004279.2018.1445474

Rupin, P., Muñoz, C., Jadue-Roa, D. S., Rivas, M., Gareca, B., Iturriaga, C., & Lobos, C. (2018). *El juego dentro y fuera del aula: miradas cruzadas sobre prácticas lúdicas infantiles en momentos de transición educativa* [Play inside and outside the classroom: Crossed-views on children's playful practices in moments of educational transition]. FONIDE: Informe final. https://centroestudios.mineduc.cl/wp-content/uploads/sites/100/2018/10/Informe-final-FONIDE-FX11651-Rupin_apDU.pdf. Accessed 19 July 2021.

Subsecretaría de Educación Parvularia. (2018a). *Bases Curriculares de la Educación Parvularia* [Curricular bases for early childhood education]. Ministerio de Educación. https://parvularia.mineduc.cl/wp-content/uploads/sites/34/2018/03/Bases_Curriculares_Ed_Parvularia_2018.pdf. Accessed 19 July 2021.

Subsecretaría de Educación Parvularia. (2018b). *Trayectorias, avances y desafíos de la educación parvularia en Chile: análisis y balance de la política pública 2014–2018* [Trajectories, advances and challenges of early childhood education in Chile: Analysis and balance of public policy 2014–2018]. https://parvularia.mineduc.cl/2018/03/05/revisa-los-avances-desafios-la-educacion-parvularia-2014-2018/. Accessed 19 July 2021.

Treviño, E., Varas, L., Godoy, F., & Martínez, M. V. (2016). ¿Qué caracteriza a las interacciones pedagógicas de las escuelas efectivas chilenas?: una aproximación exploratoria [What characterizes the pedagogical interactions of effective Chilean schools? An exploratory approach]. In J. Manzi & M. R. García (Eds.), *Abriendo las Puertas del Aula: Transformación de las Prácticas Docentes* [Opening the classroom doors: Transformation of teaching practices] (pp. 185–220). Ediciones UC-CEPPE.

Treviño, E., Godoy, F., Rozas, F., Fajardo, G., Wyman, I., Cisternas, P., Arbour, M. C. (2018a). Cachapoal: el camino de la mejora y la consolidación de UBC [Cachapoal: The path for improvement and consolidation of UBC]. In E. Treviño, E. Aguirre, & C. Varela (Eds.), *Un Buen Comienzo para los niños de Chile* [A good start for the children of Chile] (pp. 257–278). Universidad Diego Portales.

Treviño, E., Mintrop, H., Villalobos, C., & Órdenes, M. (2018b). *What might happen if school vouchers and privatization of schools were to become universal in the U.S.: Learning from a national test case—Chile*. https://nepc.colorado.edu/publication/chilean-voucher. Accessed 19 July 2021.

Treviño, E., Varela, C., Rodríguez, M., & Straub, C. (2019). Transformar las aulas en chile: superar la desconexión entre la enseñanza actual y los modos de aprender de los estudiantes [Transforming the classrooms in Chile: Overcoming the disconnect between current teaching and students' ways of learning]. In A. Carrasco & L. Flores (Eds.), *De la Reforma a la Transformación. Capacidades, Innovaciones y Regulación de la Educación Chilena* [From reform to transformation. Capacities, innovations and regulation of Chilean education] (pp. 173–216). Ediciones UC.

Treviño, E., González, A., Muñoz, C., & Castillo, F. (2020). *Estudio de evaluación del curso "Mejora de interacciones en el aula para apoyar el desarrollo de lenguaje en educación parvularia" de JUNJI* [Evaluation study of the JUNJI course "Improving interactions in the classroom to support language development in early childhood education"].

Marigen Narea is an Assistant Professor at the School of Psychology from the Pontificia Universidad Católica de Chile also acting as a Principal Researcher at the Centre for Advanced Studies on Educational Justice. She has a PhD in Social Policy from the London School of Economics and Political Science; MA in Education and International Development from Boston University and MA in Educational Psychology from the Pontificia Universidad Católica de Chile.

Her research is focused on early childhood interventions and policies, educational program evaluation and child development.

Felipe Godoy is an associate researcher at Centre for Advanced Studies on Educational Justice from Pontificia Universidad Católica of Chile, and PhD candidate at Monash University. Formerly, he served as head of the Research department at the Division of Early Childhood Education, in the Ministry of Education of Chile, and he has worked as researcher at the Centre for Comparative Education Policies from Diego Portales University. His research has focused on early childhood education policies, teaching practices and impact evaluation of early childhood teachers' professional development programs.

Dr. Ernesto Treviño is the Director of the Center for Educational Transformation, Principal Researcher at the Center for Educational Justice, and Associate Professor of the Faculty of Education at the Pontificia Universidad Católica de Chile. He is interested in understanding of educational inequalities in Chile and Latin America, and studies of the interaction between policy and practice in schools and classrooms to promote the integral development of students.

Chapter 4
Lessons Learnt on the Transition from Preschool to Primary School in Mexico

Benilde García-Cabrero, Angel Urbina-García, Robert G. Myers, Anisai Ledesma-Rodea, and Marla Andrea Rangel-Cantero

Abstract This chapter showcases some of the pioneering studies conducted in Mexico that explored how transition from preschool to primary school is experienced by different stakeholders within the socio-political context of Mexican education. Overall, the Mexican education system seems to offer limited continuity between the preschool/kindergarten and the primary school with important implications for children's personal development and school transition. Longitudinal studies reveal that intervention programs informed by international research seem to support positively the development of children's skills having a long-term effect. Cross-sectional intervention programs seem to help children develop interpersonal and academic skills that help them navigate this transition. Some parents, teachers, and headteachers seem to recognise the importance of this period of change; however, they do not seem to deploy effective strategies to support this change. Implications of Mexican educational policies during this transition are discussed.

B. García-Cabrero (✉) · A. Ledesma-Rodea · M. A. Rangel-Cantero
National Autonomous University of Mexico, Mexico City, Mexico

A. Urbina-García
University of Hull, Hull, UK
e-mail: m.urbina-garcia@hull.ac.uk

R. G. Myers
Hacia una Cultura Democrática. A.C. (ACUDE), Mexico City, Mexico
e-mail: rmyers@acudemx.org

© The Author(s), under exclusive license to Springer Nature Switzerland AG 2022
A. Urbina-García et al. (eds.), *Transitions to School: Perspectives and Experiences from Latin America*, International Perspectives on Early Childhood Education and Development 37, https://doi.org/10.1007/978-3-030-98935-4_4

Introduction

The first five years of life are critical to children's development as they lay the foundation for their subsequent personal and academic development which are built through experiences in the environments in which children participate. From a biosocial perspective, these early experiences help establish important neural connections that foster language, reasoning, problem solving, social skills, behaviour, and emotional health (Mustard, 2007; Parisi et al., 2019). Therefore, early childhood education settings are particularly important in child development since they promote curiosity and exploration, and allow the development of cognitive, social, motor, and emotional skills. Early childhood education centres in Mexico aim to promote holistic child development without a particular focus on preparing children to enter primary school. Nevertheless, these centres offer important experiences that can help children start formal schooling (Smith & Glass, 2019); although, entering primary school does not come without challenges.

Moving from preschool to first grade of primary school has been internationally recognised as a challenging process for children's academic and personal life (Fabian, 2013; Perry et al., 2014; Urbina-Garcia, 2019). There are multiple factors that shape the type of experience the child will have when entering primary school. These factors include their developmental stage and temperament, home and community experiences, having attended initial and/or preschool education, the social and cultural context that frames these contexts, and the rules or expectations that children's social context set out for this transition. This process is experienced not only by children but also by their mothers, fathers and/or close relatives, impacting the lives of everyone involved (Jindal-Snape, 2016; Myers et al., 2008). Scholars have investigated a wide range of variables involved in the transition process which have led to the current knowledge and understanding of the topic around the world, although most of this body of research comes from developed countries. In Latin American countries such as Mexico, few empirical studies have focused on this transition process. While the Mexican government made preschool level mandatory for all children aged 3–6 as a requirement to enter primary school in 2004 (McConnell-Farmer et al., 2012), the scarce number of Mexican studies (including Spanish and English language) has limited the development of effective educational policies and guidelines to support students' school transition. This has implications since there is a culture in Mexico of not using the latest research to create public policies (Castillo-Alemán, 2012), with policies developed based on political interests (Alemán & Hiruma, 2013), which needs to be challenged through a robust research base.

This chapter showcases longitudinal and cross-sectional studies carried out in Mexican preschool centres and primary schools and offers a critical analysis of the socio-political context of Mexican education and educational policies which frame the preschool and first grade of primary school and the transition between these.

The Transition to School in Mexico: Educational System and Social Context in Mexico

The total population of Mexico is 127.6 million (Sistema Nacional de Información Estadística y Geográfica (INEGI), 2020) and predicted to reach 130 million by 2050 (Álvarez-Mendiola, 2006). Throughout the country's history, several government institutions have been created to meet the needs of one of the most populated countries of the world and address social issues including health and education. In Mexico, there are many subsystems which offer education and childcare services for children ranging from 45 days to 6 years old to support parents who work full time (McConnell-Farmer et al., 2012; Rivera & Guerra, 2005). These subsystems— SEDESOL (Social Development Secretariat), DIF (National System for Integral Family Development), SEDENA (National Defence Secretariat), IMSS (Mexican Institute for Social Security), and ISSSTE (Social and Security Services Institute for Government Workers) operate under SEP's (Secretaría de Educación Pública) regulations, but each institution also has its own internal regulations and guidelines for its educational services. Historically, the creation of these institutions and further scope going from a 'childminding' to a more 'educational' approach was highly influenced in the 70–80s by the Head Start educational programs created in the US (Rivera & Guerra, 2005). Public primary school education on the other hand, is by law, regulated and provided by the government to all children aged 6–12 years. Both early childhood and school educational levels are public and subsidised by the government; hence, parents do not pay any fees. However, in the last three decades, the creation of private preschool centres and primary schools (where parents must pay a fee) has skyrocketed in Mexico due to the alleged low quality of education provided by the public system (Cázares, 2015). The basic education provision in Mexico lasts 12 years. The preschool level includes three years of instruction (3–5 years old). Primary education (6–12 years old) comprises six years of compulsory instruction which allows access to secondary school (12–15 years old), that lasts three years (Secretaría de Educación Pública (SEP), 2012).

How Transitions Operate Within the Mexican System: A Web of Discontinuities?

While preschool education has been mandatory in Mexico since 2004, there are data revealing that not all children attend preschool (Pérez-Martínez et al., 2010). There are children who attend nursery prior to starting preschool and other children who transition to preschool coming straight from home. In Mexico there are urban and rural schools as well as private and public schools. A careful analysis of the continuities and discontinuities in the current curricula reveals an emphasis on using a play-based learning approach (Secretaría de Educación Pública (SEP), 2017) to promote children's personal development at preschool level. In contrast, there is a heavy emphasis on academic development at primary school level (i.e., literacy-related skills) following a problem-based approach (Pérez-Martínez et al., 2010). Public preschool centres promote children's development of cognitive, social, emotional, and motor skills; however, such emphasis is not geared towards a specific final outcome – that of learning how to read and write to pass subject tests/exams (Gómez-Meléndez et al., 2018). This aim seems to be inconsistent with what the primary school expects children to do. Public primary school provision aims to support children to develop literacy skills to pass subjects tests/exams (Rodríguez-Gómez, 2015; Scott et al., 2018). Whilst in preschool level children do not need to sit exams/tests, primary school children do, which is indeed a school procedure for a child to gain access to the second year of primary school (Secretaría de Educación Pública (SEP), 2012).

Mexico's education expenditure is the second-highest among OECD countries; however, investment *per student* is the lowest (Organisation for Economic Co-Operation and Development (OECD), 2017). According to the latest OECD (2017) report, preschool level enrolments significantly improved in Mexico over 12 years between 2005 and 2017, reaching 87%, similar to the average for OECD countries. Mexico and Hungary are the only countries to start compulsory education at the age of 3, whereas all other countries start at 4, 5 or 6 years. All OECD countries, but Mexico and Ireland, report programs or activities (e.g., open doors, parent information sessions, taster days) to facilitate children's transitions to the primary school (OECD, 2017). Those OECD countries reporting to support children for transitions, implement between 5 and 8 transition activities.

All countries have similar numbers of children in preschool and first grade, except for Mexico and Turkey – where there is an abrupt change in the size of the class (going from 30 to 48 and 20 to 40 children respectively). Interestingly, out of 22 OECD countries, only Mexico and New Zealand did not report specialised training for teachers to support the transition. According to independent reviews commissioned by the OECD, the definition of goals and the teaching methods used in Mexico's preschool education "are not great" (OECD, 2004 p. 51), are too "instructive" rather than "constructive", and the profile of what children "should be like at the moment of their transition into primary school has not been agreed upon nor operationalized" (OECD, 2004 p. 48). The same report goes on to say that the Mexican authorities' decision to have a curriculum-related division of initial education (0–3 years.) and preschool education (4–6 years.) negatively impacts preschool children's learning. In fact, this division runs contrary to usual practices in OECD countries (e.g., Sweden, Norway, Finland, New Zealand, United Kingdom) where all educational programs are aligned to have a "common curriculum, teacher profile and learning goals" (OECD, 2017 p. 49). The Mexican transition from preschool to school seems to be complicated given the lack of coherent curriculum and pedagogically-related approaches for the first grade of primary school curriculum.

Children's Transition: A Follow-Up Study from Preschool to 5th Grade of Primary School

This section analyses one of the few but most important longitudinal studies undertaken in Mexico regarding the transition to school of a group of preschoolers that attended an innovative program: the High/Scope Preschool Curriculum (Epstein & Hohmann, 2012). In essence, the High/Scope curriculum promotes children's direct interaction with objects, events, and ideas, making children's interests and choices the basis of it. On the other hand, teachers, caregivers, and parents offer physical, emotional, and intellectual support, always keeping a balance between child's initiative and adult's input (Epstein, 2007).

In an attempt to explore the effectiveness of the High/Scope curriculum in Mexico, a group of researchers adapted and implemented it in the Mexican context, to offer potential solutions to address the most pressing needs of the Mexican preschool education, including: (1) the design of effective strategies for the introduction of educational innovations (García-Cabrero & Espriu, 1987, 1991); (2) the development of programs for teaching staff tasked with introducing educational innovations (Barocio, 1997); (3) the development of assessment systems to determine the effectiveness in facilitating transition from preschool to primary school (García-Cabrero & Pérez, 1990; García-Cabrero et al., 1992); and (4) the long-term impact of the program.

García-Cabrero et al. (1992) conducted a study of school transition that involved the follow up of a sample of five cohorts of children (3–6 years old) who participated in the High/Scope curriculum in Mexico City. The first cohort was followed up from 1st to 5th grade in primary school, the second till 4th grade, the third up to 3rd grade, and the fourth and fifth, till 2nd and 1st grades, respectively.

This study of school transition is a pioneer project in the Mexican context for several reasons: (1) it was the first one to adopt an experimental approach to adapt and validate an educational innovation; (2) there were no precedents of conducting follow-up studies to analyse the transition process from preschool to primary school; and (3) it was the first one to place an emphasis on, and measure, socioemotional skills, besides cognitive skills as the basic components of an optimal transition. By the time the High/Scope Preschool Curriculum was implemented, the official program emphasised cognitive skills as described by Piaget to make sure children would acquire representation skills and logico-mathematical skills as pre-reading-writing and pre-mathematics that would facilitate formal learning of these skills.in primary school.

Participants

The study followed and assessed 139 students from the experimental groups (who experienced the High/Scope Curriculum) and 131 from the comparison groups (who had followed the official public preschool curriculum) totalling 270 students (26, 35, 43, 89, 77, respectively from the first to the fifth cohort) (García-Cabrero et al., 1992). Participants from the experimental groups were followed to the primary schools where they were enrolled, and then, researchers randomly selected a matched boy or girl of the same group who had not experienced the High/Scope Curriculum.

Measures

Academic Achievement was measured through the final score assigned by the teachers of each grade in each of the five years of follow-up of both the experimental and comparison groups. The IDEA (Inventory of Academic Achievement) test (Macotela et al., 1991) was also used to measure academic achievement in the third generation of graduates.

Socioemotional development was measured through the subscales: social adaptation and autonomy; interaction with peers; and pride about their work (self-efficacy) of the COR (Child Observation Record) (High/Scope Educational Research Foundation, 1992). Teachers rated students' socioemotional development through observations over a week using a checklist of 20 items (not achieved, in process, achieved).

Also, compliance with each of the 11 Cognitively Oriented Curriculum (COC) (Banet et al., 1979; Weikart et al., 1971) original goals were assessed through the percentage of children reaching each goal at the end of each school year (García-Cabrero & Pérez, 1990). The 11 goals are oriented mainly to one of two domains: cognitive domain (four goals); or socioemotional domain (seven goals). The attainment of the goals was measured three times a year during the preschool years, and was assessed once a year (through observation of the teacher in charge) at the end of each primary school year during the follow up study.

Semi-structured interviews with primary school teachers were conducted to find out if they perceived differences in social adaptation and academic performance between children from the experimental and comparison groups.

Results

Readiness for school revealed that once the COC was implemented with high fidelity (third cohort of students), children from the experimental groups outperformed those from the comparison groups and these differences were statistically significant.

A chi-square test was used to test the differences in levels of accomplishment of the COC goals. Data revealed that most of the students (70% on average) from the experimental groups in all cohorts were in the highest level of attainment of the goals. Results were statistically significant for eight of the eleven goals measured.

Also, academic achievement results of students of the five cohorts who participated in the follow up study of the experimental and comparison groups, showed that during the five years of follow up, experimental group students outperformed students of the comparison group. To assess the differences in performance between mean achievement of both groups, the Wilcoxon rank sum test with continuity correction was used (W = 47,888, p-value <0.001).

Models of Data Analyses

Several models of the relationship between goals, socioemotional skills, pride in their work, and performance were tested. We present three of them, because of their importance for preschool to primary school transition.

Model 1

The first model tested the relationship between the achievement of students predicted by three variables: social adaptation and autonomy, pride in their work, and group (experimental, control) to which they belong.

Data showed that the three variables predict achievement in a statistically significant way, which allows us to assert that the experimental group students' achievement was influenced by the variables Social Adaptation and Autonomy and Pride in their Work. These data are relevant to studying the factors that affect a successful transition from preschool to primary school.

Model 2

This model explains the performance in mathematics through the percentage of achievement obtained in Goal 2 (skills to define and solve problems). Data showed that the categories of 66.6% and 100% of achievement of Goal 2 are significant to explain achievement in mathematics during primary school. The high percentages of compliance of Goal 2 predict high performance in mathematics and the differences with the control group are significant. In other words, having participated in the experimental group, and having achieved high compliance with Goal 2, predicts high performance in mathematics.

Model 3
This model assessed the relationship between the percentage of achievement of Goal 5 (Expressive skills: talk, write, dramatise and represent graphically) and achievement in Spanish.

Data showed, that high percentages of compliance with Goal 5 predicts better performance in Spanish. In other words, being part of the experimental group, and having achieved high compliance levels (66% and 100%) in Goal 5, predicts a high achievement in Spanish.

Analysis of data from interviews with primary school teachers of the schools where children were followed revealed that an important group of students from the experimental groups were sent to special groups for gifted students. Also, teachers reported that almost 50% of children from these groups learned to read in the first three months of first grade in primary school, versus 35% of children from the comparison groups, and by the end of second grade, 100% of students from the experimental groups completed the process of reading and writing, versus 77% of the students from the comparison groups. The transition of students from the experimental groups to primary schools was considered very acceptable and no behaviour problems were reported by the teachers. Also, these students were considered to show a high degree of initiative and autonomy, as measured by the socioemotional questionnaire that teachers completed after observing children.

In the third cohort of students, 86% of children in the experimental group were in the highest category of peer interaction (collaborative work), versus 75% of those in the comparison group. In the pride in work category, 57% of the children in the experimental groups vs. 50% of those in the comparison groups achieved the highest category. The differences between groups in the different levels of teamwork and pride in work, were analysed through a chi-square test; the results show significant differences in favour of the experimental children of the third cohort. The results found in the relationship models between variables show that the High/Scope curriculum promoted the development of skills that allowed students to transition successfully to the primary education level, fostering both their cognitive and socioemotional development.

Recent Studies on the Transition from Preschool to School in Mexico

Myers et al. (2008), through a series of studies on the transition from preschool to primary school in Mexico, have found that the main emphasis of educational public policies is on ensuring that children are well-prepared to enter primary school, rather than getting schools ready to facilitate children's transitions. Myers et al. (2008) conducted a qualitative study to analyse the factors related to the preschool-primary transition in Mexico and found different challenges that children have to face to move successfully between home and preschool, and from preschool to primary school:

Change may require children to start communicating and learning in a language that is not their mother tongue, as most of the primary school teachers do not speak any of the 67 indigenous languages officially recognised in Mexico. Usually, the adult-child relationship at home or preschool tends to be informal and supportive, while in primary school adult-child relationships can be less supportive, more formal, and less personal (Lye, 1996).

When children start primary school, they arrive in an environment which is mainly literacy-driven and formal, rather than a play-based orally driven environment with which children were familiar. At school, the child has to interact with a group of children initially unknown to them, while previously their interactions were limited to family members and some friends.

Challenges like these can indeed make children's entry to school difficult, especially during the first few months. However, in some cases, the adaptation process can take longer, and can have a negative impact on their learning, leading to a sense of failure and low self-esteem, which could also lead to dropping out from school (Myers, 1992; Myers et al., 2008; Peters, 2010). Nevertheless, it is important to acknowledge that most children, not only navigate the new environment successfully, they thrive at primary school (Jindal-Snape, 2016).

Myers et al. (2008) conclude that the transition process can be approached from a variety of theoretical and practical perspectives and identify that indeed, there are multiple factors that determine the type of experience the child will have when entering elementary school. Delgado et al. (2015), Delgado-Fuentes (2011), and Delgado-Fuentes et al. (2014) reported a comprehensive study on the transition between preschool and primary school in Mexico which took place over five months during the 2009 and 2010 school year. This case study research involved the observation of the interactions of teachers and children from urban, rural, and indigenous communities, focusing on the affective components of the transition from home to preschool and from preschool to primary school. The researchers argued that successful transitions require adapting to both the academic and emotional demands of the new settings. This work focused on investigating specific characteristics of teaching practices used in five preschools and five primary schools that could promote familiarisation to the school context and facilitate their transitions. Findings revealed that teachers conducted three different types of activities across both levels: (1) unplanned or vaguely focused activities (with no clear goals and rules, inconsistent routines from one day to the other, no time limits for each activity) that do not help children transitioning to preschool or primary school comprehend and integrate to the school context; (2) organised activities that help to comprehend this context and to build a learner's role; and (3) organised activities that help to comprehend the context, build a learner's role, and promote autonomy in learning. The best practices (organised activities) were found in some of the preschools, whereas there was a lack of good practices in primary schools. The first two types of activities prevailed in primary schools, whereas the third type was unfortunately, scarce. In preschool classrooms where the third type of activities prevailed, teachers' actions were essential in supporting children to adjust to the new school environment and to promote their involvement in school activities which positively impacted their motivation to attend and learn. The involvement of children in formulating classroom rules, planning activities, reflecting on and evaluating learning processes, were found as most relevant for allowing children to adapt and succeed in their new context.

Delgado et al. (2015), defined transition as a process that involves social adaptation as one of the dimensions that are required for children to get 'ready' for primary school, as well as taking into account the differences between the two educational levels. The study proposed a way of understanding this process and the ways teachers can help to facilitate it. Grounded theory (Charmaz, 2006) was the methodological approach used in this study which considered a new system within Bronfenbrenner's (1979) ecological model, − the nanosystem − that represents the activities within the classroom, whose structure and development allow children to understand what school is about and what role they are expected to play.

The Effectiveness of a Transition Program; and How Headteachers/Teachers View the Transition

Research on transitions reveals that not only children, but also their parents, experience a school transition (Griebel et al., 2017; Jindal-Snape, 2016; Puccioni, 2015; Wickett, 2017; Wildenger & McIntyre, 2011). Teachers and headteachers are seen as key stakeholders who can support families to facilitate the transition (Balduzzi et al., 2019). Considering this framework, this section presents a series of empirical studies reported in Urbina-Garcia and Kyriacou (2018) and Urbina-Garcia (2019, 2020) which have been instrumental in understanding how the transition to primary school is experienced by pupils aged 5–6, how teachers can support families, and how parents and headteachers perceive the preschool transition in Mexican public schools.

In the first study, Urbina-Garcia (2020) explored the extent to which an intervention program could support preschool children's transition to first grade of primary school. The senior leadership team from one public preschool contacted academics from an internationally recognised public university in Mexico and requested support for families during the transition to primary school – given a perceived lack of children's academic 'readiness'. Drawing from the international literature, this study followed a quasi-experimental design having an experimental and a control group (from different schools). Each group comprised 20 children ($N = 40$) from 5 to 6 years old ($M = 5.6$) with their corresponding teacher and teaching assistant ($N = 4$). The views of the children's parents on the effectiveness of the program were also gathered.

Measures

Children's cognitive, social, and motor skills were assessed using the *Assessment and Evaluation Programming System for Infants and Children* (AEPS) (Bricker et al., 2002), a criterion-referenced test with sound psychometric properties as reported in previous studies (Noh, 2005). Children's skills were measured considering a 3-point scale: "0 = Does not have the skill"; "1 = Uses the skill inconsistently" and "2 = Uses the skill consistently". The main teacher and teaching assistant's practices that promote early literacy were assessed with a self-report questionnaire adapted from the *"Inventory of Early Literacy Practices"* (Neuman et al., 2000) including 40 items on a 3-point rating scale: "0 = Does not use the practice"; "1 = Inconsistent use of the practice" and "2 = Consistent use of the practice". Parents' perceptions on the effectiveness of the program were gathered via three open-ended questions: (a) What factors will you consider for choosing the primary school to which your child will attend? (b) In which way do you support your child in this transition? and (c) What have you talked about with your child regarding the primary school? Parents' satisfaction with the program was rated with a single-item on a 5-point scale (1 = Very Dissatisfied to 5 = Very Satisfied).

Intervention

The leadership team reported that children lacked literacy-related skills which they thought were necessary for transition to an outcome-based curriculum with high academic demands. Whilst this result reflected a concern mainly focused on children, the intervention also included parents, main teacher (the teacher who is responsible for the class) and teaching assistant, to ensure a greater impact. The transition program included a number of transition activities (e.g., reading books about changes in life; allowing children to write labels for 'window', 'table', 'door'; children drawing the primary school they visited)" reported in previous studies as effective to support preschoolers' transition (Claes, 2010; Hedegaard & Fleer, 2013; Peters, 2010). These activities were adapted by considering the local cultural practices and educational policies of the school (taking children out from the school is forbidden by Ministry of Public Education policies given the high rates of crime and violence in the city, hence a safe visit to a close primary school was carefully-planned and authorised). A group work plan was created between the researcher, the teacher, and teaching assistant to deliver the program that lasted 6 months with three *in-classroom* sessions per week. The intervention included activities that were considered to promote children's (a) early literacy (cognitive domain); (b) social skills; (c) fine motor skills; (d) home-school involvement; and (e) school-school links. A full description of the program is available in Urbina-Garcia (2020).

Results

Statistically significant differences were found (between experimental and control groups) which suggests that the intervention program did help children develop cognitive, social, and fine motor skills. Addressing the needs reported by the leadership team, it was observed that the inclusion of literacy-related activities significantly supported children's development of cognitive and fine motor skills (learning the alphabet, shapes, sizes and forms; writing labels and own name; writing stories from home; writing what visiting a primary school feels like). The constant use of group activities also helped improve children's social skills (initiate conversations about the primary school visit; exchange ideas; work collaboratively) which will be useful once in primary school. The visits to a primary school helped children improve their understanding of what a primary school looks like – by using the draw-and-tell method during group activities. The main teacher and teaching assistant (experimental group) acknowledged the importance of this change and started using new practices that promote literacy-related skills (allowing children to label objects in classroom, write their names in their work, tell a story brought from home, express how they see the primary school everyone talks about at home). Home-school activities helped parents acknowledge the importance of this transition for their child and learn what their child can and cannot do in the classroom. Parents reported to be talking to their child more frequently about the primary school.

In another study, Urbina-Garcia and Kyriacou (2018) explored teachers' use and type of transition practices and children's most common problems in classroom as reported by the teachers. They also investigated headteachers' and parents' perceptions around children's transition to primary school. They recruited 15 preschool and primary school teachers *(N = 30)*; ten parents (five preschool and five primary school), and five headteachers. They also aimed to find associations between teacher's demographic data, the use of transition practices and reported children's problems.

Research Design

A mixed-method research design was used for this study (questionnaire, rating scale, and semi-structured interviews). Two different surveys and semi-structured interviews were developed based on an extensive literature review on the transition to school. Both surveys aimed to measure the use, type, and frequency of teachers' transition practices comprising 38 items on a 5-point Likert scale (1 = Never to 5 = Always). The children's problems rating scale comprised 12 most common problems identified in the literature to be rated on a 5-point Likert type format (1 = Not at all true to 5 = Yes, very true*)*. The semi-structured interview aimed to obtain headteachers' and parents' perceptions comprised 10 open-ended questions. Quantitative data were analysed via descriptive statistics and one-way ANOVA looking for significant variations between preschool and primary school teachers. Pearson correlation was also computed to investigate potential associations among variables. Qualitative data were analysed via NVivo, performing a thematic analysis following the procedure described by Terry et al. (2017).

Results

Findings revealed that both groups of teachers frequently used more practices to establish home-school links (providing important information to parents, organising 'open doors', information sessions), while practices aimed at establishing school-school links (visiting primary school, inviting primary school teacher) were not a common practice. Primary school teachers seemed to implement transition practices on a more frequent basis than their preschool counterparts. Both groups of teachers reported moderate-to-frequent problems in their classroom mostly related to children's behavioural and attentional patterns. However, primary school teachers reported to have slightly more problems in classroom than preschool teachers. The most frequently reported problems focused on children's difficulty following directions, showing behavioural problems (cannot stay seated) and difficulty taking turns. Statistical correlations between preschool teachers' demographics, their practices, and children's problems suggested that teachers with more specialised training courses (annual mandatory training provided by the Ministry of Public Education regarding pedagogical activities, classroom management, assessment among other areas) reported more problems related to children having difficulties respecting teacher's authority, taking turns, carrying out the assigned classroom activities, and staying focused in classroom activities. Similarly, primary school teachers with higher academic qualifications were associated with reporting children with problems following directions, remaining seated for long periods of time, and understanding school-tasks. These findings may reflect teachers' expectations of how children should behave in each educational level.

Results showed that preschool parents were concerned about developing their child's personal and academic skills in preparation for first grade, whereas primary school parents were concerned about their child's lack of behavioural self-regulation skills. Parents seemed to be aware of the change from a play-led to a more academic-led routine and the challenge this would represent to children; however, they did not know how to support them. One way in which all parents reported supporting their child was by sending him/her to English language lessons or enrolling him/her in a private preschool to foster literacy-related skills. These findings are important as they seem to reflect parents' understanding of equipping their child to face academic demands in primary school – by making their child bilingual. These results support the notion that parents think that literacy skills are the most important aspects for their child to be ready to enter primary school. These novel findings in Latin American contexts seem to echo evidence found in Hong Kong (Chan, 2012; Li et al., 2013). Headteachers' perspectives revealed that for some of them, this transition does not really represent a challenge for children, and it was evident, that headteachers were not aware of practices to support their staff or children. These findings contrast with Noel's (2012) results where headteachers in Australia were reported to be aware of the importance and implications of this transition and with Njenga's (2015) results from Kenya where headteachers showed a positive attitude towards supporting families.

Discussion and Conclusions

This chapter aimed to analyse the sociocultural context surrounding the transition to school in the Mexican public system. It also showcased pioneering studies on the preschool transition which have been conducted in Mexico in the last three decades. Firstly, our analysis showed that the lack of empirical studies, specific educational policies, guidelines, and educational programs may suggest that the transition to school is not a topic that is prioritised by Mexican academics, politicians, and practitioners. Future research should be conducted to establish whether this is indeed the case and if it is, analyse the reasons behind it. Secondly, these studies have laid the groundwork to learn and analyse critically how this transition is experienced by Mexican children and what gaps need to be addressed in this respect. Specifically, these studies have shown that an effective intervention should aim to support children to develop greater autonomy, independence, and self-confidence. Findings showed that it is important to help children develop cognitive skills (to face academic demands regarding reading, writing, and mathematics) and interpersonal skills (socioemotional) to facilitate children's transition to a new academic environment, rules, roles, and identities. Some of these interventions showed that children who received an intervention that aimed to promote cognitive skills, performed better in academic-related tasks. However, these seem to be underpinned by the development of socioemotional skills, which is consistent with research elsewhere (Denham et al., 2014; Fabian, 2013; Okonduugba et al., 2020; Wong, 2015). It is important to note that these interventions support the notion that children must have a set of academic and personal skills to enter the first grade of primary school. The notion that schools should be ready for children was not explored. Future research should look at the way in which schools can be made ready for each child and their unique preferences and needs. The transition to school frameworks of the studies conducted in Mexico, also included the need to consider not only factors related to children like readiness for school, but also contextual factors (Besi & Sakellariou, 2019), highlighting the important role of the families, schools, and communities, which is being recognised by a growing body of research (Hannah et al., 2010; Lau & Power, 2018; Mayer et al., 2010; Salmi & Kumpulainen, 2019).

These studies offer evidence of the need to work with the significant adults (parents, teachers, headteachers, and teaching assistants) to establish collaborative work, which seems to be essential to promote a sense of community. Interesting differences were found between preschool and primary school teachers' perspectives regarding children's 'problems'. Findings revealed that primary school teachers identified children with behavioural problems (cannot stay seated) and children with difficulty taking turns, more frequently compared to preschool teachers. This difference may be due to higher expectations of primary school teachers given the traditional pedagogical approach used in the first grade of primary school (sit down, pay attention, listen to the teacher) and given that preschool children were used to learning by play. These results seem to be consistent with previous research conducted mostly in developed countries (Denham et al., 2014; Hatcher et al., 2012; LoCasale-Crouch et al., 2008) which found that behavioural problems are more common in primary school compared to a preschool classroom. From the perspectives of parents, results showed that parents should be given information about the importance of their child's transition. Working closely with parents seems to lead to a better understanding of how best to support their child's transition. Findings from these studies should be taken with caution given the small sample size and given that causality could not be established. Nevertheless, these findings show a positive association between a psycho-educational intervention and the development of personal and academic skills which could inform future studies. Finally, the studies on transition conducted in Mexico reveal that what is required to facilitate children's transition to school are not only special practices or interventions to help in the development of children's skills, but also specific educational policies that consider supporting all stakeholders involved. Future research on transitions should look at whether we need to prepare children for school or prepare schools for children or perhaps, we should be advocating for both. Also, the need to include a fine-grained analysis of interactions at a nano level, beyond what Bronfenbrenner (1979) describes as micro-level within the classroom, to reveal the characteristics of teachers' practices, that help or hinder children to make a successful transition, has been highlighted. Future research will help inform educational polices to ensure that the demands referred to by Myers et al. (2008), are not excessively challenging for children. Excessive demands may result in states of anxiety and feelings of low self-efficacy preventing children from making a successful transition to primary school.

References

Alemán, G. D. C., & Hiruma, A. A. (2013). *La Reforma y las Políticas Educativas: impacto en la supervisión escolar* [The reform and educational policies: Impact on school supervision]. Flacso México.

Álvarez-Mendiola, G. (2006). Lifelong learning policies in Mexico: Context, challenges and comparisons. *Compare, 36*(3), 379–399.

Balduzzi, L., Lazzari, A., Van Laere, K., Boudry, C., Režek, M., Mlinar, M., & McKinnon, E. (2019). *Literature review on transitions across early childhood and compulsory school settings in Europe*. ERI.

Banet, B., Weikart, D. P., & Hohmann, M. (1979). *Young children in action*. High/Scope Press.

Barocio, R. (1997). *La Formación Docente para la Innovación Educativa* [Teacher training for an innovative education]. Editorial Trillas.

Besi, M., & Sakellariou, M. (2019). Factors associated with the successful transition to primary school. *European Journal of Education Studies, 5*(10), 64–75.

Bricker, D., Waddell, M., Capt, B., Johnson, J., Pretti-Frontczak, K., Slentz, K., & Straka, E. (2002). *Assessment, Evaluation, and Programming System for infants and children (AEPS(R)), curriculum for birth to three years*. Brookes Publishing Company.

Bronfenbrenner, U. (1979). *The ecology of human development: Experiments by nature and design*. Harvard University Press.

Castillo-Alemán, D. (2012). Las políticas educativas en México desde una perspectiva de política pública: gobernabilidad y gobernanza [The Mexican education policies from a public policy perspective: Government and governmentality]. *Revista Internacional de Investigación en Educación, 4*(9), 637–652.

Cázares, L. C. (2015). La mercadotecnia en el servicio educativo privado en México [The marketing in private education service in Mexico]. *RIDE Revista Iberoamericana para la Investigación y el Desarrollo Educativo, 6*(11), 486–498. https://www.redalyc.org/articulo.oa?id=498150319029. Accessed 18 August 2021.

Chan, W. L. (2012). Expectations for the transition from kindergarten to primary school amongst teachers, parents and children. *Early Child Development and Care, 182*(5), 639–664. https://doi.org/10.1080/03004430.2011.569543

Charmaz, K. (2006). *Constructing grounded theory: A practical guide through qualitative data analysis*. SAGE.

Claes, B. (2010). *Transition to kindergarten: The impact of preschool on kindergarten adjustment* [Ph.D. dissertation]. Alfred University. https://aura.alfred.edu/bitstream/handle/10829/2666/Claes%2C%20Bethany%202010.pdf?sequence=1&isAllowed=y. Accessed 31 July 2021.

Delgado, M., Peral, A., & Valle, C. (2015). La transición del preescolar a la escuela primaria ¿cómo aprenden los niños a leer el contexto escolar? [The transition from preschool to primary school. How do children learn to read in the school context?] In N. Del Rio (Ed.), *La Primera Infancia en el Espacio Público* [Early childhood in the public space] (pp. 108–122). Universidad Autónoma Metropolitana.

Delgado-Fuentes, M. A. (2011). The transition from preschool to primary school: How do children learn to interpret social settings? In I. Candel Torres, L. Gómez Chova, & A. López Martínez (Eds.), *Proceedings of 4th international conference of education, research and innovation* (pp. 723–733). ICERI/IATED. https://library.iated.org/view/DELGADOFUENTES2011TRA. Accessed 25 May 2021.

Delgado-Fuentes, M. A., González, A., & Martínez, C. (2014). La transición del preescolar a la primaria: El papel de las familias y el rol activo de los niños [The transition from preschool to primary school: The role of families and the active role of children]. In A. Bazán Ramírez & N. I. Vega Alcántara (Eds.), *Familia-Escuela-Comunidad. Teorías en la Práctica* [Family-school-community. Theories in practice] (pp. 333–355). Universidad Autónoma del Estado de Morelos.

Denham, S. A., Bassett, H. H., Zinsser, K., & Wyatt, T. M. (2014). How preschoolers' social–emotional learning predicts their early school success: Developing theory-promoting, competency-based assessments. *Infant and Child Development, 23*(4), 426–454. https://doi.org/10.1002/icd.1840

Epstein, A. S. (2007). *The intentional teacher: Choosing the best strategies for young children's learning*. National Association for the Education of Young Children.

Epstein, A. S., & Hohmann, M. (2012). *The high scope preschool curriculum*. The High Scope Press.

Fabian, H. (2013). *Children starting school: A guide to successful transitions and transfers for teachers and assistants*. David Fulton Publishers.

García-Cabrero, B., & Espriu, R. M. (1987). El curriculum con orientación cognoscitiva [The cognitively oriented curriculum]. *Revista Latinoamericana de Estudios Educativos, 16*(1–4), 11–16.

García-Cabrero, B., & Espriú, R. M. (1991). Validación de un programa de educación preescolar con orientación cognoscitiva [Validation of a cognitively oriented preschool program]. *Revista Latinoamericana de Estudios Educativos, 21*(4), 115–147. http://www.cee.edu.mx/rlee/revista/r1991_2000/r_texto/t_1991_4_05.pdf. Accessed 18 August 2021.

García-Cabrero, B., & Pérez, M. M. (1990). *Evaluación de las Metas del Curriculum con Orientación Cognoscitiva* [Assessment of learning outcomes of the cognitively-oriented curriculum]. Facultad de Psicología.

García-Cabrero, B., Pérez, M. M., & Rentería, M. (1992). Efectos a Largo Plazo de un Curriculum de Educación Preescolar con Orientación Cognoscitiva [Long-term effects of a cognitively-oriented preschool education curriculum]. In J. Flip & A. M. Cabello (Eds.), *Mejorando las Oportunidades Educativas de los Niños que entran a la Escuela* [Improving the learning opportunities of children when entering primary school] (pp. 179–196). Editorial ARGÉ limitada.

Gómez-Meléndez, L. E., Cáceres Mesa, M. L., & Zúñiga Rodríguez, M. (2018). La evaluación del aprendizaje en la educación preescolar: aproximación al estado del conocimiento [The assessment of learning processes in preschool education: Approaching a state of knowledge]. *Conrado, 14*(62), 242–250.

Griebel, W., Wildgruber, A., Schuster, A., & Radan, J. (2017). Transition to being parents of a school-child: Parental perspective on coping of parents and child nine months after school start. In S. Dockett, W. Griebel, & B. Perry (Eds.), *Families and transition to school* (pp. 21–36). Springer.

Hannah, E., Gorton, H., & Jindal-Snape, D. (2010). Small steps: Perspectives on understanding and supporting children starting school in Scotland. In D. Jindal-Snape (Ed.), *Educational transitions: Moving stories from around the world* (pp. 51–67). Routledge.

Hatcher, B., Nuner, J., & Paulsel, J. (2012). Kindergarten readiness and preschools: Teachers' and parents' beliefs within and across programs. *Early Childhood Research & Practice, 14*(2), 1–17.

Hedegaard, M., & Fleer, M. (2013). *Play, learning, and children's development: Everyday life in families and transition to school*. Cambridge University Press.

High/Scope Educational Research Foundation. (1992). *High/Scope Child Observation Record (COR) for ages 2½–6*. High/Scope Press.

Jindal-Snape, D. (2016). *A-Z of transitions*. Palgrave.

Lau, E. Y. H., & Power, T. G. (2018). Parental involvement during the transition to primary school: Examining bidirectional relations with school adjustment. *Children and Youth Services Review, 88*, 257–266. https://doi.org/10.1016/j.childyouth.2018.03.018

Li, H. C. W., Mak, Y. W., Chan, S. S., Chu, A. K., Lee, E. Y., & Lam, T. H. (2013). Effectiveness of a play-integrated primary one preparatory program to enhance a smooth transition for children. *Journal of Health Psychology, 18*(1), 10–25. https://doi.org/10.1177/1359105311434052

LoCasale-Crouch, J., Mashburn, A. J., Downer, J. T., & Pianta, R. C. (2008). Pre-kindergarten teachers' use of transition practices and children's adjustment to kindergarten. *Early Childhood Research Quarterly, 23*(1), 124–139. https://doi.org/10.1016/j.ecresq.2007.06.001

Lye, D. N. (1996). Adult child–parent relationships. *Annual Review of Sociology, 22*(1), 79–102. https://doi.org/10.1146/annurev.soc.22.1.79

Macotela, S., Bermúdez, P., & Castañeda, I. (1991). *Inventario de Ejecución Académica: Un modelo diagnóstico-prescriptivo para el manejo de problemas asociados a la lectura, la escritura y las matemáticas* [Academic Performance Inventory: A diagnostic-prescriptive model for the management of mathematics and literacy-related problems]. Facultad de Psicología. U.N.A.M.

Mayer, K. L., Amendum, S. J., & Vernon-Feagans, L. (2010). The transition to formal schooling and children's early literacy development in the context of the USA. In D. Jindal-Snape (Ed.), *Educational transitions. Moving stories from around the world* (pp. 85–103). Routledge.

McConnell-Farmer, J. L., Cook, P. R., & Farmer, M. W. (2012). Perspectives in early childhood education: Belize, Brazil, Mexico, El Salvador and Peru. *Forum on Public Policy Online, 2012*(1), 1–27. https://files.eric.ed.gov/fulltext/EJ979437.pdf. Accessed 18 August 2021.

Mustard, J. F. (2007). Experience-based brain development: Scientific underpinnings of the importance of early child development in a global world. In M. E. Young & L. M. Ricardson (Eds.), *Early child development: From measurement to action* (pp. 43–86). The World Bank.

Myers, R. G. (1992). El niño y sus ambientes de aprendizaje. In J. Filip & A. Cabello (Eds.), *Mejorando las Oportunidades Educativas de los niños que entran a la escuela* [Improving the learning opportunities of children when entering primary school] (pp. 33–51). Editorial ARGÉ limitada.

Myers, R. G., Flores, B., & Peters, M. (2008). *La transición de educación preescolar a la primaria en México y su relación a logros educativos: un estudio exploratorio* [The transition from preschool to primary education in Mexico and its relationship to educational attainment: An exploratory study. 1]. Hacia una Cultura Democrática, A.C. (ACUDE).

Neuman, S. B., Bredekamp, S., & Copple, C. (2000). *Learning to read and write: Developmentally appropriate practice*. NAEYC.

Njenga, A. V. W. (2015). *Assessment of head teachers' leadership practices in enhancing transition from preschool to lower primary in public primary schools in Limuru sub county, Kiambu County, Kenya* [Doctoral dissertation]. Mount Kenya University. https://erepository.mku.ac.ke/handle/123456789/2035. Accessed 31 July 2021.

Noel, A. (2012). Easing the transition to school: Administrator's descriptions of transition to school activities. *Australasian Journal of Early Childhood, 36*(4), 44–52. https://doi.org/10.1177/183693911103600407

Noh, J. (2005). *Examining the psychometric properties of the second edition of the Assessment, Evaluation, and Programming System for three to six years: AEPS test 2nd edition (3–6)* [PhD dissertation]. University of Oregon.

Okonduugba, A., Christian, S., Agah, J., Ugwu, G., Ifelunni, C., Ezema, V., et al. (2020). Effects of caregivers' training program on preschoolers' socio-emotional readiness for transition from kindergarten to primary one in Rivers State. *Global Journal of Health Science, 12*(5), 1–30. https://doi.org/10.5539/gjhs.v12n5p30

Organisation for Economic Co-Operation and Development (OECD). (2004). *Early childhood education and care policy: Country note for Mexico*. https://www.oecd.org/education/school/34429196.pdf. Accessed 31 July 2021.

Organisation for Economic Co-Operation and Development (OECD). (2017). *Starting strong V: Transitions from early childhood education and care to primary education*. OECD Publishing. https://doi.org/10.1787/9789264276253-en

Parisi, G. I., Kemker, R., Part, J. L., Kanan, C., & Wermter, S. (2019). Continual lifelong learning with neural networks: A review. *Neural Networks, 113*, 54–71. https://doi.org/10.1016/j.neunet.2019.01.012

Pérez-Martínez, M. G., Pedroza-Zúñiga, L. H., Ruiz-Cuéllar, G., & López-García, A. Y. (2010). *La educación preescolar en México. Condiciones para la enseñanza y el aprendizaje* [Preschool education in Mexico. Conditions for teaching and learning]. Instituto Nacional para la Evaluación de la Educación (INEE). https://www.sep.gob.mx/work/models/sep1/Resource/8004/3/images/educacion_preescolar.pdf. Accessed 18 August 2021.

Perry, B., Dockett, S., & Petriwskyj, A. (Eds.). (2014). *Transitions to school-international research, policy and practice*. Springer.

Peters, S. (2010). *Literature review: Transition from early childhood education to school*. Report to the Ministry of Education. http://ece.manukau.ac.nz/__data/assets/pdf_file/0008/85841/956_ECELitReview.pdf. Accessed 31 July 2021.

Puccioni, J. (2015). Parents' conceptions of school readiness, transition practices, and children's academic achievement trajectories. *The Journal of Educational Research, 108*(2), 130–147. https://doi.org/10.1080/00220671.2013.850399

Rivera, F. L., & Guerra, M. M. (2005). Retos de la educación preescolar obligatoria en México: la transformación del modelo de supervisión escolar [Challenges of compulsory preschool education in Mexico: Transforming the school supervision model]. *REICE-Revista Electrónica Iberoamericana Sobre Calidad, Eficacia y Cambio en Educación, 3*(1), 503–511. https://www.redalyc.org/articulo.oa?id=55130150. Accessed 18 August 2021.

Rodríguez-Gómez, R. (2015). El proyecto educativo SEP-SNTE y la prueba ENLACE [The educational project SEP-SNTE and the ENLACE test]. *Revista Mexicana de Investigación Educativa, 20*(64), 309–324. https://www.redalyc.org/articulo.oa?id=14032722015. Accessed 18 August 2021.

Salmi, S., & Kumpulainen, K. (2019). Children's experiencing of their transition from preschool to first grade: A visual narrative study. *Learning, Culture and Social Interaction, 20*, 58–67. https://doi.org/10.1016/j.lsci.2017.01.007

Scott, D., Posner, C. M., Martin, C., & Guzman, E. (Eds.). (2018). *The education system in Mexico*. UCL Press. https://doi.org/10.14324/111.9781787350724

Secretaría de Educación Pública (SEP) [Ministry of Public Education]. (2012). *Sistema Nacional De Información Educativa* [National educational information system]. http://www.snie.sep.gob.mx/indicadores_y_pronosticos.html. Accessed 31 July 2021.

Secretaría de Educación Pública (SEP) [Ministry of Public Education]. (2017). *Aprendizajes Clave para la educación integral* [Key learnings for comprehensive education]. https://www.planyprogramasdestudio.sep.gob.mx/descargables/APRENDIZAJES_CLAVE_PARA_LA_EDUCACION_INTEGRAL.pdf. Accessed 31 July 2021.

Sistema Nacional de Información Estadística y Geográfica [National Institute of Statistics and Geography] (INEGI). (2020). *Características educativas de la población* [Educational characteristics of the population]. The Mexican Government. https://www.inegi.org.mx/temas/educacion/ Accessed 31 July 2021.

Smith, N., & Glass, W. (2019). Ready or not? Teachers' perceptions of young children's school readiness. *Journal of Early Childhood Research, 17*(4), 329–346. https://doi.org/10.1177/1476718X19875760

Terry, G., Hayfield, N., Clarke, V., & Braun, V. (2017). Thematic analysis. In C. Willig & W. Stainton-Rogers (Eds.), *The SAGE handbook of qualitative research in psychology* (pp. 17–37). SAGE. https://doi.org/10.4135/9781526405555.n2

Urbina-Garcia, A. (2019). Preschool transition in Mexico: Exploring teachers' perceptions and practices. *Teaching and Teacher Education, 85*, 226–234. https://doi.org/10.1016/j.tate.2019.06.012

Urbina-Garcia, A. (2020). An intervention programme to facilitate the preschool transition in Mexico. *Frontiers in Education, 5*(95), 1–13. https://doi.org/10.3389/feduc.2020.00095

Urbina-Garcia, A., & Kyriacou, C. (2018). Children's problems during the preschool transition: Views of Mexican teachers. *European Scientific Journal, 14*(22), 154–172. https://doi.org/10.19044/esj.2018.v14n22p154

Weikart, D. P., Rogers, L., Adcock, C., & McClelland, D. (1971). *The cognitively oriented curriculum: A framework for preschool teachers*. University of Illinois.

Wickett, K. (2017). Are we all talking the same language? Parents, practitioners and teachers preparing children to start school. In S. Dockett, W. Griebel, & B. Perry (Eds.), *Families and transition to school* (pp. 175–191). Springer. https://doi.org/10.1007/978-3-319-58329-7

Wildenger, L., & McIntyre, L. (2011). Family concerns and involvement during kindergarten transition. *Journal of Child and Family Studies, 20*(4), 387–396. https://doi.org/10.1007/s10826-010-9403-6

Wong, M. (2015). Voices of children, parents and teachers: How children cope with stress during school transition. *Early Child Development and Care, 185*(4), 658–678. https://doi.org/10.1080/03004430.2014.948872

Benilde García-Cabrero is Professor of Educational Psychology at the Universidad Nacional Autónoma de México. She has worked as a consultant and coordinator of international educational/research projects in matters of educational assessment, curriculum development, civic education, socio-emotional skills and technology-enhanced learning for several organisations, such as the Mexican Ministry of Education, the Council for Educational Development (CONAFE), the former National Institute for Educational Evaluation (INEE, now MEJOREDU), UNICEF, UNESCO and UNDP. Working with these organisations has led to the production of a vast body of empirical evidence regarding the improvement of quality education in Mexican urban and rural schools. She has published extensively in the form of scientific articles, national reports, international reports, books and book chapters and is a member of a range of professional national and international bodies. She is currently a member of the Editorial Board of the International Journal of Educational and Life Transitions and of the Scientific Committee of the Revista Internacional de Educación Emocional y Bienesta*r* (International Journal of Emotional and Wellbeing Education, RIEEB).

Angel Urbina-García is an international educational psychologist and an expert in child development with more than 15 years of experience in academia having worked in Asia, Europe and America in the field of psychology and education working with students from 50+ countries. He has held leadership positions in world-class universities and is an international researcher with significant experience in conducting research across continents using a mixed methodology and following a psycho-educational approach. He has led important international research projects with research grants from the prestigious British Academy, Leverhulme Trust, British Council and the UK's Global Challenges Research Fund. He pioneered the research on the preschool to school transition in Latin American contexts, and has now created an important international network of researchers from South East Asia (e.g., Vietnam, Cambodia, Laos, Thailand, Singapore, Hong Kong, Australia, New Zealand etc.), North America (e.g., Mexico and United States) and Latin America (e.g., Chile, Honduras, Brazil, Cuba, Argentina, Ecuador and Colombia) to conduct cross-cultural cutting-edge research. His research findings have been disseminated widely at international world-class conferences and have been published in international peer-reviewed journals. He sits on the Editorial Board of the *International Journal of Educational and Life Transitions,* and is a reviewer for several international world-leading peer-reviewed journals. He also works closely with the Regional Bureau for Education in Latin America and the Caribbean: OREALC/UNESCO Santiago de Chile.

Robert G. Myers earned a bachelor's degree from Oberlin College, a master's degree from Stanford University and a Ph.D.in Economy from the University of Chicago. He was an assistant professor of comparative education at this university, Program Officer for the Ford Foundation in Canada and Colombia, and Director of an Evaluation Study on the investment of the FORD Foundation in higher studies abroad for nationals of Third World countries. He has also been Division Director for the High/Scope Educational Research Foundation and Coordinator of the Consultative Group on Early Childhood Care and Development. Since 1997 he has been an Independent Advisor on Early Education. He has overseen initial and/or pre-school education evaluation projects in Peru (USAID), Nicaragua (UNICEF), India (Aga Khan Foundation) and Kenya (Aga Khan Foundation). He participated in the field work for the mid-term evaluation of PRODEI in Mexico, and has participated as a professor in evaluation courses (Nicaragua and Mexico). He is a member of the Society of Comparative Education and has been a member of the Board of Directors for 6 years. Currently, he is an independent educational researcher at "Hacía una Cultura Democrática, A.C." (ACUDE) [Towards a Democratic Culture, A.C.]. Mexico.

Anisai Ledesma-Rodea holds a B.A. in Psychology from the Faculty of Higher Studies Iztacala and an M.A. in Psychology with a focus on digital technologies applied to education from the National Autonomous University of Mexico (UNAM). Currently, she is a Ph.D. student in the Educational Psychology and Development programme at UNAM. She has worked as an instructional designer in a number of online courses and textbooks and has delivered courses and workshops for teachers of different educational levels focused on the development of digital skills used in education. She has designed intervention programmes in the areas of language and early literacy. Currently, she works as an assistant researcher in the project "Effects of a training program on social-emotional skills for high school mathematics teachers" led by Professor Benilde Garcia.

Marla Andrea Rangel-Cantero holds a B.A. in Psychology from the National Autonomous University of Mexico (UNAM). She has participated in the research project "Challenges in the school permanence of at risk of abandonment or academic underachieving students of the Faculty of Psychology (UNAM)". She has actively collaborated in the development of instructional manuals for teachers for programs such as ChildFund Mexico. She has also worked as an assistant teacher at the Faculty of Psychology, and has participated as academic supervisor of the program of early initiation to research in Psychology (PiTIP). Currently, she participates as an assistant researcher in the project "Effects of a training program on social-emotional skills for high school mathematics teachers".

Chapter 5
Characteristics of Cuba's Early Childhood Educational and Scientific Experience

Odet Noa Comans

Abstract In this chapter, the Cuban educational experience is presented, based on the scientific investigation *Approach to the characterization of the preschool Cuban child*, carried out by the Latin American Reference Center for Preschool Education (CELEP) during the last two decades. The value of this investigation lies in knowing the characteristics of the first 6 years of life in order to implement quality education with a positive influence on the transition to primary school. The research emphasises results about socio-affective development, since teachers do not always consider this across both pedagogical and affective domains. The analysis is fundamentally qualitative, based on an extensive bibliographic search which illustrates Cuban reality. The results reflect the predominance of positive emotional states in both boys and girls. Play is still a fundamental activity, but it has to be well conducted in order to make children gradually 'ready' for 'study activities', that will be very important in the school stage. The chapter aims to provide valid information for teachers, pedagogues, psychologists, and professionals who are already trained or are in training, as well as families, in order to contribute to successful educational practices in the transition process.

Early Childhood Education in Cuba

The Cuban early childhood education system is financed, coordinated, and regulated by the National Preschool Education Directorate of the Cuban Ministry of Education. It is a national system, specified in all of the provincial and municipal directorates throughout the country. Local implementation of the national system means that early childhood education in Cuba reaches the community level, with

---

O. N. Comans (✉)
University of Havana, Havana, Cuba

actions or tasks in early childhood implemented in each jurisdiction, based on specific geographic, demographic, and sociocultural conditions (Rios et al., 2016).

There is a nationwide curriculum, organised into five dimensions of education and development: education and social-personal development education and development of motor skills; education and development of the relationship with the environment; education and development of communication; education and aesthetic development (Cáceres Suárez & Benavides Perera, 2019). One of the strengths of the curriculum is that the educational policy to be followed is based on scientific research. The aim of the curriculum is to achieve maximum possible overall development of each child from birth to 6 years of age (Gallo et al., 2018). Early childhood education provision serves more than 99% of the Cuban child population through two modalities: an institutional one in kindergartens and in the preschool grade of primary schools; and a non-institutional one through the socio-community program *Educate your child* (Alliance for Human Development, 2021).

There are kindergartens in all Cuban provinces with priority access given to children of working parents. Children who attend kindergarten are between 1 year of age (when they can walk independently) and 5 years of age. However, the demand for educational care is greater than the capacity of the institutions, which is why *Educate your child* program was created. *Educate your child* serves approximately 68% of the Cuban child population between 0 and 6 years of age, with families prepared to educate their own children. Among the program's key features are:

- It is coordinated by the Cuban Ministry of Education, with intersectoral participation.
- It was founded 28 years ago.
- It is designed for non-working mothers and fathers.
- Its objective is to prepare families, based on their knowledge and experiences, to carry out educational activities with their children from 0 to 6 years old in the home setting.
- It is focused on the family and the community as the leading protagonists in the children's care and development. It is a social program of integrated educational care that deals with the diverse aspects of the development of children, such as health, nutrition, intellectual and socio-affective development, and protection, in an integrated, intersectoral, and participative manner.
- It is implemented as a 'joint activity' in communities and homes. The staff who run the program act as promoters and advisors. Collaboratively with the family, they organise learning activities.
- The program is implemented at community level throughout the entire country, generally with two-weekly frequency. Joint activities last approximately 1 h daily.
- Staff in the program are volunteers and receive specialised professional training towards a Bachelor's Degree in Early Childhood Education.
- The program model has been replicated in different countries of the region. It is a low-cost and highly efficient alternative to centre-based programs, and is flexible and adaptable to the particular needs and situations of different families.

- The program is attended by groups of children between the ages of 2 and 3 and between 4 and 5 years and their families. There is also an individual modality for children with special needs or other needs that do not allow them to attend group sessions. This individual modality is conducted at children's homes by program staff together with the families.

Some of the success factors of the *Educate your child* program (Laire, 2016) are:

1. The impact of early care on the further development of the person.
2. The enormous potential of the family in their children's education, especially during the early years.
3. The search for non-formal approaches to early childhood education as a result of the difficult domestic economic conditions which commenced in the 1990s.
4. The extension of paid maternity or paternity leave, which allows the working mother or father to stay with their child at home during the first year after birth.
5. The need to cater for families in rural and remote areas with non-institutionalised early childhood education opportunities.
6. A decrease in the number of children not achieving expected outcomes.
7. Improvement of academic performance in primary school.
8. Contribution to the preparation of families to educate their children in COVID-19 conditions (Castro et al., 2020).

Any beneficial impacts are dependent on the quality of early childhood education (ECE), which should provide a learning environment for all children to succeed in acquiring social, emotional, cognitive, and linguistic skills (García-Carrión & Villardón-Gallego, 2016).

When a child enters any educational program in early childhood from the home context, there is a transition process. If the early childhood program is very different from what occurs within the family circle, the transition can become difficult. How difficult it will be depends, among other things, on the characteristics of the program. Given this, it might be presumed that a non-formal program such as *Educate your child* would facilitate an adequate transition for the child (Peralta, 2007).

The current Cuban pedagogical theory is drawn from a cultural historical approach which, fundamentally, adopts a humanistic and optimistic position where personality is not seen as innate, with its formation and development closely linked to educational and cultural experiences (Menéndez & Peña, 2019). Development is understood to be a process that occurs as a result of education. It is continuous and builds on previous development. Each stage creates the foundational basis for the next. The achievements in each new stage have their beginnings in the previous stage in which they appear as potential achievement in future. In any development, specific social conditions must be taken into account at each stage (Burke, 2006).

Early childhood education in Cuba is considered the basis of the national educational system. It is responsible for the development of children from 0 to 6 years of age with the aim of their transition into the primary school where their education until the age of 11–12 years will be continued. Basic secondary and upper secondary levels conclude children's school education (Menéndez & Peña, 2019).

Considerations of the historical-cultural conception of early childhood education allow us to make some reflections about transitions in Cuba:

- Highlighting the children's social interaction, from which they appropriate the maternal and spiritual culture, it can be affirmed that children actively participate in the rhythm and quality of their transitions.
- Transitions can be considered as key moments in the sociocultural learning process, through which children modify their behavior based on what they learn through social interaction with their environment (Burke, 2006).

There are three different types of transitions that arise from consideration of cultural-historical theory:

1. those that occur in the family space;
2. those from the family-social environment to an institution; and
3. the transition that is made to the primary school (Peralta, 2007).

In Cuba, these three types can be exemplified as:

1. From the family space to the *Educate your child* program. In the first year of the child's life the family attend an appointment at the family doctor's office which exists in each community. The doctor and nurse are also promoters of the *Educate your child* program and offer educational guidance to families on the development of their babies.
2. From the family space to the group or individual modality of the *Educate your child* program, starting at the second year of life.
3. From the family space to the kindergarten.
4. From the kindergarten to the preschool group of primary school.
5. From the preschool group to the first grade of primary school.

Cuban Educational Policy on the Process of Transition to Primary Education

Cuban educational policy guarantees an affective, coherent, and developing educational process. The need for continuity of children's development has been foreseen in the early childhood education curriculum. One of the most important components is the preschool diagnosis.

To determine how well children who graduate from early childhood to primary education are prepared, a set of diagnostic tasks is carried out. These explore the development achieved in areas directly related to the knowledge and skills they will acquire in the first grade. For example, the diagnostic tasks explore certain content from the curriculum dimensions of education and development of communication, education and development of the relationship with the environment, education and personal social development, and education and aesthetic development. Together, this content contributes to the learning of writing, reading, and mathematics which children will experience when they start first grade (Menéndez & Peña, 2019).

The preschool diagnosis is applied by the early childhood educator, accompanied by first grade teacher. They are advised to complement the result of the tasks with individual annotations, partial and final evaluations about the knowledge, habits, abilities, and norms of relations with the world of each child, as well as ways of learning during the child's journey through early childhood. Such an approach is consistent with suggestions about collaboration between preschool and school settings which moves beyond the sharing of information about children to joint initiatives that foster shared pedagogies and classroom practices (Hugo et al., 2018).

Diagnosis at the preschool level articulates and gives continuity to the educational process at both levels of education, also contributing to the educational transition from preschool to primary school. The pedagogical diagnosis undertaken of the children at the end of the sixth year of life allows the educator to evaluate the effectiveness of the curriculum and the child's mastery in applying it, as well as the characteristics of the students and educators that have influenced the entire pedagogical work. The diagnosis guarantees the assessment of the skills, habits, and capacities of the children as a consequence of the educational experiences they have. It is, in turn, an effective way for the first grade teacher to become familiar with their future students in the different spaces in which they plan to be, regardless of the final process of application of the diagnostic tasks (Menéndez & Peña, 2019).

Knowing the characteristics of each child's development as they move from the playful preschool context to a fully schooled context is important in order to avoid unfavourable breakdowns in the educational process. During this move, changes occur in the system of relationships among the child and adults and among the children themselves. Play remains a fundamental activity and it is important for it to be continued effectively in order for children to prepare gradually for studying, which is seen as the most important part of the school stage (López & Siverio, 2016).

The Cuban educational system reiterates this approach with the Ministry of Education in Cuba regulating

> the consolidation of the continuity and articulation of early childhood, primary and special education, as well as the intersectoral, inter-institutional and community coordination for educational care, with the gradual transition of a level of education to another, that favors the concatenation between them, as well as between the educational modalities, years of life, cycles. This is conditioned by ways of working, methods, means and processes. (MINED, 2018)

Approach to the Characterisation of the Cuban Preschool Child. A Look at Scientific Research

This section of the chapter is based on information collected through an extensive desk review of previous research about the characteristics of Cuban preschool children. The investigation entitled *Approach to the characterization of the Cuban preschool children* was carried out in Cuba (López et al., 2011).

The main objective of the project was to explore the characteristics of children aged 0 to 6 years and to contribute to the training of families and educators who are responsible for the children's education. The results of this study have been used in a range of Cuban research, providing a theoretical and methodological platform for studies of Cuban early childhood education. For example, it provided the basis for the study of Cuban children's access to and use of digital technologies (Comans, 2020).

Methodology and Procedure

The study of the characterisation of Cuban preschool children was designed to consider annual cross sections through six areas of children's development: motor; language; intellectual; socio-affective; social personal; and growth and health. It used a longitudinal design with cross sections considered in each year of life. Descriptive approaches were used, in order to identify the particularities of the development of children at these ages.

The research was carried out in seven provinces of Cuba: Guantánamo; Santiago de Cuba; Sancti Spíritus; Villa Clara; Habana; Ciudad Habana; and Pinar del Río. These locations were intentionally included, based on the requirements: to cover the three regions of the country; availability of personnel at provincial level with the required preparation for the execution of tasks; and an assessment of social development and education achieved in these territories.

In each province, a sample of 600 children distributed equitably in a main municipality and in a marginal urban one was selected, totalling 4200 children altogether. The sample was stratified by 3 months in the first year of life; by 4 months in the second year; and, in the case of the third year of life, the age interval between 2 years and 8 months and 3 years and 15 days, that is, four and a half months. To carry out the research, a national group was formed under the organisation and direction of the Latin American Reference Center for Preschool Education (CELEP). This team brought together specialists from different areas of child development, representing the following organisations and institutions: CELEP; the National Institute of Sports, Physical Education and Recreation (INDER); the University of Pedagogical Sciences *Enrique José Varona*; the City of Havana; the Faculty of Psychology of the University of Havana; and the Ministry of Public Health (MINSAP). The national group was made up of subgroups that studied the different areas of development mentioned above. The selection of researchers was determined by the experience of each one in the specific aspects of the study. In order to carry out the study in different provinces, it was necessary to establish in each province a research team made up of methodologists, managers and teachers from the higher pedagogical institutes with a general preparation in child development, especially relating to preschool aged children, and with a deeper and more specific knowledge in the explored areas. In each municipality, a leader was selected among the field researchers by development area. These people coordinated and controlled the work of the team members in conjunction with the head of the research at the municipality level.

Preliminary analysis of existing sources and research was carried out to determine the indicators and aspects to be assessed in each sphere of development, the procedures for analysing the results, as well as the orientation and control of the work of the provincial teams. The methods and instruments for data collection were interviews, direct observation, and pedagogical situations. Interviews were conducted with families. Both parents were interviewed whenever possible. The aim was to collect opinions from both parents around the following topics: motor skills; intellectual development; language development; socio-affective development; and health care of their children across the ages from 0 to 6 years. The interview targetting the socio-affective area aimed to explore relationships between parents and children.

Interviews were conducted in the home setting. Field notes were made about the family structure, material conditions, and organisation of the home. Generally, the research team followed a pre-structured interview guide, with around 42 questions. The guide provided opportunity for questions to be re-phrased or the asking of follow-up questions. During the visit, observation data were also collected about the child's social behaviours, emotional reactions, and communication at home, mainly with their mother and father.

The pedagogical situations were a group of experimental tasks. Their general objective was to explore children's achievements across each developmental area in each age group. An example of an experimental task in the socio-affective area was called *the activity collaboration*. This task aimed to collect information about relationships, adult-child communication, their behaviour, and expressions. The indicators of the child's socio-affective development were assessed by the field researcher, according to a rating of YES (achieved) or NO (not achieved).

In addition to this, the methods of data collection were piloted to assess the degree of understanding of the instruments by the parents and the field researchers and to make the necessary adjustments before their final application. The piloting in each stage was carried out in La Lisa municipality of La Havana.

Results

Some of the results (López et al., 2011) from this study are described below. Analysis was reported according to each child's age in each of the developmental areas listed. Differences were found and reported, with special emphasis on the socio-affective area.

One important result was that, depending on the developmental characteristics of the children, transitions can be more or less difficult. The level of challenge was largely seen to depend on a child's emotional state and their affective development (Laire, 2016).

As part of the characterisation of socio-affective development in children from 0 to 3 years of age, the following results were noted:

- prevalence of positive mood;
- the most frequent emotions were joy and pleasure, which were expressed through smiles, mimes, gestures, and movements. Curiosity towards animals was also seen and, to a lesser extent, anger and anguish; and
- collaborative relationships with family and other close adults.

The socio-affective development of children from 4 to 6 years old was distinguished by:

- the manifestations of positive emotions are gaining variety and richness in their expression;
- the main feelings and emotions are love, joy, pride, shame, solidarity, and aesthetic feelings;
- there was a prevalence of verbal expression of these affective states;
- interest in the recognition of the adult in the activity increases and the presence of the feeling of sympathy expands; and
- self-evaluations begin, although the evaluations made by adults of their actions are still of great importance to the children.

One of the most significant results of the research was that it has shown the dynamism of child development, which is in constant evolution.

When going from 1 year of life to another and as part of the development process there are three phases:

1. consolidation of the learning and emergence of new learnings;
2. strengthening of these new learnings; and
3. beginning of the consolidation of the acquired learning. (López et al. 2011).

During each year of life, time must be given so that children, in their own way, consolidate what has already been acquired and incorporate new formations. The results obtained from this study have contributed to the elaboration of a more relevant curriculum for Cuban early childhood education and to a more adequate direction of the educational process by educators and families (Laire, 2016). These results have informed the country's educational policy (Menéndez & Peña, 2019). The process included challenges such as putting more emphasis on socio-affective education from early childhood education to facilitate their transitions to school.

Conclusions

Based on the results of the reported scientific research, it is concluded that the transition from one stage of education and development to another must occur naturally and gradually; adequate preparation must be guaranteed, for children, as well as for teachers and family members involved.

Across the study, the predominance of positive emotional states in boys and girls was described. The positive behaviour could be a tendency in Cuban children. However, the manifestations of positive emotions are very diverse and their expressions range from a little interaction with unfamiliar adults to caring a lot about what adults think of them, largely dependent on children's age.

Play is still a fundamental activity that has to be well conducted in order to prepare children gradually for another activity that is seen as the most important of the school stage, namely, study activity. If a child experiences the adult evaluation as a natural and happy process, he/she will associate the evaluation experience with positive emotions and this could be very favourable for school readiness.

In conclusion, guidelines are recommended that, although they are being materialised in the Cuban context, need further scientific research to be undertaken and applied to the practice of education for children from 0 to 6 years old. The recommended guidelines include:

- transition and continuity of children's development should be reflected in the early childhood education curriculum;
- an effective and coherent, educational process throughout the transition period to be guaranteed;
- teachers and families to continue to be seen as major contributors to transition to primary school;
- the diagnosis of levels of development shown by boys and girls starting school learning to be carried out in nuanced ways which allow teachers to access data to assist them in organising, guiding, and directing their pedagogical work;
- teacher preparation to be strengthened to make the first grade of primary school more like preschool; and
- the families in the different care modalities to be educated in the diagnostic process, with the aim of moving beyond just wanting good results for their children to expecting realistic assessments of their children's development.

References

Alliance for Human Development. (2021). *Educate your child.* http://ahd.ca/our-projects/cuba-exclusive-birth-study/educate-your-child-program/. Accessed 19 July 2021.

Burke, M. T. (2006). *De preescolar a escolar* [From preschool to school]. Official Report of the International Congress of Early Childhood Education. Latinoamerican Center of Early Childhood Education.

Cáceres Suárez, Y., & Benavides Perera, Z. (2019). La evaluación del desarrollo integral de los niños de la primera infancia desde lo social-personal [The evaluation of the integral development of early childhood children from the social-personal point of view]. *Varona. Revista Científico Metodológica, 69*, e6. http://scielo.sld.cu/scielo.php?script=sci_arttext&pid=S1992-82382019000200006&lng=es&tlng=es. Accessed 19 July 2021

Castro, P. L., Campo, I. C., Demósthene, L., Leyva, M., Álvarez, L., Ríos, I., et al. (2020). *Familias y educandos retornamos a clase con nuevos saberes y retos. Guía de apoyo para familias y educadores* [Families and students return to class with new knowledge and challenges. Support guide for families and educators]. Instituto Central de Ciencias Pedagógicas-UNICEF.

Comans, O. N. (2020). *El uso de los audiovisuales como medio de desarrollo en la primera infancia* [The audiovisual use as a means of development in early childhood] (Vol. 27, pp. 21–37). Perfiles de la Cultura Cubana. http://www.perfiles.cult.cu/articulos/2-Perfiles-num27-Noa%20Comans_O.pdf. Accessed 19 July 2021.

Gallo, M. A., Quintero, O., Cáceres, Y., Pentón, D., Menéndez, C., Díaz, M., et al. (2018). *Programa educativo de cinco a seis años de edad* [Educational program for ages five to six]. Editorial Pueblo y Educación.

García-Carrión, R., & Villardón-Gallego, L. (2016). Dialogue and interaction in early childhood education: A systematic review. *Multidisciplinary Journal of Educational Research, 6*(1), 51–76. https://doi.org/10.17583/remie.2016.1919

Hugo, K., McNamara, K., Sheldon, K., Moult, F., Lawrence, K., Forbes, C., et al. (2018). Developing a blueprint for action on the transition to school: Implementation of an action research project within a preschool community. *International Journal of Early Childhood., 50*(2), 241–257. https://doi.org/10.1007/s13158-018-0220-1

Laire, C. (2016). *Early childhood development in Cuba*. UNICEF Oficina Regional para América Latina y el Caribe. https://www.unicef.org/cuba/media/591/file/early-childhood-development-cuba-2016.pdf. Accessed 19 July 2021.

López, J., & Siverio, A. M. (2016). *El diagnóstico: Un instrumento de trabajo pedagógico: De preescolar a escolar* (Tercera edición) [The diagnosis: An instrument of pedagogical work: From preschool to school (3rd ed.)]. Editorial Pueblo y Educación.

López, J., Siverio, A. M., Burke, M. T., Rios, I., Valdés, M., Hernandez, M., et al. (2011). *Informe de la aproximación a la caracterización del niño preescolar cubano* [Report of the approach to the characterization of the Cuban preschool child]. Cuban Academy of Sciences.

Menéndez, C., & Peña, P. (2019). *Folleto de orientación para la aplicación de tareas diagnósticas para niños y niñas que egresan de la primera infancia* [Guidance leaflet for the application of diagnostic tasks for children graduating from early childhood]. Ministerio de Educación.

MINED. (2018). *Preparación del curso escolar* [Preparation of the school year]. Ministry of Education.

Peralta, M. V. (2007). *Transiciones en educación infantil: Un marco para abordar el tema de calidad* [Transitions in early childhood education: A framework to address the issue of quality]. O.E.A Symposium, Washington, DC. http://educacioninicial.mx/wp-content/uploads/2017/11/TRANSICIONES-EN-EDUCACION-INFANTIL.pdf. Accessed 19 Aug 2021.

Ríos, I., Díaz, M., Pérez, M., Travieso, I., De la Vega, I., Brito, et al. (2016). *Por una educación de calidad en la primera infancia. Programa de superación para directivos y educadoras* [For quality early childhood education. Improvement program for managers and educators]. Editorial Nomos-UNICEF.

Odet Noa Comans is a researcher and associate professor in the field of education and Early Childhood Development. She has been a technical teacher advisor for the Latin American Reference Centre for Preschool Education (CELEP) and the Central Institute of Pedagogical Sciences (ICCP) Cuba. She collaborates with the Faculty of Psychology of the University of Havana and the University of Pedagogical Sciences "Enrique Jose Varona" Cuba. Odet maintains professional relationship with UNESCO, she did a CONFINTEA research internship in 2017 at the Institute of Educational Planning (IIEP) and collaborates with the "UNESCO Chair" Initiative with Deusto University. Her main research interest is on family roles in early childhood education, with particular emphasis on parental mediators around audiovisual media and their impact on children's development. She has published her work nationally and internationally. Currently, she is finalising her PhD at Deusto University in Spain. She is the Vice-President of the Cuban Committee of the World Organisation for Early Childhood Education (OMEP).

Chapter 6
Play-Study Unit: The Pedagogical Conduct of Year One in Maringa, Brazil

Ágatha Marine Pontes Marega and **Marta Sueli de Faria Sforni**

Abstract In Brazil, Year One is the threshold where the transition between playing and study activities starts. This chapter describes a research project in Maringá, Brazil, focused on the teaching organisation of Year One in the primary school. The study was foregrounded on theoretical perspectives advanced by Vygotsky, Leontiev and Elkonin, which position play and study as activities that trigger children's holistic development and have a fundamental role in Year One. The point of departure for the experiment was the convergence of play and study, articulated around the conceptual theme of 'means of transport'. The experiment followed stages of observing children's play and introducing subject content related to the transport theme to promote children's awareness of social roles. The experiment recognized that play and study do not have the same structure but can have the same content focus. The study highlighted how subject content introduced at school can prompt children to go beyond the reproduction of daily relationships that commonly occur in free play and broaden their knowledge of the world through access to scientific knowledge. Results of the study note the pedagogical importance of integrating play and study in Year One. The investigation highlighted the importance of conducting further research to investigate how transition processes integrate play and study in Year One.

Á. M. P. Marega (✉)
Universidade de São Paulo (USP), São Paulo, Brazil
e-mail: agathamarega@usp.br

M. S. de Faria Sforni
Universidade Estadual de Maringá Brasil, Maringá, Brazil

© The Author(s), under exclusive license to Springer Nature Switzerland AG 2022
A. Urbina-García et al. (eds.), *Transitions to School: Perspectives and Experiences from Latin America*, International Perspectives on Early Childhood Education and Development 37, https://doi.org/10.1007/978-3-030-98935-4_6

Introduction

The enactment of Act 11.114, published on the 16th May 2005, (Brasil, 2005) and Act 11.274, published on the 6th February 2006 (Brasil, 2006), extended the period of basic education from 8 to 9 years and made children's enrolment in school from their sixth year mandatory. The extension of the school period is one of the aims of the Brazilian Education Plan (PNE), promoting comprehensive fundamental schooling for everybody between the ages of 6 and 14-years. It makes possible a longer schooling period for Brazilian children. The inclusion of 6-year-old children in basic schooling was greatly debated by parents, teachers, and researchers in Brazil.

Within the agreement-disagreement debate, at the Act's approbation by Parliament, the theme of children's transition to basic education featured strongly. This was based on the understanding that children's early education was related to playing, whereas basic education ruptured this tradition and inserted children within the formal requirements of schooling. On the one hand, people insisted that 6-year-old children should remain within the children's early education conditions where infancy is respected and games and play would continue to feature within children's educational lives. Beneath such an opinion, there is the concept that, in elementary education, study requirements are greater, with no space for playing and games. On the other hand, educators held that Year One primary is an important moment for the development of 6-year-old children since a new social place is open to them and studies emerge as a new and highly relevant activity.

Many feared that children's inclusion in mandatory education would place them very early in formal and routine teaching situations, robbing them of space and time allotted to childhood. "Will the child cease to play in Year One?" "Which curriculum will be adapted to Year One primary?" "Has the 6-year-old child the maturity to participate in basic (elementary) education?" These were important questions at that time and implicitly expressed the idea that playing and studying were antagonistic activities which could not occupy the same space.

Fourteen years after the publication of the Act, research work is necessary on this transition period so that pedagogical pathways may be discovered that would contribute towards children's development: "How would pedagogical conduct be administered during this particular school year?" "What is actually important for children's development at this age?" "Would it be playing, an activity proper to children, or the study of school subject matters?"

In this chapter, we report theoretical and practical research that the authors have developed in a Year One class to investigate play and study activities within pedagogical conduct. The current research is based on the theoretical perspectives of historical and cultural psychology, especially the works of Vygostky, Leontiev and Elkonin. The experiment was undertaken in a government-run school in Maringá, Brazil.

Transition Period and Activities of Children's Development

Feelings of 'suffering', 'loss' or 'fear of the novelty' are experienced in the transition from one determined schooling stage to another. Some parents or guardians are worried about the future new stage and fear that the children will not follow the new routine. Children may also have the same fear, even though, as a rule, they have a great curiosity about the novel school space and joy in their admittance. In their opinion, the primary school means having homework to do, keeping exercise books, having new friends. In other words, a new world to be discovered.

To facilitate the children's transition from early childhood to basic education, several schools have introduced the practice of celebrating a welcome week within the new school space. The new routine, the school premises and the professionals working there are presented, coupled to several activities to integrate the newcomers. According to Sforni (2019), the welcome week is an important activity, although it must be understood as one (but not the only one) of many necessary activities. It is a mere moment of showing change and not a complete transition process. When seen externally, change has a fixed date. However, "from the subjective point of view, or rather, from the point of view of the person who experiences change, it is not something with a duration of one day or one month, but it involves a period before and after the fact in itself. Therefore, it is necessary to speak of a transition *process*" (Sforni, 2019, p. 285). In Leontiev's words (2004, p. 315), transition requires a "rationally conducted process, of directed education" so that change triggers development, rather than be a hindrance to development.

The transition from play activity to study activity occurs during the period in which children are enrolled in Year One of primary school. An in-depth study of the characteristics of these activities will help us to undertake the pedagogical processes involved in this transition.

Playing activities derive from the experiences that children have participating in adult life and in undertaking activities done by adults, even though they do not have the power to undertake the corresponding activities themselves. Since they do not have the conditions to materialize them effectively, they produce playful situations to exercise their social role. For example, when they play at being physicians, children penetrate the adult world pretending to be doctors, patients, or nurses. Through 'sham' social roles, children appropriate the contents of human relationships and develop. When children play at 'pretending to be', they model relationships between people (Elkonin, 1987).

According to Elkonin, study activities occur at the precise moment when children are inserted within a systematised teaching system. Access to writing allows the occurrence of knowledge not merely through the direct interaction of people, objects, and phenomena, but also through the appropriation of knowledge on the different sciences. According to Elkonin (1969), enrolment in the primary school has a new social meaning to children: children have their first social function in the school, or rather, the role of students, with duties, rights and responsibilities. When Year One students undertake their new social role, they still have their own ways of thinking and acting from the experiences lived during childhood and kindergarten years. Simultaneously, they are aware of school tasks that, normally, differentiate them from the former experience, such as subject matter determined by areas of knowledge, individual activities, a greater number of activities in their exercise book, the use of handbooks, and formal assessments. These differences are augmented by a school organization with stricter rules with regard to punctuality, discipline, and accountability.

The novelty that accompanies basic (elementary) education comprises study activities aligned with subjects and specific teaching-learning methods. Such activities generate the students' development and a new formation is produced: the initial bases of awareness and theoretical thought. This formation is provided by learning the notions of the different sciences that make up the school curriculum. Learning demands specific methods that involve high levels of abstraction, generalization, and mental planning (Davidov, 1988).

According to Leontiev (2004), the change of place that student-agents occupy is the motivating force in the development of their psyche. However, it is not the place in itself that determines the agents´ development but the activities that are developed by them in the new place. Consequently, admittance to the mandatory primary school causes reorganisation in 6-year-old children, but does not immediately cause a change in their psychic activity. So that study activities may have meaning for children, they should be pushed or motivated by necessity. In other words, so that children start studying, they should be motivated by a need to study which is not exactly felt. When the necessity to study arises, playfulness is still present as a motif for children's activities.

Therefore, one is usually aware of some moments reserved for free play during the first years of school and an attempt to reconcile study with play. In this case, playing is frequently employed as a tool to teach certain subject matter, such as pedagogical games to learn the letters of the alphabet, hopscotch to count numbers, music to memorise information and others. However, when they become a resource of learning, playing and games become distanced from their original function.

We must not conceive the above as the addition of two activities and reserving time and space for each. It is useless to integrate the two activities formally within the classroom context and keep them without any communication. How may one rationally conduct such transition? Theoretical studies show that, in spite of the differences, there is no dichotomy between playing and study activities. However, it was not clear how to organise teaching for children of this age group so that there would be a convergence between the two activities.

We have considered that the rational conduct of the transition process would start within a mutual relationship in which the two activities interpenetrate and interact. The following didactic experiment was undertaken to analyse, in practice, a type of teaching organisation with this feature.

Didactic Experiment: Subject Matter in a Play-Study Unit

Several studies have provided theoretical bases to analyse the organisation of teaching of Year One primary and provide structure for the didactic experiment.[1] The Year One classroom where the experiment was conducted is located in a municipal government school and comprised 24 students. More than half the students had attended municipal early childhood education centres; two students had been enrolled in the educational institution for the first time; and a small number came from private infant/early childhood education schools. Slightly more than 50% of the children were 6 years old. The experiment was performed in ten sessions, with 2 h each, over 1 month.

We analysed the curricular outline of Year One to choose the subject matter that would prompt students in the discovery of new human activities and make possible new themes/arguments for games (Moya et al., 2019). We selected the subject matter 'means of transport' from the different curriculum contents and used it as a theme/argument within the game of social roles for the didactic experiment. The choice was due to two factors:

1. although it is a subject matter within the everyday life of the children, the human activity that surrounds it seems to be significant to broaden their knowledge beyond day-to-day experience;
2. 'means of transport' is a concept with great possibilities of generalisation.

The derived ideas (car, driver, plane, ship, bicycle, and others) may easily be inserted in 'once-upon-a-time' situations and connect formal content and playful activities.

For the sake of analysis, we organised the sessions into three thematic stages, with common aims (Table 6.1).

Children's manifestations were observed and registered during the experiment. According to Vygotsky (2004), in the wake of the plurality of facts, we are normally aware of what lies within our interest, or we are guided by a succession of facts. However, scientific observation requires that researchers select beforehand the facts that they would observe according to the aims of their investigation. Scientific observation does not merely serve "to describe facts, but to explain them, or rather, to discover their causes and bases" (Vygotsky, 2004, p. 434). Our observation was

Table 6.1 Didactic experiment: Content of the social role games

1st step	Observation of games by children with toys related to means of transport;
2nd step	Introduction to subject matter 'means of transport' with music, stories, images and film strips; and
3rd step	Social roles mediated (argument 'plane') with thematic objects.

---

[1] The didactic experiment was structured using Vygotsky's genetic-experimental method, with interest in the genesis and the development of higher psychological functions.

directed towards a relationship between teaching activities and students' learning evidenced by playful activities.

In the first step of the didactic experiment, we perceived that the children were playing with toys related to means of transport, with the mediation of the teacher. The following toys were available: a cattle-truck, several types of cars, miniature transport kit, Formula One car, truck, bucket truck, construction truck, motorbike, jet plane, pink car with jet-ski and coloured building blocks. This step was used to observe whether the toys would stimulate the children in creating characters and roles within games; how the children-toy relationship would be established; and which themes and subject matter would appear in the game.

According to Japiassu (2007), the game's ontogenetic development consists of multiple phases:

1. imitation or manipulation of the objects;
2. pretending, with personification;
3. pretending with personification and projection;
4. projected pretending; and
5. daydreaming.

The situations perceived in the games developed by the children mostly corresponded to the imitation or handling of the objects, such as the movement of the jet plane by friction, the movement of the truck around traffic lights or the construction of a garage with the coloured blocks to harbour the jet plane. These are activities that belong to the first step of the ontogenetic development of games, as described by Japiassu (2007). Generally, the games with toys mobilised playful activities governed by the objects and showed that games in themselves do not make possible the game of social roles, or rather, they are not objects that orient the game but the subject matter that the children have on a particular theme or argument.

Some games correspond to pretending activities with personification and projection (Japiassu, 2007). We underscore three situations with these characteristics:

1. several girls started a game with the pink car, the jet-ski, and strawberry-shaped dolls to which roles were attributed; however, they soon changed the game and started to play with a beauty parlour, with one of them pretending to be the manicurist and the others the clients;
2. other children took other roles, such as housewives, residents on a premise or invaders of a castle. However, they did not demonstrate specific attitudes in these roles, or rather, representation was rather generic; and
3. several children took the role of the interlocutor and the pilot of a racing car, the pilot of an army helicopter and the role of mother and son/daughter.

Themes may be also perceived in the games: castle, farm, army, war, Formula One race, hotel, beauty parlour, and shopping. Except in the army, beauty parlour, and Formula One race themes, the children failed to adopt social roles, such as shopkeeper or hotel receptionist. In the games involving the themes of army and Formula One race, developed by two children, we identified a type of projected pretending. This occurs when the child does not use their body in the game but 'animates' the objects. According to Japiassu (2007, p. 35), children "construct an imaginary plot and materialise the 'cinema director' since they coordinate, and simultaneously observe, the development of the events in the sites imagined".

Generally, in the situations under analysis, it became evident that, although children were interested in the toys, the latter did not trigger a theme/argument related to the 'means of transport' subject. At the end of the first step, we observed that:

1. the toys generally provided activities immediately linked to the objects or to planned constructs;
2. toys evoked certain themes to the games – for example, the jet plane triggered a game with a pilot and enemy armies – but sufficient subject matter is necessary on the theme for the development of the game; and
3. the themes/arguments for the game were directed by the set of subject matter that the students had, or rather, by the knowledge that they had on the real phenomena.

According to Elkonin (1998), the developmental dynamics of the game are divided into two groups: the group of object relationships in which the game's content lies in the activities with the objects and the group of personal relationships in which the game's subject matter lies within the representation of roles related to social relationships. We perceived that, as a rule, the toys failed to create the representation of roles related to human activities.

Consequently, Elkonin's (1998) conclusion may be restated: toys do not foreground the game; the subject matter that children have on a determined theme foregrounds the game. These children had never experienced war and probably they had never witnessed a jet plane fire a missile. However, these subject matters, albeit distant from their immediate life, are provided by the social media and are imitated by the children.

Although children experience many human activities, they reproduce only some of them. For instance, children pretend to be manicurists, to be at war, to be mother and son/daughter, or rather, they imitate that part of reality that is enhanced in their daily life: the beauty industry, violence, and daily relationships. Games reveal that children's worlds are not 'a fantasy island', but the reproduction of the social universe with all its contradictions.

We also observed that social media have appropriated a central role in the formation of students´ thought. This observation reinforces the school's need to have a more active role in enhancing students' cultural universe by providing them with new subject matter. When the school fails to provide new subject matter to play with, when the school thinks it is 'respecting' children's freedom when it gives mere space for free playing, it is leaving children in the grip of the only mode of seeing and knowing the world normally provided by the cultural industry.

Consequently, the role of schooling is to enrich children's cultural repertoire so that they may have new subject matter and new roles to be enacted in their games. Study activities may be the condition for the advancement of children's knowledge about the world and broadening their possibilities for the representation of human activities.

To end the first step of the experiment, we had another meeting. The children were divided into three groups and the following themes were drawn: bus, plane and ship. During the games, we perceived that the children were not concerned with the role rules represented by them. Situations between passengers and driver, between pilot and flight attendants, or pedestrians and drivers were not extant. Generally, the students were concerned with sounds or movements produced by the means of transport.

Consequently, the game of social roles related to the theme 'means of transport' did not occur since the students did not have the required subject matter to represent them.

After the analysis of step one of the experiment, in which the children acted freely with the objects, we organised the intervention stages to direct the game pedagogically. Our aim was to introduce different content related to means of transport and analyse the manner in which games occurred after our intervention. We linked the subject matter to literacy situations that are part of the pedagogical tasks of Year One primary school. The subject matter 'means of transport' is a scientific concept to be developed and should be taught theoretically. At this stage, we used different types of music, stories and images related to the subject matter.

We started the second step of the didactic experiment with the music "The plane", by Toquinho, where the personified plane speaks about itself. We discussed such subject matter as the aim of the trip, whether the trip was a work trip or just for fun, the size of the aircraft, its speed and weight. Consequently, owing to the music, we encouraged the children to talk on other means of transport they knew to help them acknowledge different categories of transport (air, sea, and land).

So that the students would approach the concept 'means of transport', we developed several related activities. For example, we used cutting and pasting activities so that the children would create posters with categories related to means of transport. Although children could differentiate air, land and sea means of transport, several could not list them as means of transport. In other words, they had not understood the features that make up a means of transport: movement, carrying passengers or cargo, and others. Lack of understanding of the concept was revealed when some children wanted to make cuttings of the sky or the sea to make the poster, reflecting the situation where

> [...] the child uses concepts but is unable to reason for their use. For example, when the small child utters the word "father", even if it uses the term in the proper context, she is not aware that it represents a type of parenthood. The use it makes of the term is linked to the person, to the object, to the thing in itself and not to the concept. (Sforni, 2004, p. 78)

So that the concept 'means of transport' is closer and more relevant to the children, we provided a sort of 'conversation' for the next meeting. We hung the posters on the blackboard and wrote the names of the 'means of transport' categories. Using a projector, we then showed the children pictures of several means of transport and the human activity related to them. Among the means of transport, the plane was chosen to continue our experiment. Since air travel is not a common thing within the daily life of the participating children, it was expected that it would give us more information in the analysis on the teaching role since their imitations would not be based on daily experience.

The following pictures were introduced: a passenger plane with its different sections (turbines, wings, axis, landing gear), a fighter jet, a supersonic plane, a pilot in the cabin, an air traffic controller, control tower, flight attendants, passengers, the crew, plane seats, passengers boarding a plane, passengers getting off a plane. As the students saw the pictures, we intervened to label the roles of those involved when required since some were unknown, such as the air traffic controller and flight attendants. Due to their uniform and the act of serving meals, the children associated the flight attendants with 'waiters', a social role which was very close to their experience.

In another meeting, two film strips[2] with plane and airport scenes were shown. We chose scenes depicting the airport environments, departure of passengers, take-off of plane, the relationship between flight attendants and passengers, the pilot's communication with passengers and others. After discussing what was happening in the scenes and the role of each person, the following invitation was given: "Let's pretend we are on a plane". Imitation of the scenes were practically without any dialogue and the students who had the role of the passengers did not manifest themselves verbally, or rather, they did not ask the help of the flight attendants and did not interact with each other. Imitation was rather timid and did not last long.

The above result showed that students were not involved in the social roles of each person on the plane. It was not a theme close to the daily life of the children, with scant subject matter in the pretending representation. The subject matter on this type of means of transport did not 'take off'. In fact, it was a key factor for the continuation of the investigation: "[...] If we want children to play at planes, soldiers, drivers, if we want that a role or another is practiced by the children, they should, above all, generalise the corresponding social functions and behavior rules" (Elkonin, 1987, p. 92).

We asked whether the game of social roles was always related to what children experienced in the home or what they saw on TV. "Can the school, through subject content, add new elements or new arguments to the children's games?" "Is it possible that the school makes clear certain behavioural norms of existing social functions beyond the daily lives of the children?"

In the first place, it seems that children only play with things they have experienced: games represent situations of daily life. According to Elkonin (1998), knowledge on the social functions of a determined person and their behavioural norms are required in order for children to enact the role. If they do not enact the roles, this is taken to mean that these social functions are not yet present in children's awareness, due to lack of sufficient knowledge of that human activity. In other words, although children know that pilots drive a plane and that the flight attendant serves

---

[2] Films were Plano de Vôo [Flightplan] and Vôo Noturno [Red Eye]. Since they are films for adults, only scenes for children were exhibited.

passengers, they are not aware of how this is done, nor do they know the relationships between the crew and the pilot, for instance.

Prior to playing the role of pilot, soldier, physician and others, small children know that pilots fly planes, soldiers fight against the enemy and shoot, the physician cures children and gives them vaccine. But the procedure in piloting planes, the relationship between the pilot and other crew members or passengers, the plane etc.; the manner in which the soldier acts, his [sic] management of weapons, his [sic] attitude with his [sic] superiors or comrades; the way the physician acts, his [sic] relationships with patients etc., all this was not sufficiently differentiated and generalised by the children (Elkonin, 1987).

Consequently, when children represent the social roles of certain people, they are also internalising social norms. However, children must learn what and how people do in order to represent the role. During our didactic experiment, we informed the children with stories, music, images and scenes of people and objects related to means of transport. We discussed the attitude of people and how they behaved on a plane.

In the third step of our didactic experiment, we organised the game of social roles on the theme 'plane', with several thematic objects. We wanted to analyse the manner in which children played after they learned more about human activities on a plane or in the airport. The objects comprised identity tags, ties, earphones, trays, oxygen masks, radio communicator, travel bags and uniform. The thematic objects actually became the most attractive elements of the game for the children. According to Elkonin (1998), the thematic objects help children in their representations and, gradually, they may be removed so that children's attention would be focused on behavioural norms of each social role rather than on the handling of the objects. Hence, Elkonin (1998) has recommended not overloading the game with unnecessary accessories.

When we reminded the children of the function of each person on a plane or an airport, we formed two groups, with approximately 10 children in each, to play in separate rooms so that we would have better conditions to observe the development of the activity. In Group 1 and in Group 2, the distribution of roles, organised by the children themselves, did not occur without conflicts. The roles of pilot and flight attendants were greatly disputed. Few children wanted to have the role of passengers and no one wanted to be the flight controller. According to Elkonin (1998), children prefer a determined role because they want to achieve their desires through representation: "In general, the preferred roles are those of people that occupy a special place in society" (Elkonin, 1998, p. 100).

We told the children that the game would be repeated several times and that all would have the opportunity of playing other roles. Thus, children who had the role of flight attendants served the passengers and this scene was repeated several times: the passengers asked for something to eat and the flight attendants served them meals. Children who represented pilots did not speak to passengers prior to departure and the flights controllers did not know exactly what to do. Perhaps, such a social role is still unknown by many people.

When these steps were covered, two issues were raised about the relationship between the playing and study activities. The first deals with the premise that the game of the social role should be enriched by subject matter. Lack of knowledge on social activities and their respective acts make it impossible for children to play roles as they are played in real life. The other issue comprises the importance of intentional and systematised teaching given by the school. Free games reveal several social problems. When no pedagogical orientation is extant, the playing activity does not necessarily promote the planned learning, highly disseminated in educational media. It is in the school that we should explore new themes for games and permit students to appropriate new subject matters.

Elkonin (1998) insists on the importance of the teacher knowing the psychological nature of games within children's development. The teacher's role involves providing themes for the game and making it possible for children to represent several social roles. If children play alone, without the teacher's help, they play with what they know and roles remain unchanged.

So that children may experiment with new roles, they have to mobilise perceptions for the details of such activity; they should be attentive to body and oral language used by the person imitated, memorise behaviour forms and imagine situations that go beyond the more immediate life context. So that this may occur, it is necessary that the teacher allows direct contact with people who have different functions or speak about these persons, making available to children several knowledge sources (Elkonin, 1998).

It would be greatly productive for children's development if they also play the roles of astronauts and extraterrestrial beings, forest guardians and endangered animals, traffic policemen and drivers, and air traffic controllers and pilots. Several subject matters and behavioural norms of different social functions would be appropriate for them and, consequently, their cultural repertoire would be greater and wider.

Final Considerations

The teaching of scientific concepts through playfulness lies within the pedagogical mediation necessary in the context of Year One primary education. This, in turn, makes possible qualitative steps forward in children's development at this schooling stage. When children learn new subject matter, they are aware of other spheres of human activities which broaden their role representations and their access to other forms of thought, abstraction, and generalisation. These are basic for later school years and for world comprehension.

Teacher intervention in games does not necessarily mean their physical presence with the children, but in the organisation of the activity, the selection of the subject matter, and the means for their incorporation to the students´ games. In other words, mediation in Year One primary education comprehends new arguments for pretending games and for teaching subject matter so that the students may have elements to play with and to study. This does not result in a stop to playing; on the contrary, it means providing the necessary substrate in children's development.

We share the presupposition of Vygotsky (2012) when he states that we cannot teach what is already known and we cannot teach only what is at the level of children's development. Progress would cease. Based on the experiment above, we conclude that when the school provides subject matter which is different from that known by children, it broadens the symbolic tools with which children react to the world through games and studies.

Although playfulness and study do not have the same structure, both have a common feature: subject matter. Activities related to subject matter demonstrate the pathway to conduct teaching rationally within Year One primary. This means that one should not strengthen the difference between these two activities, opposing them, one linked to pleasure and the other to duty, reserving space for one and then for the other. The unity of the two within the subject matter should be enacted, gradually evaluating giving pleasure through knowledge, and emphasising the richness of the novel place occupied by primary school students.

Playfulness and study are different activities but equally important in Year One primary school. One should not make a choice. When we only teach subject matter to children, we would be removing what is proper to childhood. When we provide only games, we would neglect the right of children to access systematised knowledge (Marega, 2010; Marega & Sforni, 2011).

Games may trigger in children the need to learn subject content which pervades their lives. Further, the learning of curricular subject matter may broaden their repertoire for games and playfulness. The organisation of teaching through the interweaving of these activities enriches both in a reciprocal manner, and rationally contributes to the transition process. Such organisation prevents a crisis that tends to occur by suddenly rupturing playfulness simply because children legally have moved to mandatory schooling.

References

Brasil. (2005). Law 11.114, 16 May 2005. http://www.planalto.gov.br/ccivil_03/_ato2004-2006/2005/lei/l11114.htm. Accessed 29 July 2021.
Brasil. (2006). Law 11.274. 6 February 2006. https://abmes.org.br/arquivos/legislacoes/Lei_11274_20060206.pdf. Accessed 29 July 2021.
Davidov, V. (1988). *La enseñanza escolar y el desarrollo psíquico* [School education and mental development]. Progreso.
de Moya, D. J., de Sforni, M. S. F., & Moya, P. T. (2019). Temas e conteúdos do jogo de papéis: Sinalizando caminhos para a atuação pedagógica com a atividade lúdica na educação infantil. [Themes and contents of the role game: signalling paths for pedagogical performance with playful activity in early childhood education]. *Revista Contexto & Educação, 34*(109), 121–133.
de Sforni, M. S. F (2004). *Aprendizagem conceitual e organização do ensino: contribuições da teoria da atividade* [Conceptual learning and teaching organization: Contributions from activity theory]. Junqueira Marin Editora.

de Sforni, M. S. F. (2019). Transições no processo de escolarização: da educação infantil ao ensino fundamental e dos anos iniciais aos anos finais do ensino fundamental. [Transition in the schooling process: From early childhood education to elementary school and from the early years to the final years of elementary school]. In *Currículo da Educação Municipal de Maringá*. Educação Infantil e Anos Iniciais do Ensino Fundamental.

Elkonin, D. B. (1969). Característica general del desarrollo psíquico de los niños [General characteristics of the psychic development of children]. In A. Smirnov, S. Rubenstein, A. Leontiev, & B. Tieplov (Eds.), *Psicología* [Psychology] (pp. 493–503). Grijalbo.

Elkonin, D. B. (1987). Problemas psicológicos del juego en la edad preescolar [Psychological problems of the game in the preschool age]. In M. Shuare (Ed.), *La psicologia evolutiva y pedagógica en la URSS* [Evolutionary and pedagogical psychology in the USSR] (pp. 83–102). Editorial Progreso.

Elkonin, D. B. (1998). *Psicologia do jogo* [Psychology of the game]. Martins Fontes.

Japiassu, R. (2007). *A linguagem teatral na escola* [Theatrical language at school]. Papirus.

Leontiev, A. (2004). *O desenvolvimento do psiquismo* [The development of the psyche] (2nd ed). Centauro.

Marega, Á. M. P. (2010). *A criança de seis anos na escola: transição da atividade lúdica para a atividade de estudo* [The six-year-old child at school: Transition from playful activity to study activity]. Universidade Estadual de Maringá. Master's Dissertation.

Marega, Á. M. P., & de Sforni, M. S. F. (2011). A criança de seis anos na escola: é hora de brincar ou de estudar? [The six-year-old at school: Is it time to play or study?]. *Revista Contrapontos, 11*(2), 143–151.

Vygotsky, L. S. (2004). *Psicologia pedagógica* [Pedagogical psychology]. Martins Fontes.

Vygotsky, L. S. (2012). *Obras Escogidas* (Tomo III) [Selected works (Vol. 3)]. Machado Libros.

Ágatha Marine Pontes Marega is Pedagogue at a Brazilian public school. She is currently pursuing doctoral studies in education at the Faculty Education of the University of São Paulo (USP). She is a member of the research group "Education, Society and Public Policy: Historical and Cultural Theory conceptions (GEPESPP/USP) registered at CNPq – National Council for Scientific and Technological Development. Has experience in schooling with particular emphasis on transition period; activities of children's development; study activity.

Marta Sueli de Faria Sforni is a professor at the Graduate Program in Education at the State University of Maringá (UEM) – Brazil. She has long advocated the importance of a public school that promotes the development of students through the learning of scientific concepts. Marta has been researching on conceptual learning; teaching organization; didactics and curriculum. She is the coordinator of the Group of Studies and Research in Teaching Activity (GEPAE) registered at CNPq – National Council for Scientific and Technological Development.

Chapter 7
The Transition from Early Childhood Education to Fundamental Education in São Paulo, Brazil: Formatives and Political (Dis)Agreements?

Patrícia Dias Prado and Angélica de Almeida Merli

Abstract This chapter presents analyses of doctoral research being conducted through the School of Education at the University of São Paulo (FEUSP) which investigates children's transition from early childhood education to fundamental education, within the Municipal Education Network of the city of São Paulo/SP, Brazil. The data have been generated through observation, monitoring and coordination of training meetings on the theme, with a target audience of professionals working in early childhood education and in the early years of fundamental education. Data include field notes, audio recordings and video (with permission), and document analysis of municipal and federal policies, informed by the field of childhood pedagogy. In addition to showing how curricula documents have addressed this transition, the joint analyses of the comments and reflections of professionals reveal the importance of: orientations to educational units, management and teaching teams to reduce disruptions in the passage of children from one step to the other; expansion of spaces for integrated training among professionals in early childhood education and fundamental education; the role of teaching and management teams in the actions of articulation between the two stages, with emphasis on pedagogical coordination; and the guarantee of the right to childhood, to play, and to the care and role of children and professionals in both.

P. D. Prado (✉)
Universidade de São Paulo, São Paulo, Brazil

School of Education, University of São Paulo (FEUSP), São Paulo, Brazil
e-mail: patprado@usp.br

A. de Almeida Merli
São Paulo Municipal Education Network (PMSP), São Paulo, Brazil
e-mail: angelicamerli@usp.br

© The Author(s), under exclusive license to Springer Nature Switzerland AG 2022
A. Urbina-García et al. (eds.), *Transitions to School: Perspectives and Experiences from Latin America*, International Perspectives on Early Childhood Education and Development 37, https://doi.org/10.1007/978-3-030-98935-4_7

Introduction

This chapter uses a number of acronyms, which are listed here for clarity.

BNCC   National Common Curriculum Base
DCNEI   National Curriculum Guidelines for Child Education
DRE   Regional Education Directorates
EB   Basic Education
EF   Fundamental Education
EI   Early Childhood Education
EMEF   Municipal Elementary School
EMEI   Municipal School of Early Childhood Education
PPP   Pedagogical Political Project
RME   Municipal Education Network
SME   Municipal Education Secretariat
UE   Educational Unit

In his discussion of childhood education in Brazil, Abramowicz (2009) presents the idea of childhood as an experience, and considers "what the elementary school proposes as a childhood experience for children" (p. 317). In Brazil, one of the consequences of the expansion of fundamental education (EF) to 9 years, resulting from the implementation of Law No. 11.274, of 6 February 2006 (Brasil, 2006), has been increased discussion about the reception of children and their families into the stage of basic education (EB). Discussion has also canvassed a need to consider early schooling for young children in early childhood education (EI) and the possibility of guaranteeing the right to childhood and play in elementary education as well as EI (Quinteiro & Carvalho, 2007).

In Brasil, the women's movements and Child Education Forums have struggled to expand and democratise EI for all. However, while EI is recognised as the first stage of basic education (EB) the public financing policy for EB did not include EI in FUNDEB (Fund for Maintenance and Development of Basic Education and Valorization of Education Professionals (Brasil, 2020)). In addition, it was argued that there was a lack of public money in underdeveloped countries to subsidise both early childhood education (EI) (for children aged 4–5 years) and elementary education (EF) (for children aged 6–14) simultaneously, and for many years, the latter was established as the stage in which more should be invested, as the return would be greater:

> Therefore, the expansion of one year of schooling is an economic educational policy, because, on the one hand, the expansion of Early Childhood Education would burden the State and, on the other, the State was already paying, in practice, in some municipalities, for this expansion. (Abramowicz, 2009, p. 319)

The economic bias was the focus for the expansion of EF. However, this was not accompanied by pedagogical actions to welcome children into the first year of EF. Children who had recently turned 6 years of age, or even younger, were referred to the EF without the school and its professionals having been minimally prepared to receive them, or to consider which inherent aspects of the education of young children should be relevant to guide the developing practices.

More than 10 years after the implementation of the 9 year EF, there is still a lack of coordination between this stage and the one before it (EI). The lack of dialogue between professionals at both stages, although the normative and curricular documents emphasise the need to reduce disruptions in the transition, is still a weakness and a point of attention to be considered by the Education Secretariats in policy proposals, as well as in training and implementation of the guidelines contained in the documents.

Recognising this gap, this chapter presents analyses resulting from ongoing doctoral research within the Faculty of Education of the University of São Paulo (FEUSP). It highlights the emerging need for reflection on the transition of children from EI to EF, based on the comments and perspectives of teachers, managers and policy-makers. The study is based on principles of qualitative research (Ludke & André, 1986) and action research, chosen for linking different dimensions of knowledge, and in the search to bridge the gap between colonising science and invisible science in the geopolitics of scientific knowledge (Sousa & Oliveira, 2018). Data collection occurred during training meetings with Municipal Education Network (RME) professionals, from both EI and EF, in São Paulo, with the common objectives of discussing and reflecting on the education of children in the two distinct spaces.

First, the meetings of an optional professional learning course in the first semester of 2018 were observed. The course was titled "The teaching practice of the childhood teacher: between ruptures, continuities and transitions", and was promoted by one of the 13 Regional Education Directorates (DREs), of the Municipal Education Network. The target audience was managers and teachers working in EI and EF.

Topics for the course meetings were organised around the following themes: childhood pedagogy; teaching; teaching identity; integrated curriculum; organisation of time, physical space/environments and interactions; and pedagogical documentation. The DRE, responsible for the course, offered 50 places: 33 registrations were made and at the last meeting there were 11 people present. The trainers used slides, with images and excerpts from the regional network's documents and selected publications as a theoretical framework, which triggered the proposed reflections and discussions.

From the second semester of 2018 to the first semester of 2020, the researchers coordinated monthly meetings of the study group "Transitions" at the School of Education, University of São Paulo, FEUSP, with the same target audience. An average of 10 professionals from EI and EF, working in different DREs in the same network, attended these meetings. Among the topics discussed were: Why is it important to talk about transition? How to be a teacher of young children in early childhood education and elementary school? Nine year elementary school and the impacts on pedagogical proposals for/with young children in EI and EF; Pedagogical documentation as a powerful tool for articulation between EI and EF; and What is necessary for professional training so that the educational concepts and proposals from EI to EF are conceived as continuities?

In both the Optional Course and Study Group investigated, data were generated through field notes and audio recordings (with some on video), following prior permission of the collaborating professionals participating in the research and of the Municipal Secretary of Education of São Paulo (SME/SP). The methodological approaches and instruments used followed the ethical procedures established for scientific research in Human Sciences, in accordance with University of São Paulo Code of Ethics. These approaches involved documentary analysis of municipal and federal policies, in the light of the production of research in the field of childhood pedagogy (Faria, 2014; Oliveira-Formosinho, 2016; Prado & Souza, 2017).

In this chapter, the focus of the analyses is the data generated in the year 2018, from the five meetings of the Optional Course and six meetings of the "Transitions" Study Group.

The Transition in the Comments of Teachers, Managers and Policies

The search for references to the theme of the transition of children from EI to EF in normative and curricular documents leads us to publications such as the National Curriculum Guidelines for Early Childhood Education (DCNEI) (Brasil, 2010, p. 29), which states that:

> Early Childhood Education institutions must create procedures for monitoring pedagogical work and for assessing the development of children, with no objective of selection, promotion or classification, ensuring: […] The continuity of the learning processes through the creation of strategies appropriate to the different moments of transition experienced by the child (transition from home/institution of Early Childhood Education, transitions within the institution, transition from daycare to pre-school and transition from pre-school to Elementary School).

In addition, the DCNEI contains an item that addresses the articulation of EI with EF, highlighting that in the transition between the stages it is necessary to: "ensure continuity in the learning and development process, respecting age specificities", without anticipating EF content (Brasil, 2010, p. 30).

More recently, the National Common Curricular Base (BNCC) was approved (Brasil, 2017). It is a mandatory document to be considered in the preparation of curricular proposals for education networks across the country, in which there are guidelines regarding the transition process from EI to EF. Item 3.3 of the BNCC highlights the necessary attention to the transition process between the stages, so that the changes occur in a balanced way, guaranteeing "integration and continuity of the children's learning processes" (Brasil, 2017, p. 51):

> It becomes necessary to establish strategies of acceptance and adaptation for both children and teachers, so that the new stage is built on what the child knows and is capable of doing, in a perspective of continuity in their educational path.

Documents from the Municipal Education Network of São Paulo, in which data were collected for the research shared in this chapter, also address the issue of transition and articulation between EI and EF.

Normative guidance n° 01, of December 2013, entitled "Evaluation in Early Childhood Education: Improving Looks" (São Paulo, 2014), highlights in its item XI – Articulation of Child Education with Elementary Education – that the benefits of learning built by children cannot be disrupted in the transition between stages. Therefore, it is necessary to plan this process and integrated pedagogical proposals, considering "the conception of child/childhood, the organization of spaces and times, the valorization of playing, the ludic and the imagination" (São Paulo, 2014, p. 26). Further:

> The transition process from early childhood education to elementary education must contemplate from the curriculum, understood as a living instrument, to the creation of adequate spaces, both in the rooms and in the external area, in addition to practices that make child/children so they can develop their children's peer cultures. (São Paulo, 2014, p. 27)

The normative orientation (São Paulo, 2014) also highlights the important role of teaching records, both in the evaluation processes (Merli, 2015; Prado & Merli, 2018), and in transition, considering that these enable EF professionals to learn about the educational work and the processes experienced by children in EI schools. In the EI units of the Municipal Education Network São Paulo, individual descriptive reports of children are prepared each semester, shared with their families during the period when the children are attending EI and sent to the EMEFs (Municipal Elementary Schools) during the children's transition to the first year of EF.

In one of the study group meetings, several comments by the professionals present highlighted the important role of reports in the transition to EF:

> If we are talking about transition, one element that will connect is the report;
> The way it was written, you can already understand the concepts;
> The report can be a tool for EMEF to get closer to children and families
> (Study Group Professionals, 10 September 2018).

In 2015, the Municipal Education Secretariat (SME) of São Paulo, published the document "Integrating Curriculum for Children in São Paulo" (São Paulo, 2015), which sought to promote reflections on pedagogical practices aimed at a transition process that articulated the work developed across both EI and EF. The document makes reference to the National Curriculum Guidelines for Basic Education (Brasil, 2013), highlighting the need to share the same conceptions and principles through the educational stages, so that there are no breaks, as:

> [...] childhood is not divided into unrelated and decontextualized compartments, as the child who goes to a new Educational Unit remains the same, and the experiences in each Unit must be diverse, elaborate and specific for small groups, but coherent and continuous, although not linear. (São Paulo, 2015, p. 26)

The curriculum document for EF in the São Paulo Network, published in notebooks by areas as curricula components, presents a common introductory section that addresses the theme of transitions between EI and EF, and between Elementary School I (years 1–5) and II (years 6–9). It highlights teachers as protagonists of the curriculum and the role of the management team in promoting articulation between the two stages: "teachers from the same area, from different areas; the same cycle and the different cycles in the curricular discussions and in the organization of the plans with a view to better serving the students of that school community" (São Paulo, 2019a, p. 21).

As in official documents of the network participating in this study, the comments of the professionals participating in the training meetings highlight the role of the management team in the transition and articulation processes between EI and EF, in addition to important reflections and questions: "How [do I] exercise my supervisory role, guiding the units, if I don't prepare for it?" (School Supervisor in Optional Course, 18 September 2018).

What does this comment suggest? One interpretation might be that the professional puts herself in the role of someone who needs to be trained in order to be able to intervene in everyday issues inherent to the function and role she occupies. Sometimes, it was the teachers who highlighted the importance of the management team in the articulation between the stages and, in relation to school supervision, and emphasised its "important role as a central axis of articulation in the territory" (EI Teacher in Optional Course, 18 September 2018).

When thinking about the role of the management team in the articulation between the stages and the necessary continuity in the educational process, some comments noted the need to address, also with managers, the specifics of working with children, with regard to spaces and times for play in EF schools. It was assumed that the right to childhood, to play and to be a protagonist is something to be guaranteed both to children and to teachers in EI and EF. In one of the Optional Course meetings, a teacher asked: "Do you address this issue of the importance of playing and spaces in meetings with EMEF managers? At EMEF, I play half hidden because I am afraid of being misunderstood" (EF Teacher in Optional Course, 9 October 2018).

The attentive look at and the appreciation of the children's right to play in EI and EF reappeared in further comments from this same teacher as something to be the focus of training for both teaching and management teams, in order to favour the articulation between the stages and within the Educational Units (UEs) themselves. In this regard, the teacher said:

> … justifying, I think that today it shouldn't be necessary in the network anymore, the city hall is so advanced in these discussions! That is why I ask for your collaboration (DRE trainers) in the training of directors, mainly from EMEFs. Justifying why you are joking is an energy that should be spared for the teacher, having to justify, having to fight, raising the flag… (EF Teacher in Optional Course, 9 October 2018).

The teacher's anguish was revealed in other moments of the Optional Course, always highlighting the importance that the concepts and guidelines for working with children were also discussed with the management teams. It was argued that, being limited only to training of teachers, the practices proposed in the educational units can be misinterpreted by professionals who do not follow the discussions, causing differences in practices and discussions to emerge within the same education unit.

Other comments revealed that there is still a need for integration between professionals from the same Educational Unit:

> Sometimes it happens at the school itself ... there is no conversation between the teachers, a more general line of work, an alignment of ideas (EF Teacher in Optional Course, 28 September 2018)
>
> If elementary school teachers had access to what is proposed, to the goals of the preschool... this is not only the CEI (Center for Early Childhood Education) for EMEI (Municipal School of Early Childhood Education) and EMEI for EMEF, this is a series for the other, that is not clear (EF Teacher in Optional Course, 2 October 2018).

From these comments, it is clear that investment in integrated work is sometimes something to be done within the institutions themselves and, in parallel, expanding understanding of articulation requires working with other educational units. In this sense, pedagogical coordination plays an essential role in continuing in-service training and establishing strategies for articulation and continuity in pedagogical actions.

In the City Curriculum: Elementary Education (São Paulo, 2019a) there is reference to the entry of children in the first year of EF and their experiences in the literacy cycle, highlighting that:

> The Literacy Cycle (1st, 2nd and 3rd year) marks the student's entry into Elementary School. For some children, it is the beginning of school life; for others, the transition towards a new teaching stage. In both cases, they are children between five and six years old who have different knowledge and experiences in their family, social and cultural contexts and who are also anxious for the construction of new learning, among them, the expansion of the use of practices of language in the context of systematic education. (São Paulo, 2019a, p. 96)

The transition of EI children to a new stage, to a new institutional context, demands that their different knowledge and experiences be welcomed in EF. This welcoming presupposes the knowledge, on the part of those who work in the early years of the EF, of the paths experienced by the children who have left EI. The records sent from the EI units to the EMEFs are powerful instruments for sharing the work done and for the consequent proposal of practices in continuity.

However, in addition to a careful analysis of these records, reflections and discussions about working with children can favour transitions with fewer disruptions. In this sense, comments like:

> I think that the concept of childhood is not very clear to teachers of EMEF (Pedagogical Coordinator of EI in Optional Course, 18 September 2018)
>
> There is a misalignment between what first year teachers expect from children who arrive from EI and the work that is done there (EI Teacher in a Study Group, 13 November 2018)

show the divergence of conceptions and practices in working with children.

Continuing inservice training that, in the Municipal Education Network in São Paulo is accompanied by pedagogical coordination, can constitute moments for the establishment of: "transition actions also for teachers, talking about the pedagogy of childhood in training" (Pedagogical Coordinator in a Study Group, 10 December 2018). Regarding the possibilities for discussing transitions in inservice training, it was pointed out that it would be essential to propose training that supports teachers in their practices, that is, "think about training, workshops, because I feel that they (teachers) no longer know how to welcome children in the transition to EMEFs" (Pedagogical Coordinator in Study Group, 10 December 2018).

Therefore, the use of inservice training moments in EF schools to discuss welcoming children from EI, favouring reflections and collective planning, is a path pointed out as providing an important strategy to overcome disruptions in the process of educational transition.

The comments of the participating professionals also highlight the field of childhood pedagogy as an area for further training. However, bringing together professionals from early childhood education and elementary education in pursuing this pedagogical approach presents challenges, particularly around the expectations of children in the first year of elementary school in areas such as literacy (Britto, 2005).

In February 2019, the Municipal Education Secretariat (SME) published two documents in which the theme of transition and articulation between the stages is also addressed. In SME Normative Instruction No. 02, of 02/06/2019, there is reference to Ordinance No. 7598/2016 (São Paulo, 2019c), in which procedures are established for the issuance of the educational documentation prepared in EI, as a way of evidencing the children's learning and development processes at the end of this stage (São Paulo, 2016).

Another document recently published by SME in São Paulo was the City Curriculum: Early Childhood Education (São Paulo, 2019b), in which there is a chapter dedicated to the theme of transitions. The chapter entitled "Articulating early childhood education and the early years of elementary education" is subdivided into five items that address aspects such as: integrative dimensions of EI and EF, curricular integration, transitions in EI and transition from EI to EF.

This document, which has integrated education as one of its basic principles, highlights the need for reflection on transitions "so that the continuity of the children's learning processes is respected and there are no sudden breaks" (São Paulo, 2019b, p. 158). There is also an emphasis on the role of the management and teaching teams, and of families and/or guardians of the children, in the sense of "building clear processes of articulation, through meetings, interviews, welcoming actions, parents school, child councils, murals, newspaper, youth press, school councils, etc." (São Paulo, 2019b, p. 159).

Emphasis on the role of management in the processes of articulation between the stages also was present in the reflections of the formative meetings surveyed, in comments such as:

If the directors do not get close to things, the pedagogical coordinator is overloaded;

A group out of tune gets sick;

For us it is complex to deconstruct this, we need to be aligned, very sure of what we are doing, to speak with a lot of coherence and propriety, because it will not be an easy job (referring to the discussion of transitions in the in-service training) (Pedagogical Coordinators in Study Groups, 4 October 2018 and 10 December 2018).

The curricular document Curriculum of the City: Child Education (São Paulo, 2019b) also presents possibilities for supporting transition processes, such as:

> [...] hold sectoral meetings to outline actions to implement the City Curriculum, analyse the continuity of PPPs (Pedagogical Political Projects), organize transition projects in the territories, articulate with the Municipal and State UEs from the perspective of the belonging of the children to the territory. It is known that it is a challenge to break with practices that have historically been constituted, but it is necessary to start by integrating managers, teachers and educators and drawing up a plan for transitions to the territory. (São Paulo, 2019b, p. 163)

In addition to actions at territorial levels, such as those pointed out in the excerpt above, there are references to the need to establish public policies for professional training, in which integrated training meetings are prioritised:

> In addition to individual, regional or group of teacher(s) initiatives, it is essential that public policies increasingly favour curricular integration, providing integrated and collective training with teacher(s) of children from 0 to 12 years old, addressing the theme transition between levels. These lines of continuity are not ready: they need to be imagined, discussed, reflected, woven, transformed into propositions that are established as milestones of this necessary integration. (São Paulo, 2019b, p. 162)

The comments of the professionals in the researched course and study group reinforce the importance of expanding formative meetings guided by the theme of integration and articulation between the stages, in order to reduce the disruptions in the process of transition from EI to EF:

> How many moments do we have to sit down and discuss with Fundamental? This is still a timid movement that we hope will expand ... making this approximation is very difficult (School supervisor in Optional Course, 10 December 2018);

> There are things that must come from the teacher, from the school, and not from the government. It is necessary to create demand for new legislation to be generated ... let us do it (School supervisor in Optional Course, 2 October 2018);

> You need to dig spaces instead of waiting for SME documents (School supervisor in Optional Course, 2 October 2018).

These comments from EI and EF professionals highlight the need to promote integrated training meetings to broaden the debate and reflections on the articulation between EI and EF. Part of the aim of these meetings could be to promote transformative approaches by encouraging participants to problematise their own practices as well as the practices of other professionals working with children from 0 to 12 years old.

As stated by Gobbi and Pinazza (2014, pp. 11–12):

> (...) education should be thought of as a promoter of children's learning, committed to respecting the manifestations of the multiple languages of children and, thus, concerned with guaranteeing girls' and boys' spaces and means in which their language expressions can be present, being understood in its entirety and complexity by all.

Faria (2014) presents reflections on the gaps in teacher training evidenced by the reality of daycare centres and preschools. Reference is made to Quinteiro and

Carvalho (2007) and research on the early years of EF, in schools in the State of Santa Catarina/Brazil that, "show the various modalities of child participation and, therefore, point out a strong criticism of teacher education that does not contemplate the young citizen and mischaracterizes him [sic] as 'without light', only as a student" (Faria, 2014, p. 162).

Regarding training courses that aim to articulate the different stages and support the transition processes, the teachers participating in the research pointed out that:

> Teachers ask 'what did you do at EMEI?', because they are unaware of the EMEI environment and the work done there (Pedagogical Coordinator of EI in Optional Course, 28 September 2018)

> Spaces need to talk so that one respects the work of the other (DRE Trainer in an Optional Course, 18 September 2018)

> I think this dialogue that is starting, but did not exist, is very important, the change in the 9-year elementary education justified the need for this dialogue (Assistant Director at EI in Optional Course, 18 September 2018)

It is necessary to look at the EMEFs and think that childhood needs to be taken care of in this context as well (School Supervisor in an Optional Course, 18 September 2018)

> To have integration, you have to be willing; if the teacher doesn't want it, it doesn't work (EI Pedagogical Coordinator in Study Group, 9 October 2018).

The perception of this need to expand the integration between professionals of the two stages in training moments is what has been driving the research presented here. It is not possible to think about the articulation between EI and EF during the children's transitions from one stage to the next, without considering the transitions of the professionals between them. It is essential, therefore, to provide spaces for discussion and integration that allow those who work with children in EI, or in EF, to get to know, discuss and reflect collectively on the specificities of small and large children, their education, as well as their own conceptions and teaching practices in childhood.

Conclusions: Document and Analyse Pathways, Favour Continuities

The expansion of elementary education to nine years established the entry of 6-year-old children to school and, at the same time, subtracted one year from their experiences in early childhood education. As a result, the debate about the work to be developed in the EF has expanded, focusing particularly on the need to consider the specificities of childhood and to ensure that the transition process is marked by continuities, through the development of strategies to overcome possible ruptures in the passage from one stage to another.

The possibilities for this to occur have been the subject of discussions and reflections in different training spaces and also in educational units that have come to have a close look at the transition and articulation between the first two stages of basic education (EI and EF). However, the perspectives present in curricular documents, norms and training spaces have pointed to the necessary expansion of integrated training between EI and EF professionals, as ways for them to discuss and reflect on the different roles assumed and pedagogical practices with children, both in early childhood schools and elementary education units.

Professionals from EI and EF who were involved in the research meetings discussed weaknesses in policy and practice, as well as needs and possibilities for articulation and the promotion of transitions with few disruptions. The growing movement of discussion on the topic of transitions was pointed out and specific actions that have been developed in different territories were reported, such as: visits by EMEI children to EMEFs; meetings organised by school supervision teams integrating EI and EF; revisions of guidance to EI families on the transition to EMEFs; projects involving children from both stages, such as meetings, exchange of letters and drawings; partnerships between the pedagogical coordination of EMEIs and EMEFs in the analysis of reports and records, and pedagogical documentation.

These findings reiterate those reported by Motta (2013, p. 17):

> That the transition between Early Childhood Education and Elementary Education works through the construction of 'bridges' that link these two segments, especially from the continuity in reading and writing activities that recognize the social function of this practice.
>
> That the children in their classes are perceived in their child dimension, not reducing them to a social role component of the child condition.
>
> That they recognize in school learning the role of mediation between spontaneous and scientific knowledge so that they effectively contribute to the construction of higher mental functions.
>
> That reintroduce the dimension of the body in the classroom without dichotomizing thought and movement.

The comments of the teachers and managers in the research meetings also reveal, among other aspects, the expectations that the professionals of one stage have in relation to the work performed in the other, showing the need to expand the spaces of integrated training among professionals in early childhood education and elementary education. They also highlight the perception of the essential role of management teams, especially pedagogical coordination, in the actions of articulation in the transition process between the two stages.

The analysis of the records sent by EMEIs to EMEFs is revealed as a potent possibility for the establishment of articulations between EI and EF. This is because the pedagogical documentation reveals paths experienced by children and teachers, in addition to sharing knowledge about the work performed and the concepts that underlie it. However, documenting and recording routes alone are not tools for reflection and training that favour continuities. Therefore, it is essential that they be taken as objects of study and analysis.

As Formosinho and Oliveira-Formosinho (2019, p. 109) emphasise:

> Professionals have the civic right and duty to monitor the development of pedagogy in everyday life and to document its consequences on learning and thus obtain information (from pedagogical documentation) that allows them to take a longitudinal look at children's learning, and not an instant verification at a predetermined and out-of-context moment.

Larrosa (2015, p. 193) points out that: "the effectiveness of educational actions is determined by its power to move from the possible to the real". The training spaces considered in this research are powerful means for reaching what sometimes appears in the comments of both education professionals and educational policies, but that has not yet reached practice.

The comments highlight proposals and reflections on the transition and articulation between EI and EF. However, in order to actually be able to innovate practices, it is essential to move from discourses to effective actions, in which children's rights to childhood, play, leadership, inventiveness, and the experiences of multiple languages (Edwards et al., 1999; Merli, 2015; Prado & Souza, 2017) are guaranteed in line with the specificities of children's education in EI and EF.

Strategies to advance from discussion to practice, expand training spaces, promote effective transition, and articulate actions between early childhood education and elementary education presuppose the profound and potent involvement of professionals not only in these settings, but also those who work in the Education Secretariats, through which public policies for professional training are promoted as a right and, in a sense of continuity, are also formative.

In this way, when all involved assume responsibility for analysing and problematising practice and for working together to support transition processes, there is the potential for positive change to occur.

References

Abramowicz, A. (2009). Educação Infantil e a Escola Fundamental de 9 anos [Early childhood education and the 9 year fundamental school]. *Olhar de professor [Teacher look]*, 9(2), 317–325. http://revistas2.uepg.br/index.php/olhardeprofessor/article/view/1467. Accessed 6 July 2021.

Brasil. (2006). *Law 11.274. February 6 2006*. http://www.planalto.gov.br/ccivil_03/_Ato2004-2006/2006/Lei/L11274.htm. Accessed 6 July 2021.

Brasil. (2010). *Diretrizes curriculares nacionais para a Educação Infantil* [National curriculum guidelines for early childhood education]. MEC/SEB. http://portal.mec.gov.br/dmdocuments/diretrizescurriculares_2012.pdf. Accessed 6 July 2021.

Brasil. (2013). *Diretrizes curriculares nacionais para a Educação Básica* [National curriculum guidelines for basic education]. MEC/SEB. http://portal.mec.gov.br/docman/julho-2013-pdf/13677-diretrizes-educacao-basica-2013-pdf/file. Accessed 6 July 2021.

Brasil. (2017). *Base Nacional Comum Curricular* (BNCC) [Common national curriculum base]. MEC. http://basenacionalcomum.mec.gov.br/. Accessed 6 July 2021.

Brasil. (2020). *Lei n. 4.113, de 25 de dezembro de 2020. Regulamenta o Fundo de Manutenção e Desenvolvimento da Educação Básica e Valorização dos Profissionais da Educação (FUNDEB)* [Law n. 4,113, of December 25, 2020. Regulates the fund for maintenance and development of basic education and valorization of education professionals]. MEC. http://www.fnde.gov.br/index.php/legislacoes/institucional-leis/item/14134-lei-n%C2%BA-14-113,-de-25-de-dezembro-de-2020. Accessed 20 April 2021.

Britto, L. P. (2005). Letramento e alfabetização: implicações para a educação infantil [Literacy and literacy: Implications for early childhood education]. In A. L. G. de Faria & S. A. Mello (Eds.), *O mundo da Escrita no universo da pequena infância* [The world of writing in the universe of small childhood] (pp. 5–21). Autores Associados.

Edwards, C., Gandini, L., & Forman, G. (1999). *As cem linguagens da criança: abordagem de Reggio Emilia na educação da primeira infância* [The hundred languages of the child: Reggio Emilia's approach to early childhood education]. Artes Médicas Sul Ltda.

Faria, A. L. G. de. (2014). Crianças pequenas e grandes, brasileiras e italianas: encontros da pedagogia da infância com a arte [Small and large children, Brazilian and Italian: Meetings between pedagogy of chidhood and art]. In M. Gobbi & M. A. Pinazza (Eds.), *Infância e suas linguagens* [Childhoods and their languages] (pp. 155–170). Cortez.

Formosinho, J., & Oliveira-Formosinho, J. (2019). Em busca de uma abordagem holística para a avaliação pedagógica [In search of a holistic approach to pedagogical assessment]. In J. Oliveira-Formosinho & C. Pascal (Eds.), *Documentação pedagógica e avaliação na Educação Infantil: um caminho para a transformação* [Pedagogical documentation and assessment in early childhood education: A path for transformation] (pp. 96–110). Penso.

Gobbi, M. A., & Pinazza, M. A. (2014). Linguagens infantis: convite à leitura [Children's languages: Invitation to read]. In M. A. Gobbi & M. A. Pinazza (Eds.), *Infância e suas linguagens* [Childhoods and their languages] (pp. 11–20). Cortez.

Larrosa, J. (2015). O enigma da infância [The enigma of childhood]. In J. Larrosa (Ed.), *Pedagogia Profana: danças, piruetas e mascaradas* [Profane pedagogy: Dances, pirouettes and masquerades] (pp. 183–198). Autêntica.

Ludke, M., & André, M. E. D. (1986). *Pesquisa em educação: abordagens qualitativas* [Education research: Qualitative approaches]. EPU.

Merli, A. de A. (2015). *O registro como instrumento de reflexão na formação docente: pesquisa-intervenção em escola municipal de educação infantil* [Registration as an instrument of reflection in teacher education: Research-intervention in a municipal school for early childhood education]. Dissertação (Mestrado). Universidade Nove de Julho, UNINOVE. https://bibliotecatede.uninove.br/bitstream/tede/992/2/Angelica%20de%20Almeida%20Merli.pdf. Accessed 6 July 2021.

Motta, F. M. (2013). *De crianças a alunos: a transição da Educação Infantil para o Ensino Fundamental* [From children to students: The transition from early childhood education to elementary school]. Cortez.

Oliveira-Formosinho, J. (Ed.). (2016). *Transição entre ciclos educativos: uma investigação praxeológica* [Transition between education cycles: A praxeological investigation]. Porto Editora.

Prado, P. D., & Merli, A. de A. (2018). Avaliação formativa na Educação Infantil: relações entre políticas públicas e práticas docentes [Formative evaluation in early childhood education: Relations between public policies and teaching practices]. *Revista Teias*, [S.l.], *19*(54), 130–147. https://doi.org/10.12957/teias.2018.36033

Prado, P. D., & Souza, C. W. de. (Eds.). (2017). *Educação Infantil, diversidade e arte* [Early childhood education, diversity and art]. Laços.

Quinteiro, J., & Carvalho, D. de C. (Eds.). (2007). *Participar, brincar e aprender: exercitando os direitos da criança na escola* [Participate, play and learn: Exercising children's rights at school]. Junqueira & Marin/CAPES.

São Paulo. (2014). *Orientação normativa n° 01: avaliação na Educação Infantil: aprimorando os olhares* [Normative guidance n° 01: Evaluation in early childhood education: Improving the looks]. Secretaria Municipal de Educação [Municipal Education Secretariat]. SME/DOT. https://www.sinesp.org.br/images/1_-_ORIENTACAO_NORMATIVA_01_2013_AVALIACAO_NA_EDUCACAO_INFANTIL_APRIMORANDO_OS_OLHARES.pdf. Accessed 6 July 2021.

São Paulo. (2015). *Currículo integrador da infância paulistana* [Integrating curriculum for children in São Paulo]. SME/DOT. https://www.sinesp.org.br/images/28_-_CURRICULO_INTEGRADOR_DA_INFANCIA_PAULISTANA.pdf. Accessed 6 July 2021.

São Paulo. (2016). *Portaria n° 7.598, de 16/11/2016: Estabelece diretrizes para a documentação educacional a ser expedida ao final da etapa de Educação Infantil para o Ensino Fundamental* [Ordinance n° 7.598 of 16/11/2016: Establishes guidelines for educational documentation to be issued at the end of the stage of early childhood education for elementary education]. SME. https://www.sinesp.org.br/index.php/179-saiu-no-doc/895-portaria-n-7-598-de-16-11-2016-orientacoes-procedimentos-e-periodos-documentacao-educacional-a-ser-expedida-ao-final-da-etapa-de-educacao-infantil-para-o-ensino-fundamental. Accessed 6 July 2021.

São Paulo. (2019a). *Currículo da cidade: Ensino Fundamental: componente curricular: Língua Portuguesa* [City curriculum: Elementary school: Curricular component: Portuguese language]. SME/COPED. http://portal.sme.prefeitura.sp.gov.br/Portals/1/Files/50628.pdf. Accessed 6 July 2021.

São Paulo. (2019b). *Currículo da cidade: Educação Infantil* [City curriculum: Early childhood education]. SME/COPED. https://educacao.sme.prefeitura.sp.gov.br/wp-content/uploads/2019/10/cc-ef-lingua-portuguesa.pdf. Accessed 6 July 2021.

São Paulo. (2019c). *Instrução normativa SME n° 02, de 06/02/2019. Aprova a orientação normativa n° 1, de 06/02/2019, que dispõe sobre os registros na educação infantil* [Normative instruction SME n° 02, of 06/02/2019, approves normative guideline n° 1, of 06/02/2019 which provides for records in early childhood education]. SME. https://www.sinesp.org.br/index.php/179-saiu-no-doc/7274-instrucao-normativa-sme-n-02-de-06-02-2019-aprova-a-orientacao-normativa-n-1-de-06-02-2019-que-dispoe-sobre-os-registros-na-educacao-infantil. Accessed 6 July 2021.

Sousa, L. S., & Oliveira, T. (2018). Cartografias da pesquisa-ação: em busca de deslocamentos da epistemologia do Sul [Cartographies of action research: Looking for shifts in Southern epistemology]. *Comunicação e Sociedade* [*Communication and Society*], *33*, 57–81. https://doi.org/10.17231/comsoc.33(2018).2907

Patrícia Dias Prado is PhD Professor at the School of Education, University of São Paulo, (FEUSP), Brazil, in the Department of Teaching Methodology and Comparative Education, (EDM), in the area of Childhood. She is involved with the initial and continuing education of teachers, researchers, and artists of childhood. She develops teaching, extension, and research in the themes of the education of bodies in difference, in the relations of age, generation, gender, race, and ethnicity. Prof Prado is deeply interested in children's cultures and the decolonization of research with children and the Pedagogy of Childhood, in the field of Social Studies of Childhood and the interface with the Performing and Body Arts, in childhood education, and in professional and human formation. She has published extensively both nationally and internationally in these areas and is Coordinator of the Research Group *Early Childhood: Languages and Childhood Cultures*.

Angélica de Almeida Merli is Pedagogical Coordinator in the São Paulo Municipal Education Network (PMSP), Brazil, holding the position of Technical Education Assistant, in the Pedagogical Division/Elementary Education Center – Campo Limpo Regional Board of Education. She has also taught Elementary School and Special Education. Holding a Master in Education, from the Universidade Nove de Julho, UNINOVE, she is a researcher of the Research Group *Early Childhood: Languages and Childhood Cultures* in the School of Education, University of São Paulo, (FEUSP), where she is also finishing her doctorate, about transition processes from Early Childhood Education to Elementary School. She has published extensively nationally in these areas. She is also a Professor of Higher Education in Pedagogy, Álvares de Azevedo Faculty, FAATESP and facilitator of the Virtual University of the State of São Paulo, UNIVESP.

Chapter 8
Playing, Participating, and Learning in Fundamental Education (Grades 1–9) in São Paulo, Brazil: What Do the Children Say?

Thais Monteiro Ciardella and **Cláudia Valentina Assumpção Galian**

Abstract The goal of this chapter is to incorporate children's views into reflection on the curriculum proposed for the early grades of fundamental education, based on what children enrolled in the early grades in a public fundamental education school in São Paulo/Brazil choose as identifying elements of the school and its practices. In a dialogue with the elements the children made known, we discuss the transitions taking place throughout the fundamental education program that bring changes in how children enact their rights to play, participate and learn at school. As core principles, the child was seen as subject and the research with children was seen as a relevant aspect to advance debates on curriculum and its specificities during the early grades of fundamental education, in the search for creating conditions that are favorable to the learning process and respectful towards children.

Introduction

In Brazil, Law n° 11.114/2005 (Brasil, 2005) established that, at the age of 6 years, it is compulsory for children to attend fundamental education schools. Previously, the age for compulsory attendance was 7 years. Moving the enrolment age back one year and consequently extending this elementary education stage to nine years points out the need for advancing early childhood education in Brazilian fundamental education schools. To date, investigating how children represent 'being in a fundamental education school' and building meanings for school and learning opportunities, are issues that have scarcely been explored by Brazilian researchers

T. M. Ciardella (✉) · C. V. A. Galian
Universidade de São Paulo, São Paulo, Brasil
e-mail: claudiavalentina@usp.br

© The Author(s), under exclusive license to Springer Nature Switzerland AG 2022
A. Urbina-García et al. (eds.), *Transitions to School: Perspectives and Experiences from Latin America*, International Perspectives on Early Childhood Education and Development 37, https://doi.org/10.1007/978-3-030-98935-4_8

(Barbosa & Delgado, 2012; Ciardella, 2019; Gesser & Furtado, 2013; Quinteiro & Carvalho, 2007).

Since the National Curriculum Guidelines for the nine-year fundamental education program (Brasil, 2010) were established in Brazil, and within the scope of curriculum studies, we have observed attempts at building school culture that take into account the transition from early childhood education (for children aged 4–5 years) to fundamental education (for children aged 6–14 across grades 1–9). Our approach has focused on respecting the right to social quality education and to students' multiple childhood and teenage years throughout this nine-year period (Brasil, 2010). To research the transitions within this scenario means to value the place childhood and children's culture occupy in the fundamental education curriculum, while drawing attention to its specificities.

In line with the official national curriculum guidelines, we point out the school's relevance in building a curriculum that ensures children's access to dialogue with knowledge that is historically built by society, the inclusion of an already existing culture, and the creation of the possibilities to give it a new meaning based on how children look at it. Valuing childhood and contact with scientific knowledge and culture are experiences that characterise the singularity of the pedagogical work with children (both in early childhood education and fundamental education) and, as such, they should guide the curriculum of fundamental education schools throughout the 9 years.

Thus, we argue that early childhood education and elementary education are articulated stages, and that the planned curricula should favour opportunities for children to live childhood at school, considering playing and participating as conditions for learning: "the child learns when it is a subject in experience, that is, when it participates in the processes lived with the body, the mind and the emotions and not as an executor of what was thought by the adults" (Mello, 2015, p. 3).

This chapter is based on research conducted in Brazil during a master's program for the School of Education, University of São Paulo, in 2019. The research consisted of dialogue between children and researchers to discuss the nature of the school – the specific practices that make the school different from other social institutions like families, churches, and work environments (Charlot, 1979, 2000, 2009; Young, 2014); the school curriculum (Gimeno Sacristán, 1998, 2005), and childhood[1] (Corsaro, 2009b; Sarmento, 2011), by supporting listening to children during their early grades in fundamental education.

This study aimed to understand the possible meanings children attribute to school experiences, as well as to identify times and spaces created by them to live their childhood years at school. To reach these goals, circles of conversation were conducted with children aged between 6 and 10 years who were enrolled in a public school (São Paulo – SP – Brazil), in 1st and 5th grades respectively. Before the circles of conversation with researchers took place, the children were able to take

---

[1] Childhood is considered to be a social category of the generational type. Children are individuals who come together through a common, socially shaped characteristic. Although children belong to the same age group, there are multiple ways to live childhood (Sarmento, 2011).

photographs of the school and record scenes that they saw as expressive of school life.

The pictures were understood as a methodological instrument that is able to invite children to prepare, investigate, and create representations of their school experiences. Gobbi (2011) conceptualises photography as an activity that is capable of making children's otherness visible: in other words, providing opportunities for children to express how they interpret the reality they are part of and build their own cultures. Thus, when using photography, children take on centrality. This is in line with the views of Sarmento (2011), who states that redefining learning processes depends on understanding the specificity of childhood and children as subjects. It also aligns with Lobo (2012, p. 75), who states that "[if] there is nothing left to say about childhood, the moment may have come for us to learn with the children what childhood has to say to us about its space and time".

To empower listening processes means to accept that research conducted with children is pervaded by understanding the complexity of childhood and by recognising methodological challenges for the researcher. The starting point for such research is the finding that research conducted with children in school situations involves "an investigation about the school that is deepened by a knowledge of childhood" (Delalande, 2011, p. 77). Thus, by analysing their photographs and positionings about them, we tried to understand the meanings children give to the institution's curriculum and what types of school and childhood relationships they build.

Corsaro (2009a, p. 85) states that, in order to access children's productions, the researcher must "spend a long time observing and participating in micro or ordinary daily life aspects of those who are the focus of the group" so that it is possible to collect variable and consistent data which can then be analysed contextually. Accordingly, we see as the main moment of the study the acceptance of the researcher as an 'atypical adult' by the group of children. According to Corsaro (2009a, p. 94), being an atypical adult means to be a 'less powerful' adult, with whom the children can really share their views, how they understand the world, and act in it. In order to strengthen this bond, we tried to take on the double challenge of approaching the children and moving away from the other adults in the school, while preferring to share recess time with the children rather than spending observation time in the staffroom. These are some of the highlights of the methodological implications that were involved in this process of strengthening the field of research conducted with children. They emphasised the attention given to the challenge of granting centrality to listening to children as subjects in the research.

Looking to the curriculum, we worked with the idea of a cultural selection that should promote opportunities for learning and valuing childhood, as stated by official guidelines regarding Early Childhood Education and the nine-year Fundamental Education grades (Brasil, 2009, 2010). This position assumes listening to children and understanding how they interpret the curriculum.

Concepts of Childhood and Curriculum for Fundamental Education School Children

The first segment of fundamental education (Fundamental 1) in Brazil encompasses five of the children's childhood years from Grade 1 through to Grade 5. With that in mind, we aimed to identify the place childhood occupies in school life by listening to the children and, through this, contribute to discussions that bring additional elements to the curriculum proposed by the school for this segment. The intention was to strengthen the idea that "the expansion of the Fundamental Education will only be considered if it is to promote childhood at schools" (Gesser & Furtado, 2013, p. 49). In addition to that, we understand that ensuring children's rights to play, participate and learn at fundamental education schools (Quinteiro & Carvalho, 2007) may strengthen what Charlot (2000, p. 80) calls a "relationship with knowledge".

We believe that emphasising children's voices in fundamental education schools also favours reflections on the curriculum proposed and developed in early childhood education. Our position emphasises the need for a more consistent debate on the continuities between these stages, in order to support the planning of schools and teachers to deal with these transitions between levels of schooling. In Brazil, there are breaks between early childhood education and fundamental (elementary) education that are marked by both physical separations – in the public school system, in most cases, children change schools when they move from early childhood education to fundamental education, as well as symbolic separations – expressed in the idea of overcoming childhood, of 'growth', as well as of the more traditional form of school organisation, around more strictly controlled disciplines, times and school spaces.

Gimeno Sacristán (2005, pp. 12–13) points out that, in the twentieth century, the image of over-schooled children was naturalised, with courses organised by adults that disregarded children as participatory subjects. Accordingly, fundamental education schools cast aside the childhood of those children and granted centrality to adults and how they organise schoolwork. This same author insists that schools, in their traditional model, disregard time, space, and the voice of children (who, in this case, are also students) in their organisation. By approaching the need for studying schooling practices, Gimeno Sacristán (2005, p. 14) states that childhood at school is a 'non-transitory' social fact and points out the need for understanding

> **how** [children] **live this task**, what difficulties and concerns they go to school with, what they find there, the desires they leave at home and at the school's doorstep, the story they have of the future that awaits them. (emphasis added)

Charlot (1979, p. 119) also reinforces the need for overcoming the view of children built by traditional pedagogy, which insists on "children's lack of finishing" and "sees children as a reference of what they should become, in other words, according to an ideal standard". Throughout his theoretical production, Charlot (1979, 2000, 2009) has been concerned about studying the formative processes that are built during schooling years, which strengthen, or not, what the author calls 'relationships of subjects with knowledge', by understanding the child as the builder of their own processes of being and becoming subject. In other words, "the relationship with knowledge is the relationship with the world, with the other and themselves, of a subject who is confronted by the need for learning" (Charlot, 2000, p. 80), within the specific space of the school institution. This institution, as Charlot sees it, is responsible for conveying to the children "explicit and stylized behavior models, in other words, models that are purer, more schematized than those which children acquire from direct social contact" (Charlot, 1979, p. 19). Further, Charlot (2000, p. 28) explains that "relationships with knowledge are located in social times and spaces that need to receive the attention of researchers, who are busy with studies about schools, so that it is possible to understand the learning context".

We approach the curriculum field by taking the relationship with knowledge as the object of analysis. Based on Young (2014), we understand that the research conducted on school curriculum cannot lose sight of the centrality of what is taught and learned at school by taking on the specificity of its function. It is through the school that children and young people realise the right to access a selection of school knowledge, which Young claims as 'powerful knowledge', since it potentially allows children and young people to analyse the world they live in, on bases that differ from those they already have in their out-of-school experiences. By relating school knowledge to the function of education, Young (2014, p. 226) states that:

> On the one hand, as educators, we have the responsibility to deliver to the next generation the knowledge accumulated by the preceding ones. This is the element of continuity between generations that distinguishes us from animals; it is a way to say that we are part of history always. But on the other hand, the purpose of the curriculum, at least in modern societies, is not just to convey accumulated knowledge; it is also to **enable the next generation to build on this knowledge and create a new one,** since this is how human societies progress and individuals develop. (emphasis added)

Thus, the curriculum is approached in this study by analysing the route that has been followed in a Brazilian public school after the official prescriptions, as well as the daily life of children, who, by following/living the 'prescribed curriculum' (Gimeno Sacristán, 1998), redefine it within the field of action. How schools organise their curriculum is understood as a simultaneous answer to the official prescriptions and to the experiences of subjects inside the school, aiming at creating favourable learning conditions. Throughout this chapter, we consider both official curriculum documents and the interpretations of children, in the search for understanding the contexts in which they play, participate, and learn throughout fundamental education. By highlighting and discussing how children understand school, we aim at adding to expanding the possibilities of this being a specific place for sheltering childhood and creating favorable learning conditions. In doing so, we contribute to the necessary debate about a curriculum that favours integration between early childhood education and fundamental education, considering the specificities of childhood. Following this, we depart from the rights regarded as essential to children – to play, participate and learn – to ask about the school/childhood relationship and its commitment to expanding the opportunities for accessing school knowledge within fundamental education.

What Do the Children Say?

Based on the dialogue with children and the elements they raised, we understand that they build critical analyses of their own school experience – which are a result of their creative and reproductive interpretations of the social world. Their creation is related to values and ideas that they produce and share when interacting with their peers.

The official guidelines issued by the Brazilian Ministry of Education (Brasil, 2007), when dealing with children's transition from early childhood education to fundamental education, select playing and participating as essential rights toward strengthening the relationship between them and school knowledge, potentially influencing the continuity of studies. Concerning playing, these guidelines point out that, at the school, this is usually observed under three different situations: adult-child play; child-child play; and playing with the purpose of teaching content. The clear devaluation of playing is common to adults in education settings, as well as the attempt at restricting it to recess time as children grow up, leading it toward "becoming increasingly defined and restricted in terms of hours, spaces and discipline" (Brasil, 2007, p. 35). Opposing this logic, and in keeping with the guidelines, we recognise playing as a "cultural dimension of the knowledge building process and human formation" (Brasil, 2007, p. 34). Playing, participating, and learning are, therefore, humanising processes.

While developing the research, we observed the school's attempt at countering rigidity toward playing, by ensuring different hours and spaces for children to play in every grade of fundamental education. This attempt did not overcome the 'play' and 'learn' dichotomy; thus children's logic seems detached from practices that aim at developing the curriculum. In the same way, children do not indicate that early childhood education meant quality time for playing, without fragmentation.

During the circles of conversation conducted in the research, children clearly differentiated 'playing' from 'doing homework', such as when Clara[2] (6 years old, 1st grade) said: "We do not play when we do homework on the blackboard". Regarding this issue, Giovani (10 years old, 5th grade) said that there is a playing time in the classroom – when they are done with what is on the blackboard and they can play and choose to chat or play *Stop*.[3] That suggests that throughout the schooling process, playing opportunities are gradually 'allowed' by adults after the children are 'done with their homework'. Perhaps in early childhood education, there

---

[2] We use pseudonyms to refer to the participants of the research: Clara, Giovani, Luany, Felipe, Paula, Otavio and Isabela.

[3] *Stop* is a pencil and paper game very popular with children, youth, and adults.

was no homework on the blackboard, but, even so, children show that these activities were used to control the time at school according to the thinking of adults.

The children brought up other arguments surrounding the transitions among the fundamental education stages and their impact on playing. Six-year-old children were mainly concerned about stating that they no longer play, perhaps referring to their view that, since they left early childhood education, they do not need to. That image of 'playing' as something that is associated with 'babies' is socially and culturally built, and is expressed in children's comments. The idea that playing is mostly for 'babies' and that 'studying' is for older children was brought up in the circle of conversation when one of the children recalled that they used to take naps in their early childhood education school, and that this does not occur in fundamental education schools. When questioned about the reason for that, the child answered: "because you can't, right? We're no longer babies. We have to study". A 6-year-old classmate added to the conversation by saying: "It's true. I even stopped taking bottles. And I'm stopping to play now". In this dialogue, children show that they believe that playing is for younger children, not children in fundamental education. By sharing this information with an adult, they may also aim to be seen to be more mature than children in early childhood education and may expect to be granted increased importance and value in return, rather than talking about their playing universe.

When looking at the school playground, 10-year-old children took pictures from different angles and reflected on playing. They pointed out that playtime is chronologically reduced as school years go by. However, they stated that they continued to play, mostly among themselves. This suggests that time, space, and playing's own plot have changed, but playing was still valued by those children. They reinforced the importance of the playground and the stories they have lived there; at the same time, they acknowledged the need for younger children to enjoy that space more:

> Giovani: In 1st, 2nd and 3rd [grades] we used to play in the playground, but in 4th and 5th [grades], since we kind of grew up, we stopped going to the playground, because playgrounds can't, like, hold us, it's more because there were, like, too many students that needed to use it more.

> Felipe (10 years old, 5th grade): But the monitor lets us play in the playground sometimes, to remember...

The time for conversations and decision-making about the organisation of this space and time at school do not seem to be shared with the children, although the National Education Council (CNE), via Report n° 11/2010 (Brasil, 2010) which provides the National Curriculum Guidelines for the 9-year Fundamental Education, established that attention is to be given to the topic of children's participation at school.

This document states that the extension of compulsory schooling is strongly related to the right to education, and the school is both a space for exercising citizenship and civil, political, and social rights, and for the "creation of new rights and spaces for expressing them" (Brasil, 2010, p. 3). These principles should guide the review of school curricula with a "democratic and participatory approach when preparing and implementing them" (Brasil, 2010, p. 2). This implies democratic and participatory management should include the children's participation – one of the pillars of the 9-year fundamental education program – when making decisions about curriculum development.

During their participation, the children interact and reproduce the explanations provided by adults (or other classmates) and reinterpret this information based on their own logic – a concept that Corsaro (2009b, p. 31) defined as "interpretive reproduction". Thus, the school, since it provides this meeting between adults and children, and children among themselves, is configured as a powerful space for participation and interaction, even when children's actions are not legitimised by adults. This is one aspect that anchors learning activity and the relationship with knowledge.

According to what the children say, we identify that, just like playing, it is not possible to identify that there was a greater participation of children in early childhood education. We identified that the perception they have about their participation has changed throughout their fundamental education grades. Thus, unlike 1st graders, who say they enjoy being the first in line, 5th graders show that they are already aware that there is an adult-centered logic at school: there is always something to be turned in and shown, and only then are they listened to.

The student/teacher relationship is also perceived in different ways: 1st graders, for instance, regarded a teacher yelling as a valid and necessary attitude to control how the children behaved. Luany (1st grade, 6 years old) stated that she would do the same to catch the attention of misbehaving children if she was in the teacher's shoes. At no time did children report feeling that adults' rigidity was greater in the 1st year and/or that they missed the teachers from the previous year. This suggests that children arrived at fundamental education school already used to this type of attitude from adults; they were quite knowledgeable about the justifications for these forms of control mobilised by the teachers.

These younger children seem to accept and legitimate adults (and their attitudes) as an expression of unquestionable authority. In turn, 5th graders criticised the teachers' position and the need they revealed for always being right:

> Giovani: Even when the teacher goes over there and, for instance writes that 5 + 3 is 7. Then the student says it isn't, but the teacher tells the student to not give his or her opinion, because he or she is a student and not the teacher. But, like, sometimes a student's opinion matters. Not just that of the teacher. If the student can't give his or her opinion, the student will end up thinking that the teacher is always right, but sometimes they are wrong.

These data and their analysis do not suggest that the school promotes participation and powerful interactions that favour children's culture. In pedagogical activities, the contact children have among themselves seemed to be constantly monitored by the adult-teacher. The representations of these adults surrounding what is configured as ideal learning conditions generally related to the need for silence, direction, and control. Moments in which children were able to work in pairs or switch places in the classroom were seen as 'rewards', apparently unrelated to the search for better learning conditions by encouraging dialogue among children. When asked about how often they worked in pairs at school, for instance, 5th graders say that this rarely occurred and laughed. Giovani stated that it is "mostly about each one, the teacher and the blackboard". Once again, it is important to emphasise that the 5th year children did not say that these moments of interaction between peers had 'diminished' over the years. Rather, it seemed to be taken for granted. This points to the consideration that the interactions between peers are insufficiently exploited to promote learning.

To incorporate children's participation in their pedagogical knowledge seems to be challenging for teachers. Centrally under their responsibility, the decisions about topics to be studied, for instance, seem to have no meaning to the children, who, in turn, seem to feel like they are the players of what is planned *for* them and not *with* them. At one point during the research, for instance, one of the 5th graders said that one of her group classmates had come from Peru, which caught the group's attention. She pointed out that the teacher should 'go through' other countries that school year. However, the countries selected to be studied had already been chosen and Peru wasn't one of them. This makes clear that those children's curiosity and interest had no influence in selecting what was to be studied.

At no point in the research did the children mention school situations that started or were conducted according to their interests. Otávio (10 years old, 5th grade) said that he would like to have more situations involving research and scientific experimentation and that he expected these situations to be part of the final years of fundamental school. He recalled only once, in early childhood education, had the teacher proposed an experience involving the cultivation of earthworms. The other children did not mention this type of experience in early childhood education, which suggests that these practices are not recurrent at this level of schooling. In this sense, the children participating in the research did not see 'ruptures' between what they lived in early childhood education and fundamental school.

Children pointed out that decisions were made exclusively by adults, which allows us to assume that a child's view is a passive element in the learning process. By following that logic, the teachers, since they are adults, can interpret the curriculum, without necessarily listening to the children. Based on the children's comments, their learning process and expectations toward the continuity of their studies could be adversely affected. It is possible that because of this, among other aspects, the children revealed their low expectations regarding what is to come in the upcoming school years, despite the National Curriculum Guidelines for 9-year fundamental education (Brasil, 2010) establishing continuity of the education process as one of their goals. However, the children did not give clues that allow us to affirm that they experienced a 'rupture' in relation to early childhood education, as if, in the previous stage, there was a search for building more shared decisions.

Overall, when questioned about what they expected for the upcoming school years, the children's answers were related to aspects that restricted the potential of school work ("doing more homework"; "finish the school") and others that are external to the school and are related to the job market ("find a job"; "to be an engineer"). First graders showed that they were mobilised for "learning more" – even with ready speeches about literacy; they stated that they liked to write stories. However, it is worth pointing out that the stories that Luany and Clara wrote recalled activities that were performed at home, with either stronger or weaker support from the family.

The children – both starting and completing the first stage of fundamental education – showed that they expected an increase in the amount of homework as they moved through different grades at school. But they did not seem to believe that "to do homework" strengthened the relationship with school content. Quite the opposite. In their statements, "to do homework" overlaps "to study", a verb that they no longer use to refer to school: "Next year I'm going to learn more because I will have more homework to do" (Clara). Throughout this conversation, Clara seems to automate the "reading, writing, and counting" process, and does not show that the school brings the opportunity for a wide range of world readings, as she states she intends to do:

Q:	And how do you imagine the other grades in fundamental education will be?
Clara:	With more homework!
Q:	But what will they be about?
Clara:	About reading, about writing, about doing math, those things that you have to know. Because we're at school, right?
Q:	I don't get it… Why do you come to school every day?
Luany:	To not be absent.
Clara:	And be educated.
Q:	So, do all the kids go to school to be educated?
Clara:	That's it, doing homework and get educated.
Q:	And after you learn how to write and read, how do you get more educated?
Clara:	Doing more homework.

These statements suggest a limited concept of learning and literacy, one that is more related to building proper behaviors than to a relationship with conceptual knowledge, while assigning little value to the literacy process in its amplitude and to the very schooling process. Still in this sense, we did not identify in the children's comments a tone of 'rupture' when they talked about working with literature built on early childhood education: they did not resent the loss of a type of approach that could potentially continue in elementary school. When we asked about the stories that children like most, they did not show memories of experiences lived in early childhood education. Rather, they seemed to have learned to separate learning reading and writing from the possibility of reading and writing stories, for example. Despite their longer school experience, 5th graders also brought few arguments that allow us to state that they understand schooling more broadly than to just "do homework". However, they criticised the mechanical propositions that related to school knowledge as something that is 'ready' and not much – or not at all – subjected to discussions. The following excerpt makes visible the disconnection between Giovani's 'desire to learn' and Paula's warning about the true organisation of schoolwork:

Q:	And what are the expectations that you two have for 6th grade? What do you hope for?
Giovani:	I hope […] to have many experiments in science. And geography, to see embossed things, look at maps. […]
Paula:	Really? We are going to spend the entire day sitting and doing homework.

No feeling of rejection toward the school was identified in the children's statements. In turn, they indicated that teaching practices would be decisive for strengthening the relationship with knowledge – "you have to learn what is important [...] but it could be more, like, let's say, more interesting" (Giovani).

The children's account about what takes place inside the school, in terms of acquiring essential resources to expand how they read the world, reveal a certain detachment between childhood and school knowledge objects. The critical analysis conducted by Gimeno Sacristán (2005) fits here, when he points out that the school prioritises certain behaviours surrounding students' acquisition of knowledge that end up being more valued than the very relationship between subject and knowledge. In doing so, the school creates a universe that is centred on its own practices and it is not configured as a space for children to experience knowledge. What we want to point out is that "learning at schools is a way to absorb knowledge, which is often just justified because of their own rituals to which one is subjected" (Gimeno Sacristán, 2005, pp. 161–162). We understand, in this sense, that the relationship between subject and knowledge needs to be addressed both in early childhood education and in fundamental education, as children do not identify 'ruptures' between these stages, but rather the continuity of a school logic that favors a hierarchical relationship between adults and children, where the relationship with knowledge is secondary. Thus, the children's expectations regarding the next school years are weakened.

Fifth graders, when referring to teenagers in more advanced school grades, often repeated that they learn nothing at school. And they added: teenagers place homemade bombs in the trash can, break drinking fountains or clog water outlets with little bathroom tissue balls, and so on. For those children, "teenagers come to school only to brawl, vandalize or… you know, date, smoke in secret" (Isabela, 10 years old, 5th grade). And they go on: "Do you think that they want to study?" In other words, the children have built an idea that teenagers only go to school to vandalise the school space and move further away from the perception that they take on a relationship with school knowledge. This construction is possibly supported by the comments of adults about older students. Accordingly, we noticed that the school's walls kept and communicated those marks only, thus reinforcing the view children had. There was a notable absence of other expressions regarding what teenagers did at school in terms of knowledge production and learning. It is within this scenario that children prepare themselves for the next transition they are to undergo – from the first grades of fundamental education (Fundamental I) to the final grades of fundamental education (Fundamental II) – and this certainly influences their expectations toward the upcoming years at school: "Everyone stays until the very end at school, but this part could be skipped and we could go straight to working" (Paula, 10 years old, 5th grade).

Final Considerations or Recommendations

The research on which this chapter is based was guided by the ideas of authors who state that extending the time children and young people spend at school "only justifies facing [...] the curriculum issue, in relation with the whole network of factors in which school attendance takes place" (Sampaio & Galian, 2015, p. 13). Accordingly, it is understood that time spent at school does not guarantee quality education if the schools do not actually create conditions for children to take ownership of essential knowledge to interpret the world in which they live and, as subjects, are active.

The 9 year fundamental education program cannot just be an extension of what already existed, as an answer to the goals undertaken in wider politics oriented to South America. It must influence curriculum changes that guarantee access to school knowledge, for personal and social transformation, which would result in actual learning and promote the continuity of studies at a school with social quality. The data reported in this study show that knowing the specificities of childhood can influence this search for quality schoolwork. It is in this sense that, by working with these data, we decided to start from listening to the children, underlining the relationship between school and childhood. Accordingly, we add that the transitions children undergo through the stages of basic education should not mean a rupture with the discussions about childhood.

We highlight that childhood demands research whose goal is to understand children within different contexts, among them, the children – students at the public fundamental education schools – by strengthening the necessary move of changing the representations about the students by listening to them. This listening process must be conducted in such a way that considers the discussions about reducing/weakening the potential the school has for fulfilling its social function, which is to grant access to school knowledge that will allow understanding the world in its complexity.

Supporting the concepts of Gimeno Sacristán (2005), the analysis highlighted the marks of school teaching that demand behaviours from the 'student'. Furthermore, by finding support in Sarmento's and Corsaro's childhood sociology, we identified and discussed the mismatch existing between childhood and school culture.

Regarding the relationship with knowledge (Charlot, 2000), the school was recognised as a mediator in the relationships of children with the social adult world, as much as it looks at children's specific activity within this space. Thus, we stated that by valuing childhood within this space, the relationship children have with the school and knowledge can be strengthened. There is still much to achieve in terms of valuing children and childhood, but this is the direction the school followed to engage with children's logic, by problematising how it looks at children and valuing the representations they build about being children in a fundamental education school. The challenge for this to be effective involves starting with their fundamental rights – to play, participate, and learn – in order to develop a school/childhood relationship that is oriented toward expanding opportunities to access school knowledge.

Inside schools, children continue to have their roles as children and students clearly separated. It is accepted that they play during the short and limited spaces created to live 'being a child' – and only there.

This image of playing as something that is associated with 'babies' is socially and culturally constructed and is expressed in the children's comments – they are markings that symbolize, in Brazil, the view that early childhood education is a space for playing and fundamental education a space to study. This division is mainly expressed in the fundamental school, but there is still a strong dispute around the early childhood schools for this stage to be anticipatory and preparatory for fundamental school, which means that we cannot claim that we have won a curriculum for 0–5 years that enhances play and interactions.

Children go through the passage of 5–6 years, strengthened by the cultural construction that playing is more for babies and that studying is for older children: "We **have** to study" Clara (6 years old, 1st grade). Likewise, throughout fundamental school, children seek to justify their games, moving them away from the children's universe and closer to the 'job market': "For example, like this, the Lego, […], it supports whoever wants to be, for example, an engineer" (Felipe, 10 years old, 5th grade). Felipe points to a conception of play that seems to seek legitimacy in the usefulness of play, in its possible contribution to an objective in the future. However, at other times, 10-year-old children return to their childhood memories and claim that playing has supported them in building relationships between peers and is part of the memories they have of the early childhood school.

The devaluation of childhood and playing is present in the Brazilian school culture: playing and participating in the learning process are separated, both in early childhood education and in fundamental education. Mello (2015) points out that the education being offered to children in both contexts is centred on mistaken and restricted practices, which do not properly use knowledge about the formation and development of children's intelligence and personality and that disregard the needs of childhood. In this way, the transitions between early childhood education and elementary education have been planned under the logic of "speeding up schooling" – a logic that remains throughout fundamental school (Mello, 2015, p. 24). For us, this means denying the early years of fundamental school as a powerful space for dialogue between children's knowledge and the knowledge that is part of the cultural, artistic, environmental, scientific, and technological heritage, in order to promote integrated development and the strengthening of learning.

On the contrary, students are subjected to an education that is marked by pedagogical practices that are based in exhausting routines and are exposed to evaluations by an adult. This traditional way of making school oriented toward forming the 'future citizen', compromises the relationships that emerge with knowledge, and contribute to an impoverished relationship with the experience of being at school (Charlot, 2000; Sampaio, 2004).

The official Brazilian documentation emphasises the importance of continuity between the stages of education. However, listening to elementary school children allows us to state that, between 6 and 10 years of age, the process of transforming children into 'students' implies distancing them from the memories of early childhood education, which is now understood as a 'less serious' time in view of the responsibility of 'studying' that is imposed. Thus, children's pathways in early childhood education are little considered in the face of the 'universe of school knowledge' that is now being presented within fundamental education. We did not have access to the totality of memories that children built about early childhood education, but we identified that the predominant culture in fundamental education is to convince children that they have 'grown up' and that, therefore, they must abandon the actions that are part of a child's repertoire. We add that this culture is a social construction, that is, it is not exclusive to this school where the research took place.

We also identified weaknesses in relation to the planning of the transitions between early childhood education and fundamental education, between the years that comprise elementary education and between the 5th and 6th year, which characterise the transition between early and final years of elementary education as children move from Fundamental Education I to Fundamental Education II. We argue that such weaknesses are the result of the disarticulation between childhood and school.

Finally, we point out the possibility for additional research to be conducted to investigate the playing aspect of children aged 6–10 years, as well as diving deeper into the debate about school knowledge specificity in fundamental education, in the search for creating learning which favours conditions that respect childhood.

References

Barbosa, M. C. S., & Delgado, A. C. C. (Eds.). (2012). *A infância no Ensino Fundamental de 9 anos* [Childhood in 9-year elementary school]. Penso.

Brasil. (2005). *Law 11.114, May 16th 2005*. http://www.planalto.gov.br/ccivil_03/_ato2004-2006/2005/lei/l11114.htm. Accessed 14 July 2021.

Brasil. (2007). *Ensino Fundamental de nove anos: orientações para a inclusão da criança de seis anos de idade* [Nine-year elementary school: Guidelines for the inclusion of the six-year-old child] (2nd ed.). Ministry of Education. http://portal.mec.gov.br/seb/arquivos/pdf/Ensfund/ensifund9anobasefinal.pdf. Accessed 14 July 2021.

Brasil. (2009). *Diretrizes Curriculares para a Educação Infantil* [Curricular guidelines for early childhood education]. Ministry of Education. http://portal.mec.gov.br/dmdocuments/diretrizescurriculares_2012.pdf. Accessed 14 July 2021.

Brasil. (2010). *Diretrizes Curriculares Nacionais para o Ensino Fundamental de Nove anos* [National curricular guidelines for nine-year elementary school]. http://portal.mec.gov.br/dmdocuments/rceb007_10.pdf. Accessed 14 July 2021.

Ciardella, T. (2019). *"As escolas são tudo igual – só muda as criança": o ensino fundamental fotografado pelos alunos* ["Schools are all the same – Only children change": Elementary education photographed by students] [Master's dissertation]. School of Education. University of São Paulo. https://www.teses.usp.br/teses/disponiveis/48/48134/tde-03102019-123443/pt-br.php. Accessed 14 July 2021.

Charlot, B. (1979). *A mistificação pedagógica: realidades sociais e processos ideológicos na teoria da educação* [Pedagogical mystification: Social realities and ideological processes in the theory of education]. Zahar.
Charlot, B. (2000). *Da relação com o saber: elementos para uma teoria* [On the relationship with knowledge: Elements for a theory]. Artmed.
Charlot, B. (2009). School and the pupils' work. *Sísifo: Educational Sciences Journal, 10,* 87–94.
Corsaro, W. (2009a). Métodos etnográficos no estudo da cultura entre pares e das trnasições iniciais na vida das crianças [Ethnographic methods in the study of peer culture and early transitions in children's lives]. In F. Muller & A. M. A. Carvalho (Eds.), *Teoria e prática na pesquisa com crianças: diálogos com William Corsaro* [Theory and practice in research with children: Dialogues with William Corsaro] (pp. 83–103). Cortez.
Corsaro, W. (2009b). Reprodução interpretativa e cultura de pares [Interpretive reproduction and peer culture]. In F. Muller & A. M. A. Carvalho (Eds.), *Teoria e prática na pesquisa com crianças: diálogos com William Corsaro* [Theory and practice in research with children: Dialogues with William Corsaro] (pp. 31–50). Cortez.
Delalande, J. (2011). As crianças na escola: pesquisas antropológicas [Children at school: Anthropological research]. In A. J. Martins Filho & P. D. Prado (Eds.), *Das pesquisas com crianças à complexidade da infância* [From research with children to the complexity of childhood] (pp. 61–80). Autores Associados.
Gesser, V., & Furtado, M. (2013). A política de ampliação do Ensino Fundamental de Nove Anos: contextualizações legais e reflexões sobre a infância neste processo [The policy of expanding the nine years elementary school: Legal contexts and reflections on childhood in this process]. In V. S. Ferreira & V. Gesser (Eds.), *Ensino Fundamental de Nove Anos*: *princípios, pesquisas e reflexões* [Nine year elementary school: Principles, research and reflections] (pp. 33–52). CRV.
Gimeno Sacristán, J. (1998). *El curriculum: uma reflexión sobre la practica* [The curriculum: A reflection on practice]. Morata.
Gimeno Sacristán, J. (2005). *O aluno como invenção* [The student as an invention]. Artmed.
Gobbi, M. A. (2011). Num click: meninos e meninas nas fotografias [In a click: Boys and girls in the photos]. In A. J. Martins Filho & P. D. Prado (Eds.), *Das pesquisas com crianças à complexidade da infância* [From research with children to the complexity of childhood] (pp. 129–158). Autores Associados.
Lobo, A. P. S. (2012). A educação infantil, a criança e o ensino fundamental de nove anos: ampliando o debate [Early childhood education, children and nine-year elementary education: Broadening the debate]. In M. C. S. Barbosa & A. C. C. Delgado (Eds.), *A infância no Ensino Fundamental de 9 anos* [Childhood in 9-year elementary school] (pp. 69–78). Penso.
Mello, S. A. (2015). *Uma proposta para pensar um currículo integrador da infância paulistana* [A proposal to think about an integrating curriculum for childhood in São Paulo]. SME/DOT.
Quinteiro, J., & Carvalho, D. (2007). *Participar, brincar e aprender: exercitando os direitos da criança na escola* [Participate, play and learn: Exercising children's rights at school]. Junqueira e Marin/CAPES.
Sampaio, M. M. F. (2004). *Um gosto amargo de escola: relações entre currículo, ensino e fracasso escolar* [A bitter taste of school: Relations between curriculum, teaching and school failure] (2nd ed.). Iglu.
Sampaio, M. M. F., & Galian, C. V. A. (2015). Escola, tempo e currículo [School, time and curriculum]. In J. Bittencourt, J. S. Thiesen, & A. Mohr (Eds.), *Projetos formativos em educação integral: investigações plurais* [Training projects in integral education: Plural investigations] (pp. 13–42). NUP/CED/UFSC.
Sarmento, M. J. (2011). A reinvenção do ofício de criança e de aluno [The reinvention of the craft of child and student]. *Atos de Pesquisa em Educação, 6*(3), 581–602. https://doi.org/10.786 7/1809-0354.2011v6n3p581-602
Young, M. F. D. (2014). Superando a crise na teoria do currículo: uma abordagem baseada no conhecimento [Overcoming the crisis in curriculum theory: A knowledge-based approach]. *Cadernos Cenpec, 3*(2), 225–250. http://cadernos.cenpec.org.br/cadernos/index.php/cadernos/article/view/238/249. Accessed 18 July 2021.

Thais Monteiro Ciardella is a University Professor (Vera Cruz Institute, Brazil) and works at Comunidade Educativa CEDAC (São Paulo, Brazil). Graduated in Pedagogia and Master in Education (University of São Paulo, 2019), Thais researches the relationship between childhood and curriculum, studying as theoretical references: Bernard Charlot, Gimeno Sacristan and Michel Young. She participates as a researcher in the group School, Curriculum and Knowledge (ECCO in Portuguese – University of São Paulo) and Nucleus for Research and Extension in Childhood studies (NPEEI in Portuguese – Vera Cruz Institute, Brazil).

Cláudia Valentina Assumpção Galian is Associate Professor, University of São Paulo, Brazil. Cláudia was a science teacher at the Elementary School for about fifteen years. In 2010, she started to work at the School of Education, teaching issues related to curriculum and pedagogy as well as developing education research. Her studies focus on curriculum and school knowledge in the Brazilian Elementary School drawing on theories from different scholars including Michael Young, Basil Bernstein, and Ursula Hoadley. She also coordinates the group School, Curriculum and Knowledge (ECCO in Portuguese - University of São Paulo).

Chapter 9
A Case Study. Transition in a Waldorf School in São Paulo, Brazil: A Process Under Construction

Maria Florencia Guglielmo, Andrea Perosa Saigh Jurdi, and Ana Paula da Silva Pereira

Abstract The chapter reports experiences of evaluations and follow-up of children transitioning from early childhood education into the first grade of a Waldorf elementary school located in the city of São Paulo, Brazil. The study analyses the institutional strategies used to enable the school's transitional process for 6 to 8 year-old children, according to the current educational policy of the country. It presents the fundamentals of the Waldorf pedagogy, emphasising activities developed in early childhood education and the relationship between the maturity level of sensory-motor skills, cognitive, and social and emotional aspects and the formal learning process according to the Waldorf pedagogy. One section of the chapter explains the experiences of assessment and monitoring of all students in transition undertaken at the Waldorf Rudolf Steiner School since 2012. Next, the national law regarding the transition between early childhood and elementary education is discussed, as well as its impact in the kindergartens and Brazilian Waldorf schools. The chapter highlights the importance of expanding the discussion about the social and emotional maturity levels of children's development in educational institutions and in society in general.

M. F. Guglielmo (✉) · A. P. S. Jurdi
Universidade Federal de São Paulo, São Paulo, Brazil
e-mail: florencia.guglielmo@ewrs.com.br; andreajurdi@gmail.com

A. P. da Silva Pereira
University of Minho, Braga, Portugal
e-mail: appereira@ie.uminho.pt

© The Author(s), under exclusive license to Springer Nature Switzerland AG 2022
A. Urbina-García et al. (eds.), *Transitions to School: Perspectives and Experiences from Latin America*, International Perspectives on Early Childhood Education and Development 37, https://doi.org/10.1007/978-3-030-98935-4_9

Introduction

The transition from early childhood education to elementary education is a crucial moment in the child's life, which has emotional repercussions as well as impacts on the school trajectory of children and their families. This transition implies a set of continuous and complex changes in academic and social performance, adaptation, and autonomy because, in addition to changing space and/or school, there are changes in relationships, time, content, and learning contexts. According to researchers, these elements can be both opportunities and challenges for the child, family, teachers, and other professionals involved in this process (Chikwiri & Musiyiwa, 2017; Erkan et al., 2018; Fabian & Dunlop, 2007; Fontil & Petrakos, 2015; McIntyre et al., 2010; O'Toole et al., 2014; Pianta & Kraft-Sayre, 2007; Rous & Hallam, 2006).

Due to these impacts, this transition must be understood from the perspective of the child, school, family, and community. Rous and Hallam (2006) place the child at the centre of the transition process, valuing their individual characteristics, but simultaneously highlighting the importance and influence of a set of factors related to the family and community. In the case of the family, their concerns, priorities, attitudes, values, cultures, and resources stand out. Factors related to the community highlight the importance of local systems and services, namely their articulation, leadership, financing, policies, and training in the area of transition. Therefore, the transition from early childhood education to elementary education must integrate a set of guiding principles that guarantee the quality of this process. Such planning highlights the value attributed to the child's development and learning.

Gould (2012) and Hanson (2005) each propose a set of principles that characterise the transition to elementary school as a process that involves the child, family, and different professionals from the school and the community. These principles are based on building positive relationships and on effective and collaborative communication between different individuals, with the result that the entire community assumes responsibility for implementing policies that take into account social, emotional and educational needs of the child, the family, and the school – and these form the basis for planning. This planning supports the social progress of the community, as it shapes the child's school trajectory, in addition to reducing stress and allowing the family and the child a comfortable and positive change from one level of education to another (Fowler & Hanzel, 1996; Pianta & Kraft-Sayre, 2007; Salmi & Kumpulainen, 2017).

Recognising the importance of transition within education, this chapter presents a report of experiences of the transition from early childhood education to elementary education in a particular situation in Brazil. The chapter is divided into three topics. The first relates to early childhood education in the Brazilian context, addressing the legislation and policies related to the topic. The second topic is the description of the experiences, based on the foundations of Waldorf pedagogy. In the third and last topic, we highlight the challenges that Brazilian legislation poses to Waldorf schools to effect the transition from early childhood education to elementary education, in ways which prioritise the social and emotional care of those involved.

Early Childhood Education in the Brazilian Context

Early childhood education as a right is a recent achievement in Brazil and sits within the context of public policies for the educational care of children from 0 to 6 years of age. From the struggles of social movements which intensified in the late 1980s, early childhood education as a right is recognised by the Federal Constitution of 1988, guaranteeing children's access to daycare centres and preschools. In the same decade,[1] *Lei de Diretrizes e Bases da Educação Nacional* [Law Guidelines and Bases of National Education] (Brasil, 1996) defines early childhood education as the first stage of basic education. For Campos et al. (2011) the legal milestones reinforced and legitimised the processes of expanding educational assistance to children aged 0 to 6 years.

Since 2000, the legal framework has changed, which has in turn changed educational networks and the organisation of basic education. Among these changes are the lowering of the age for starting elementary education – from 7 to 6 years of age – and the introduction of compulsory schooling from 4 years of age. Thus, in Brazil, we now have compulsory basic education from the age of 4 years, with children aged 4–5 years attending early childhood education and those aged 6–14 years enrolled in elementary education. Extending the duration of elementary education to 9 years automatically shortens the duration of early childhood education to 2 years, forcing managers, educators, and the school community to reflect and create strategies that enable the school transition of children aged 6.

Campos et al. (2011) emphasise the importance of expanding the critical debate on the age of admission to elementary education. They argue that some school failures (such as difficulties learning skills, difficulties with literacy and/or numeracy, poor organisational skills, and socioemotional challenges) seem to be linked to children's reported immaturity at the time of entering elementary education. Further, it is argued that this could be avoided by increasing awareness on the part of the professionals, families, and public managers involved, about the importance of respecting the developmental time of each child and their sensory, motor, cognitive, affective, and social aspects (social and emotional skills), in addition to the child's chronological age.

The text of the *Base nacional comum curricular* [Common National Curriculum Base] (Brasil, Ministério da Educação, 2017) provides guidance on planning the transition from preschool to elementary school. When the transition happens within the same institution, the school must create forms of articulation between teachers

---

[1] In 1990, the *Estatuto da Criança e do Adolescente* [Child and Adolescent Statute (ECA)] (Brasil, 1990), created by Law No. 8069/1990, presents the principle of full protection and ensures equal conditions for access and permanence in a free public school, located near the student's residence.

at both stages to ensure that children are able to continue their particular learning and developmental processes. However, when the transition takes place between preschools and schools which are separate institutions, the document recommends that records and reports be shared among teachers of the respective schools, allowing elementary education teachers to know the development and learning processes experienced by children in preschool.

The Common National Curriculum Base (Brasil, Ministério da Educação, 2017) is a normative document that defines the essential learning skills that all students must develop throughout the different stages and modalities of basic education. Principle 3.3. – entitled *Transitions* – predicts that the continuity of learning processes for children depends on strategies appropriate to the different transitions experienced by the child (home/daycare; daycare/preschool and preschool/elementary education). The document also establishes that preschool education and elementary education institutions must develop transition programs to ensure alignment between the curricula and pedagogical practices of both schools. It is in this sense that we share below the experience of the Waldorf Rudolf Steiner School.

Analysis of the Transition in a Brazilian Waldorf School

Waldorf pedagogy was created in 1919 by the Austrian philosopher Rudolf Steiner with the foundation of the first school in Stuttgart, Germany. Today, there are 1182 Waldorf schools in 66 countries and 1911 kindergartens in 69 countries (Freunde der Erziehungskunst Rudolf Steiners, 2021). In Brazil, Waldorf pedagogy has existed since the foundation of the first school in the city of São Paulo in 1956. In 2019, the Federation of Waldorf Schools in Brazil (FEWB) registered approximately 270 federated schools.

Steiner (1988) based his pedagogical proposal on the recognition that the human being is constituted of bodily, psychic (cognitive, affective and volitional), and spiritual elements. These elements are in a mutable relationship throughout human life, influencing each other. For Steiner, knowing the different stages of development and maturation of these aspects was essential for education to realise the full potential of students. Based on this assumption, Rudolf Steiner, together with the first Waldorf teachers, developed a curriculum that encompasses the different characteristics and stages of development of children and young people, taking into account the type of experience and content that best suits their needs (Steiner, 2003). In short, Waldorf pedagogy is characterised by proposing teaching content and methodology according to each age group.

According to Waldorf pedagogy, each cycle of human development lasts approximately 7 years and has qualitatively different characteristics with regard to bodily, psychic, and spiritual aspects (Lievegoed, 1994). By adapting to these phases, education offers children and young people the best conditions to develop their skills and abilities. Aiming at a comprehensive education, Waldorf pedagogy offers a diversity of subjects that provide students with a wide range of experiences and possibilities for expression (including painting, music, crafts, gardening, and carpentry).

The curriculum is not fixed; it remains flexible to encompass historical and social differences, different cultural contexts, as well as the characteristics of each room, and the specific needs of students. Creatively reconciling knowledge about the different age groups and their characteristics with the needs of the reality in which the student lives is a challenge for the contemporary Waldorf teacher. The curricular changes need to be in line with the image of human development cultivated in Waldorf schools in order to be consistent with its pedagogical proposal (Bach Júnior & Guerra, 2018).

Waldorf early childhood education complies with the same principles listed above and maintains methodological differences in relation to elementary education and high school. The classrooms are mixed, usually with children aged between 3½ and 7 years old. It is possible to cultivate coexistence between different age groups in this space. The goal is to offer a warm and cosy environment that refers to home. The coexistence of children of different ages offers rich opportunities for them to interact while practising multiple roles (the oldest, the youngest, the leader, the follower, and so on), thus favouring the development of their social skills.

The activities undertaken throughout the day include the care and cleaning of the common space, such as gardening and cooking. Tasks are related to everyday life, and children can imitate and freely introduce them into their own games (Steiner, 2013). Other activities developed at the Waldorf preschools include drawing, painting, storytelling, music, and handicrafts. Free play inside or outside the classroom takes up a lot of school time, allowing children to develop their own experiences and exercise their fantasy skills spontaneously. Literacy occurs in the first grade of elementary education, rather than in preschool.

The period of early childhood education is marked by the development of many new skills in relation to the environment. Since the detailed description of these skills is not part of the scope of this text, we will present only the children's achievements at the end of preschool so that references for their transition to formal education in Waldorf schools can be considered.

Preschoolers at Waldorf School

From a bodily point of view, by the end of early childhood education, significant changes have occurred for the child – arms and legs have stretched, losing the rounded shapes that usually predominate in the body of younger children. Another indication of physical maturity is the exchange of temporary teeth for permanent ones.

Children of this age group who are encouraged to move freely have developed body mastery and security. Children's drawing also gains structure, showing how the child establishes the notion of space through free movement. Sensory and motor experiences are also decisive for the formation of an integrated image of their own corporeity, which can be recognised in the way they represent the human figure in their drawings.

Most preschool children also show that they have developed some notions of time and process. Their concentration when performing activities increases and memory strengthens.

Playing also gains a new configuration, when it is marked by organisation and planning. Preschool children are able to guide actions based on their own goals. In the context of mixed classes, it is also possible to see how older children assume a leadership and care position in relation to younger children, showing resourcefulness to solve their social difficulties and deal with frustration. These social skills are acquired through daily living in the space of preschool and in the family nucleus.

For Waldorf pedagogy, early childhood education is the privileged space where these skills can develop through social interaction between peers and teachers, in games and artistic, manual, and corporal experiences. These experiences allow children to explore their environment actively, strengthening their self-esteem and confidence. These achievements will be required, particularly when entering elementary education, as they allow the child to adapt appropriately to their new social and cultural context. From the point of view of Waldorf pedagogy, the acquisition of these social and emotional skills is one of the indications that the student is ready for formal education. Good emotional, affective, and social development provides the basis for a better adaptation to the new school situation than cognitive performance taken in isolation (Kern & Friedman, 2008). Children who have acquired social and emotional skills deal better with the challenges and frustrations inherent to learning and new social situations. When the time for the child's transition from early childhood education to elementary education in a Waldorf school approaches, all the elements mentioned above are observed by the educators.

Greubel (2018) points out that each child acquires the skills mentioned above in relation to their environment and at their own pace. From the Waldorf pedagogical perspective, it would be impossible to establish a cut-off date for admission to elementary education, as provided by the Brazilian national legislation, as this would involve disregarding individual differences in child development. Observing each student and their characteristics is the mechanism through which it can be inferred, albeit without absolute certainty, whether the child is ready to begin formal education without losing their spontaneity, driven by an authentic desire to learn (Banning, 2009). In this context, each Waldorf school develops its own internal process to deal with this very delicate moment, taking into account the elements mentioned above and the social and legal context of its country.

Steiner pedagogy advocates that the first child development cycle (7 years) is completed around 6½ or 7 years of age. In Brazil, February is the beginning of the school year. This means that, in order to maintain consistency with the criteria used by this pedagogical proposal, children who turn 6 in the second half of the year raise doubts in relation to transition and demand care from the professionals responsible for observing them. In many cases, it is recommended that they stay in preschool in order to allow them to complete their early childhood developmental processes smoothly.

Planning the Transition from Early Childhood Education to Elementary Education at Waldorf School

Having established these parameters, we now describe the transition process with children at the Waldorf Rudolf Steiner School. The school embraces children, families, and teachers in their transition process through different institutional actions that are implemented based on the demands of the school community. The process is constantly evaluated and modified.

At the Waldorf Rudolf Steiner School, which incorporates preschool and elementary school, the first-grade rooms are composed of students from the school's six early childhood education rooms, children from other Waldorf kindergartens and a small number of children from schools with other pedagogical bases.

Initially, children who are candidates for the first school year are observed collaboratively by preschool and elementary education teachers. These teachers observe students in their own environment. After this observation, teachers jointly decide to transfer the child to elementary education or keep him/her for another year in preschool. As a consequence, the children could be admitted to school at 6 or 7 years of age. The information collected during the visit to the room is communicated to the parents who also participate in the decision making.

From 2012, with the creation of the pedagogical support area, there was an addition to the group responsible for supporting children in transition. A professional in the field began to observe all of the preschool children destined to attend the school throughout the second half of the year. A partnership was established with the Elementary Education Enrolment Committee, which consists of teachers and other professionals, such as occupational therapists. Preschool students at other Waldorf schools close to the institution are included in the transition process through visits made by a Pedagogical Support team. During these meetings, conversations are held with teachers to analyse the specific needs of students and, in some cases, to keep in touch with families, doctors, and therapists. This institutional mediation work makes it possible to strengthen ties with other Waldorf schools.

Experience moments are also organised by the school's Enrolment Committee twice a year, in which all candidates for the first grade participate so that through games they can be observed by elementary education teachers and members of the Pedagogical Support team within the institution's own space. The objective is to prepare a conscious and careful passage for the children, so that future teachers and Pedagogical Support professionals are aware of the necessary reception for students of future first grade groups.

The work with the transition revealed to the teams that not all teachers at the institution understood school readiness in the same way as it is understood by Waldorf pedagogy: as a set of sensory, motor, cognitive, affective, and social skills (social and emotional skills), as well as encompassing the child's chronological age. Of particular concern was the persistence of the idea that the child would mature over the first year of school, even though the evidence of monitoring these children throughout their school life shows that this sometimes occurs with suffering and to the detriment of their self-esteem and wellbeing.

In 2019, a professional from the school's Pedagogical Support team started a pilot project specially focused on transition with children from preschool. In the first semester of the year, she entered all the preschool rooms at the school, watching the children in their own environment and becoming familiar with the routine of the rooms. In the second semester, she brought together groups drawn from the 48 children applying for the first grade of 2020. Groups of six students were formed with children from all classrooms, and their configuration changed with each meeting. This change in the constitution of the groups was due to the internal organisation of the preschool rooms, but it had the positive consequence that at the end of the process all the children knew each other.

Once a week, the professional performed activities in the school's gardening space with each group. The location was chosen as it allowed children to move freely. Many circle games were held, some that required agility and balance, such as climbing on fabrics ('spider web'), climbing on wooden stumps, or jumping rope. In gardening, the children built a small boat made of wood, sanded, nailed, and painted the boat sails with watercolor, chose branches for the mast, and so on. Simultaneously with this activity, the children heard a story about sailors who courageously go out to conquer new worlds. The image of the journey into the unknown and the discovery of a new world was intentionally included with the aim of offering children a symbolic framework for their transition between the stages of education. At the end of this activity, everyone played together before going back to their classrooms.

In the beginning of 2020, the teachers of the first grade rooms commented, with the Pedagogical Support team, on how the children had started the year prepared, safe, and ready for work. The project was also rated by the preschool teachers as very positive and they recommended that it should be incorporated into the actions already implemented by the institution.

Elementary education teachers are also responsible for monitoring the transition process. At the beginning of each school year, the preschool teachers, the Pedagogical Support team, and the teachers of the first grade rooms share important information about some students, allowing them to prepare an environment appropriate to the students' needs. At the beginning of the second semester, Pedagogical Support professionals make visits to the first grade rooms for 3 days, attending classes and observing children in their new environment. These observations are subsequently shared with the teachers, enabling an expanded understanding of the children and supporting the teaching work.

Families are also included in the transition process at the Waldorf Rudolf Steiner School. An important part of the transition work involves conversations between teachers and family, sometimes with the presence of a Pedagogical Support professional, in order to explain the importance of preschool experiences and offer greater security in relation to the retention of their children for another year at preschool.

Since 2018, lectures have been organised with the same purpose at the beginning of each school year for the families of children who are candidates for elementary education. Initially restricted to the institution's families, in the following year they started to include parents of children from other kindergartens, in order to share the pedagogical perspective on school readiness and the importance for the transition of the family's partnership with the institution. These meetings reinforce the importance of activities developed in preschool education for the training of students and draw attention to the negative impact of early schooling supported by studies such as those by Kern and Friedman (2008).

It is worth mentioning that the Covid-19 pandemic that occurred in 2020–2021 has made it impossible to monitor preschool children as reported in this text. The suspension of face-to-face classes has prevented direct contact with students, families, and partner institutions. The team responsible for the transition at the Waldorf Rudolf Steiner School projects the need for more intensive monitoring of children, families, and future teachers throughout 2021–2022 in an attempt to minimise the potential impacts of social isolation.

The Challenges of School Transition in Waldorf Schools and the Brazilian Legislation

The Common National Curriculum Base (Brasil, Ministério da Educação, 2017) defines early childhood education as the beginning of the educational process. It is the space for the development of basic skills, described by the document as:

> (…) the mobilization of knowledge (concepts and procedures), skills (practical, cognitive, social and emotional), behaviours and values to solve complex demands of everyday life, full exercise of citizenship and work. (Brasil, Ministério da Educação, 2017, p. 8)

These competencies can develop from two main axes that structure the pedagogical practices within the scope of early childhood education: interaction and play. The educator's role is to offer children experiences that enable them to know themselves and each other and, establish relationships with nature and with their cultural context. The document describes the five fields of experience to be covered by the practices of early childhood education: one that encompasses the formation of one's own identity in relation to others and the expansion of their cultural references; a field dedicated to artistic experience that includes the possibility of self-expression; another field linked to free movement and corporal experimentation; the field of language development in speech, thought and imagination; and, finally, a field that allows the development of the notions of time and space, and the possibility of relating different objects.

The five fields of experience should enable children who finish the cycle of early childhood education to have the following skills: to be able to demonstrate empathy and confidence, to engage in attitudes of cooperation and mutual respect, showing interest in other cultures and ways of life; in the field of movement, being able to self-care, controlling their body in games and other activities, developing manual skills; be able to express themselves freely in activities such as painting and drawing; being able to express ideas, desires and feelings through language; retelling stories; establish comparative relationships between objects, different materials, relate numbers and quantities; and be able to report important events about their own history and that of their family members. The Common National Curriculum Base (Brasil, Ministério da Educação, 2017) points out that the synthesis of learning should be indicative, not a condition of access to elementary education.

Waldorf kindergartens offer children the conditions to develop the skills mentioned above through their pedagogical principles. The problem experienced by Waldorf kindergartens in implementing the policies outlined in this document is the strict delimitation of the early childhood education age group, 4–5 years and 11 months, imposed by the national curriculum document.

Over the past few years, Waldorf schools and preschools have encountered difficulties in the transition from early childhood education to elementary education. The decrease from 3 to 2 years of the early childhood education cycle lowered the cut-off age group, forcing younger children to enter the first grade. In an attempt to maintain consistency with the child development and specific needs of each child, Waldorf schools have tried in various ways to ensure that the transition takes place at the right time, but the pressures from teaching supervisors[2] are high, and smaller institutions feel fragile in supporting a discussion about the need for their students to stay for another year in preschool.

One solution found by the schools was lawsuits brought by the parents, asking for the possibility of the child staying for another year in preschool. This solitary action resolves isolated situations and, despite the number of successful cases, there is no guarantee that the family will be able to stay. This alternative also highlights the country's social differences. Many families do not have the financial means to undertake processes such as lawsuits, and are unable to guarantee their children the experiences appropriate to their age group according to the pedagogy of their choice. This creates considerable tension, since the Brazilian Constitution (Brasil, 1988) guarantees parents' freedom in choosing the pedagogical proposal that best meets their needs.

In 2018, the Federal Supreme Court (Supremo Tribunal Federal, 2018) decided the minimum age for entering elementary education for all children was 6 years, and applied to children who turn 6 before March 31. Although the decision was made to prevent the access of under-age students, in practice this made it very difficult to keep older children in preschool. The measure states that admission must take place *from* the age of 6, but has been interpreted as if admission should occur *at* the age of 6.

The Federation of Waldorf Schools in Brazil (FEWB) has promoted debates to discuss the topic with representatives of the federated schools. The objective is to propose a consultation with the National Education Council that allows maintaining the Waldorf pedagogy for transition between grades. At the same time, there is a

---

[2] Teaching supervisors are responsible for supervising and inspecting the educational institutions assigned to them, providing technical guidance and assisting in the correction of administrative and pedagogical flaws. (Governo do Estado de São Paulo – Diretoria Regional de Ensino, 2020)

concern about the loss of important experiences on the part of children in preschool with regard to the development of social and emotional skills, which have a great impact on their future life. This situation affects the country's contemporary childhood and demands a broader discussion on the part of society.

Final Considerations

It is understood that the experience of the Waldorf Rudolf Steiner School in monitoring the transition from preschool to elementary education can be replicated in other public or private school institutions in order to ensure a better reading of the legal documentation and respect for the autonomy of pedagogical proposals. The positive results of the experience of the last years demonstrate that the benefits of this support network, formed by collaborative work between several entities (families, teachers, and different school institutions), can be used in other educational contexts and become the object of future academic research.

It should also be noted that the discussion on the age range for admission to elementary education, according to the Waldorf pedagogy, encompasses issues of a broader scope for Brazilian education, highlighting the role of early childhood education in the development of social and emotional skills and in the establishment of a meaningful relationship with learning – which, it is believed, can be hindered in a poorly planned transition. Finally, an in-depth debate on this issue can change national public policies with positive impacts on the quality of contemporary childhood.

References

Bach Júnior, J., & Guerra, M. G. M. (2018). O currículo da pedagogia Waldorf e o desafio da sua atualização [The Waldorf pedagogy curriculum and the challenge of updating it]. *Revista e-Curriculum, 16*(3), 857–878. https://doi.org/10.23925/1809-3876.2018v16i3p857-878

Banning, N. (2009). *First grade readiness: Resources, insight and tools for Waldorf.* Waldorf Early Association of North America.

Brasil. (1988). *Constituição da República Federativa do Brasil* [Constitution of the Federal Republic of Brazil]. Senado Federal. http://www.planalto.gov.br/ccivil_03/constituicao/constituicao.htm. Accessed 30 July 2021.

Brasil. (1990). *Estatuto da Criança e do Adolescente* [Child and Adolescent Statute] Lei n° 8069, de 13 de junho de 1990. http://www.planalto.gov.br/ccivil_03/leis/l8069.htm. Accessed 30 July 2021.

Brasil. (1996). *Lei de Diretrizes e Bases da Educação Nacional* [Law guidelines and bases of national education] Lei n° 9394, de 20 de dezembro de 1996. Dispõe sobre as Diretrizes e Bases da Educação Nacional. MEC. http://www.planalto.gov.br/ccivil_03/leis/l9394.htm. Accessed 30 July 2021.

Brasil, Ministério da Educação. (2017). *Base nacional comum curricular: educação é a base* [Common national curriculum base: Education is the foundation]. MEC. http://basenacionalcomum.mec.gov.br/abase/. Accessed 30 July 2021.

Campos, M. M., Bhering, E. B., Esposito, Y., Gimenes, N., Abuchaim, B., Valle, R., & Unbehaum, S. (2011). A contribuição da educação infantil de qualidade e seus impactos no início do ensino fundamental [The contribution of early childhood education quality and its impacts at the beginning of elementary education]. *Educação e Pesquisa, 37*(1), 15–33. https://doi.org/10.1590/S1517-97022011000100002

Chikwiri, E., & Musiyiwa, J. (2017). Challenges and gaps in children's transition from early childhood development to grade one in Zimbabwe. *International Journal of Educational Administration and Policy Studies, 9*(7), 91–102. https://doi.org/10.5897/IJEAPS2017.0510

Erkan, N. S., Tarman, I., Sanli, Z. S., Kosan, Y., & Omruuzun, I. (2018). First grade students' perceptions of their preschool and elementary school experience. *International Journal of Progressive Education, 14*(5), 1–13. https://doi.org/10.29329/ijpe.2018.157.1

Fabian, H., & Dunlop, A.-W. (2007). *Informing transitions in the early years. Research, policy and practice*. Open University Press.

Fontil, L., & Petrakos, H. H. (2015). Transition to school: The experiences of Canadian and immigrant families of children with autism spectrum disorders. *Psychology in the Schools, 52*, 773–787. https://doi.org/10.1002/pits.21859

Fowler, S., & Hanzel, R. (1996). Planning transitions to support inclusion. In K. Allen & I. Schwartz (Eds.), *The exceptional child: Inclusion in early childhood education* (pp. 171–202). Delmar Publishers.

Freunde der Erziehungskunst Rudolf Steiners. (2021). *World list.* https://www.freunde-waldorf.de/fileadmin/user_upload/images/Waldorf_World_List/Waldorf_World_List.pdf. Accessed 30 July 2021.

Gould, T. (2012). *Transition in the early years. From principles into practice*. Latimer Trend & Company.

Governo do Estado de São Paulo – Diretoria Regional de Ensino. (2020). *Atribuições da equipe de supervisão* [Supervisory team assignments]. https://desul2.educacao.sp.gov.br/ese/. Accessed 30 July 2021.

Greubel, S. (2018). Las ramificaciones sociales y de desarrollo de la transición del jardín de infantes a la escuela primaria [The social and developmental ramifications of transition from early childhood education to primary education]. *Research on Rudolf Steiner Education, 8*(2), 78–88.

Hanson, M. J. (2005). Ensuring effective transitions in early intervention. In M. J. Guralnick (Ed.), *The developmental systems approach to early intervention* (pp. 373–400). Paul H Brookes.

Kern, M. L., & Friedman, H. S. (2008). Early education milestones as predictors of lifelong academic achievement, midlife adjustment, and longevity. *Journal of Applied Developmental Psychology, 30*(4), 419–430. https://doi.org/10.1016/j.appdev.2008.12.025

Lievegoed, B. (1994) *Desvendando o crescimento* [Phases of childhood]. Editora Antroposófica.

McIntyre, L., Eckert, T. L., Fiese, B. H., Di Gennaro Reed, F. D., & Wildenger, L. K. (2010). Family concerns surrounding kindergarten transition: A comparison of students in special and general education. *Early Childhood Education Journal, 38*, 259–263. https://doi.org/10.1007/s10643-010-0416-y

O'Toole, L., Hayes, N., & Mhathúna, M. (2014). A bio-ecological perspective on educational transition. *Procedia – Social and Behavioral Sciences, 140*, 121–127. https://doi.org/10.1016/j.sbspro.2014.04.396

Pianta, R. C., & Kraft-Sayre, M. (2007). *Successful kindergarten transitions. Your guide to connecting children, families & schools*. Paul H Brookes.

Rous, B. S., & Hallam, R. A. (2006). *Tools for transition in early childhood. A step by step for agencies, teachers & families*. Paul H Brookes.

Salmi, S., & Kumpulainen, K. (2017). Children's experiencing of their transition from preschool to first grade: A visual narrative study. *Learning, Culture and Social Interaction, 20*, 1–10. https://doi.org/10.1016/j.lcsi.2017.10.007

Steiner, R. (1988). *A arte de educar I: O estudo geral do homem, uma base para a pedagogia* [The art of education I: The general study of man, the basis for pedagogy]. Editora Antroposófica.

Steiner, R. (2003). *A arte de educar II: Metodologia e didática* [The art of education II: Methodology and didactics]. Editora Antroposófica.

Steiner, R. (2013). *Os primeiros anos da infância: material de estudo dos jardins de infância Waldorf* [The early years of childhood: study material for Waldorf kindergartens]. Editora Antroposófica.

Supremo Tribunal Federal. (2018). *Plenário julga válida data limite para idade de ingresso na educação infantil e fundamental* [Plenary judges valid deadline for the age of entry into early childhood and elementary education]. http://www.stf.jus.br/portal/cms/verNoticiaDetalhe.asp?idConteudo=385446. Accessed 29 May 2020.

Maria Florencia Guglielmo is an occupational therapist and professor of pedagogy in both graduate and post-graduate courses at Rudolf Steiner College (São Paulo). She is the coordinator of the pedagogical support area at the Waldorf Rudolf Steiner School. She is a doctoral student at the interdisciplinary graduate programs of the Health Sciences Department at the Federal University of São Paulo. Her main areas of interest include special needs education, mental health, and Waldorf education.

Andrea Perosa Saigh Jurdi is an associate professor at the Department of Health, Education and Society at the Federal University of São Paulo. She trained as a specialist in special education and early intervention and held a post-doctoral position in childhood studies at the Education Institute of the University of Minho. She is the coordinator of the Childhood, Education, and Health Research Group. She is a researcher at the interdisciplinary graduate programs in health sciences and in the masters program in health sciences teaching – professional modality. Her main scientific interests focus on the areas of early intervention, special educational needs, and child mental health. She guides masters and doctoral students and is the author and coauthor of several scientific articles.

Ana Paula da Silva Pereira is Assistant Professor at the Department of Psychology of Education and Special Education and Coordinator of the Master in Special Education, specialization in Early Childhood Intervention; researcher at the Research Center on Education (CIEd); and member of the Supervisory team of the Northern Regional Subcommittee of the Portuguese Early Childhood Intervention System. She coordinates the Luso Brasileiro Project on Early Intervention in Autism Spectrum Disorder and is a member of the national project team: Robotics and Autism Spectrum Disorder, and the international project: Vocational Training for Physiotherapists about Family-Centered and Play-Based Approaches in Early Childhood Intervention. Her main scientific interests focus on the areas of autism spectrum disorder, early intervention, transitions, and special educational needs. She supervises Master's and PhD students and is the author and coauthor of several scientific articles.

Chapter 10
Experiences and Explorations of Transitions to School

Sue Dockett and Bob Perry

Abstract In this concluding chapter we synthesise the previous chapters and explore what can be gleaned about the transition to school in Cuba, Chile, Brazil, and Mexico. Before we examine this in detail, we provide an overview of the COVID-19 crisis and its potential impact on transition to school, arguing that a broad focus on transitions and strategies to promote the wellbeing of all involved matters now more than ever. We follow this with an update – drawn from chapter author reports and documentation – of the impact of COVID-19 on transitions experiences in each of the countries. The chapter concludes with analysis and synthesis of the themes, issues and directions identified across the previous chapters.

Introduction: COVID and Transition

As noted in the introduction to this book, the editors appreciate the efforts of the chapter authors in preparing manuscripts during the very challenging COVID-19 pandemic. Across the four countries represented by chapter authors, the impact of COVID-19 has been both severe and long-lasting. As of July 2021, Mexico, Brazil, and Chile reported some of the highest worldwide levels of mortality from COVID (Johns Hopkins University, 2021). While mortality rates in Cuba have been lower, the recent resurgence of the pandemic has seen infection rates rise (World Health Organisation (WHO), 2021). In all four countries, there have been major impacts on people's lives and ways of life, their health, and finances. That chapter authors have been able to submit manuscripts during these challenging times is impressive and reflects their commitment to enhancing the understanding of transitions to school in their countries.

S. Dockett (✉) · B. Perry
Charles Sturt University, Albury, NSW, Australia
e-mail: sdockett@csu.edu.au; bperry@csu.edu.au

© The Author(s), under exclusive license to Springer Nature Switzerland AG 2022
A. Urbina-García et al. (eds.), *Transitions to School: Perspectives and Experiences from Latin America*, International Perspectives on Early Childhood Education and Development 37, https://doi.org/10.1007/978-3-030-98935-4_10

The World Health Organisation declared the COVID-19 pandemic in March 2020 (WHO, 2020). The education sector has been one of many aspects of daily life that has been impacted by decisions to close schools and early childhood settings. In many contexts, face-to-face interactions were replaced by strategies to promote virtual and/or remote learning. In turn, several of these strategies have generated additional challenges – particularly in contexts where families have limited or no access to electronic devices or the internet (World Bank, 2021a, b). In the context of early childhood education, the closure of physical premises has challenged educators and families to consider what might constitute appropriate educational expectations for children in diverse families and communities (Campos & Vieira, 2021; OMEP Executive Committee, World Organisation for Early Childhood Education, 2020; Park et al., 2020; Pramling Samuelsson et al., 2020; Spiteri, 2021). The pandemic has also highlighted, and sometimes further compounded, structural and social inequalities in educational provision and access (UNESCO, 2021) across countries in the Caribbean and Latin American regions. For example, children living in areas characterised as disadvantaged are reported to have limited access to electronic devices and the internet (World Bank, 2021a). Despite this, these countries have implemented a range of strategies to promote education both during the pandemic and as schools and early childhood settings go through the processes of re-opening.

It could be tempting to suggest that, in such challenging times, educational transitions are insignificant in the larger scheme of events. However, we propose the exact opposite: in times of dislocation and disconnection it is even more important to consider what is happening for young children and their families, how current experiences have the potential to impact future experiences and outcomes and how communities can work together to provide appropriate, timely and relevant support.

While it is certainly the case that closures have prevented attendance at schools and early childhood settings, it has long been recognised that children learn both inside and outside educational institutions. However, in many contexts, academic concerns are exacerbated by lack of access to resources, including digital access; the loss of support related to child and family wellbeing; impacts on children's nutrition; increasing inequalities related to economic status, disability, and gender; and increases in abuse and violence towards children (Economic Commission for Latin America and the Caribbean (ECLAC)/United Nations Educational, Scientific and Cultural Organisation (UNESCO) (ECLAC/UNESCO), 2020).

In some circumstances, there is reference to 'learning loss' or 'lost schooling' (Chen et al., 2021; Engzell et al., 2021) as children have not been able to attend the physical early childhood setting or school. The World Bank (2021b) also notes that "most children have lost substantial instructional time and may not be ready for curricula that were age- and grade-appropriate prior to the pandemic". Others note that academic achievement has been impacted negatively in some areas for children experiencing disadvantage, but that this impact was not experienced by all children or across all curriculum areas (Gore et al., 2020). Berger (2021) puts this in perspective when he notes that

Our kids have lost so much – family members, connections to friends and teachers, emotional well-being, and for many, financial stability at home. And, of course, they've lost some of their academic progress.

While the last point is not insignificant, Berger argues that over-emphasis on learning loss has the potential to focus attention on perceived deficits, rather than the resilience shown by many children, families, educators, and communities. Indeed, Jindal-Snape (Times Educational Supplement, 2021) reminds us that a great deal of learning occurs in a range of environments and that discourse focusing on deficits does little to recognise the efforts of children, families, and educators during this time. In rejecting the language of 'learning loss' both authors instead stress the importance of considering the social and emotional aspects of life – such as a sense of safety, self-worth, and belonging – and the importance of welcoming children to early childhood settings and schools as a means of helping them feel personally connected to these educational settings. These aspects are also integral elements of transition experiences that are the most relevant and appropriate (optimal) for each individual (Dockett & Perry, 2014).

These exhortations are in line with several studies that consider how the wellbeing of children, families, and teachers has been impacted by increased anxiety, isolation, illness, financial stress, the demands of educating children at home, and/or new modes of delivering teaching (Broadway et al., 2020; Eadie et al., 2021; Gore et al., 2020; Mochida et al., 2021; Pascal & Bertram, 2021). Starting school, or returning to school during, as well as after the pandemic, can contribute to, as well as challenge, the wellbeing of those involved.

In 'usual' circumstances, young children and their families experience considerable change as they start school or early childhood education or return to these environments after a substantial break. For example, they experience changes in the environment, the structure of the day, expectations, and opportunities for interactions. Again, in 'usual' circumstances, there can also be continuity as families, educational settings, and communities continue to support children's learning and as children build on prior experiences. Amid the current pandemic, some of these changes have been amplified and some of the potential continuities disrupted. Understanding transitions and working proactively to help all involved manage the changes, while at the same time promoting continuity, is an essential facet of supporting wellbeing.

There are many potential short- and longer-term impacts of the pandemic that are yet to emerge. Indications are that these impacts will disproportionately affect children and families living in challenging circumstances. When children have opportunities to return to early childhood and school education, supporting their wellbeing should be a primary concern (Cowie & Myers, 2020; Hoffman & Miller, 2020). This will require agencies and organisations from many different sectors to work collaboratively to support children, families, educators, and communities. One tranche of strategies to offer such support will need to focus on educational transitions for young children. The underlying purpose of these strategies will be to build and strengthen connections with education and, in doing so, generate a positive sense of value and belonging for children – and their families – that promotes ongoing engagement with early childhood and school education.

As in most countries around the world, the COVID-19 pandemic promoted many changes in the provision of early childhood and school education. In the following section, we share research and reports alongside the perspectives and experiences of the chapter authors about recent events.

Responding to COVID-19

The Ministry of Education in **Chile** (2020) instituted a range of programmes and strategies which aimed to support children, families, and educators during the pandemic. These included creating on-line learning platforms for children in the early years of school and providing access to resources for teachers and families (Organisation for Economic Co-Operation and Development (OECD), 2020a). Some resources were distributed in print in isolated areas, as well as online and through social media. As well as focusing on academic materials, a range of resources to support the wellbeing of children, families, and educators was developed. Adaptation of the food programme for kindergartens and schools involved the delivery of food baskets across the country, although the reach and comprehensiveness of this change to the programme is not clear.

The Undersecretariat of Early Childhood developed a web page with access to resources for early childhood teachers and launched the campaign *Porque nos necesitamos, Yo te acompano* (Because we need each other, I'll accompany you at home). This campaign shared videos and activities that could be undertaken at home. The National Board of Kindergarten (Junji) also distributed resources for families promoting home-based activities for children aged 0–2 and 3–6 years (Ministry of Education, 2020).

These resources were necessary as all schools and preschools in Chile were closed during the 2020 academic year. While some reopened in 2021, there have also been closures and then re-openings as localities experienced additional quarantine restrictions. During the pandemic, educators across early childhood and school contexts reported losing contact with the children, with many unable to maintain interactions (Elige Educar, 2020). Teachers of transition level cohorts reported difficulties contacting children during the lockdown periods, with only one third of teachers indicating that they were able to contact and monitor children's participation and learning during 2020 (Un Buen Comienzo, 2020). Teachers, as well as families, reported feeling overwhelmed and stressed with their experiences of education by distance (CEDEP, 2020; Elige Educar, 2020).

Distant or online schooling has increased social inequalities as children from poorer families have had less access to electronic devices and internet. Younger children have also been left behind as the software for online education used in Chile is language based, and often not designed for children in the early childhood years. As a result of limited access to online resources, preschool children in Chile are reported to have had fewer structured learning experiences in 2020 than previous years (Centro UC, 2021), and educational disparities across socioeconomic groups are reported to have increased.

While many of the resources distributed through government programmes have sought to maintain bonds between children and their teachers and/or educational setting, there have been some major challenges around transition. For example, when preschools and schools re-opened, many children started attending these institutions without prior knowledge or experience of the settings. As well, many children started attending these settings online, without meeting their teachers or classmates in person. As schools and early childhood settings reopened, some children were able to attend for a brief time, before these settings again were forced to close. Researchers and educators are concerned that such small periods of personal interaction have not been sufficient to build the relationships that underpin optimal transitions (Dockett & Perry, 2014; Jindal-Snape, 2018). Further, there is concern that transition in the early childhood years has not been a major topic of consideration during the pandemic, even though there is mounting evidence that children are struggling with all the changes.

At the time of the pandemic, **Brazil** was a country already dealing with a struggling economy, political crises, high levels of poverty and unemployment, and wide inequities across educational provision and access (Campos & Vieira, 2021; Human Rights Watch, 2021; OECD, 2021). The COVID-19 pandemic exacerbated this situation, with measures such as the closure of schools and early childhood settings having major impacts on families living in vulnerable and precarious contexts across diverse geographic locations. As responsibilities for managing the health emergency were vested in states and municipalities, the impact was felt differently across the country.

The closure of schools and early childhood settings had a major impact on the everyday lives of children and families. School educators made use of podcasts and on-line material (UNICEF, 2020a), such as *Educação em Rede* (Network Education) (Nova Escola, 2021), which provided resources to support distance education. However, these strategies also highlighted the digital divide across the country, with many children and families having no access to either the internet or electronic devices (Núcleo Ciência pela Infância (NCPI), 2020) and educators facing challenges in adjusting materials for online delivery (UNDIME Brasil, 2021).

School closures also saw disruption to the national school feeding programme, a primary source of nutrition for approximately 40 million children across the country (Lourenço et al., 2021). The disruption to this programme also impacted the livelihoods of many farmers, for whom the programme was a major source of income, further exacerbating social and economic inequalities. Municipalities adopted different strategies to distribute food kits or vouchers to families. However, these did not reach all families (Instituto Rui Barbosa, 2020). Other consequences of the suspension of face-to-face classes included increasing drop-out rates for the children experiencing disadvantage and increased rates of domestic violence (UNICEF, 2020a). The re-opening of schools has not necessarily alleviated these challenges.

The closure of early childhood settings resulted in social isolation for many children, as they lost contact with their friends and educators and experienced times of sadness, frustration, and confusion (Campos & Vieira, 2021). Rather than rely on distance learning, educators of young children often sought ways to connect personally with families and to engage families in the implementation of activities. As a consequence, the workload of teachers increased, despite often reduced working conditions and salary (Gestrado, 2020). The expectations of families also increased. Tasks associated with educating young children fell to women "mainly mothers, but also grandmothers or older siblings. It seems that those who are in charge of children's education at school and at home continue to follow the dominant gender hierarchy in society during the pandemic" (Campos & Vieira, 2021, p. 130). Emphasising the gendered impact of the pandemic across Latin America and the Caribbean, Miranda (2020, p. 10) notes:

> The closing of schools and childcare services increases stress levels on all families, especially single-parent households and those headed by women. The lockdowns have exacerbated the impacts of unequal pressure on women and girls to do care work.

Even with schools and early childhood settings re-opening, families reported feeling hesitant about sending their children to school or early childhood settings. While substantial progress has been made in making schools and early childhood settings hygienically safe for children, difference in infrastructure means that this remains a challenge in some areas (UNICEF, 2020a).

As in Chile, the topic of transition to school does not seem to have garnered a great deal of attention or planning in Brazil. While many teachers have made efforts to remain connected to children from their class groups, making and retaining such connections is more difficult when educators and children do not know each other, as is often the case when children start school. Despite the efforts of teachers, many children have been isolated from their peers and adults outside the family. Much focus has been directed towards the re-opening of schools and early childhood settings, yet there have been few attempts to plan transitions in ways that value children's experiences and perspectives or that recognise the changed relationships among families, early childhood settings, and schools.

Schools and early childhood settings were closed in **Mexico** for an extended period from March 2020. In-person classes were replaced with *Aprende en Casa* (Learning from Home) (Government of Mexico, 2020) that relied heavily on television programmes purposefully crafted for each school level and which were broadcast through the day. The Learning from Home programme included a series of activities for preschool-aged children and was available in both Spanish and English. The televised lessons and activities were accompanied by online platforms and radio podcasts, and textbooks and workbooks were made available online for children.

While the production and broadcast of materials was a major achievement, concerns were raised about the actual reach and accessibility of the materials and the models of teaching and learning promoted. With only 63% of children aged 3–6 years having access to remote learning, and fewer than a third of parents – 29%

of those reported in a survey (World Bank, 2021a) – being available to work through the televised programmes with their children, many children and families ceased to engage with the educational programme. By May 2020, schools had lost contact with 20% of children (Secretaria de Educación Publica, 2020). The accessibility of the overall programme was also hindered by limited content available in indigenous languages and concerns around the discrete subject-based transmission modes of delivery and focus on textbooks promoted by distance education, as opposed to the more interactive modes of face-to-face pedagogies (Dietz & Cortés, 2021).

The closure of schools and early childhood settings has implications for the health and wellbeing of children and families, as well as educators. Consistent use of screens to present and or follow classes on television is often accompanied by limited physical activity, and attendant risks of obesity, and other consequences for physical and mental health, such as irritability, anxiety, and lack of concentration (Idele, 2021; UNICEF, 2021b). As in other countries, changes to the nature of work for early childhood educators, including requirements to manage new health protocols, prepare and deliver materials for remote learning, and engage with families in different ways have contributed to increased professional demands (Atiles et al., 2021). Concerns have also been raised about the mental health of parents, particularly mothers, as they were expected to assume roles of both parent and teacher (Guerrero et al., 2020).

The closure of Mexican schools and the move to distance education has highlighted – and in many cases, exacerbated – a range of structural inequalities in education. These include unequal access to the internet and electronic devices (OECD, 2020b); the absence of safe spaces in homes – especially for girls who often are required to take on care responsibilities or who may experience violence and abuse (UNICEF, 2020b); food insecurity (Gaitán-Rossi et al., 2021) and poor hygiene conditions (OECD, 2020c).

While the Mexican government has announced that "well-being as well as sensitivity to diverse contexts will be a priority in its school re-opening strategy" (OECD, 2020a, p. 29), no specific strategies were identified to support the transition to school. Proposals to focus on socioemotional, as well as academic support, as schools re-open will be important. However, to date, these proposals have not considered the impact of limited opportunities for children to build relationships with their peers and educators as they experience their transition to school, nor have they addressed the nature of relationships among families, schools and communities that will be required to build and maintain trust in the safety of schools and early childhood settings.

Even before the pandemic hit, **Cuba** was experiencing a challenging economic situation – with shortages of many resources exacerbated by the US blockade. 2020 was also the year in which Cuba experienced two major hurricanes – Laura (August) and Eta (November) (UNICEF, 2020c).

As in other countries, Cuban schools closed in March 2020 and classes moved from in-person to distance modes, utilising programmes on national television and the publication of materials on social media sites. While most schools re-opened in September 2020, closures have occurred again in 2021 with growing numbers of

COVID-19 cases (UNICEF, 2021a). To replace face-to-face classes, the Ministry of Education developed a series of programmes which were televised nationally (Ministerio de Educacion de Cuba/Fondo de las Naciones Unidas para la Infancia, 2021). Teachers also utilised social media to share materials as well as telephone communication to maintain contact with children and families (Anderson & Delgado, 2021).

Despite the closure of schools, and with heightened hygienic measures, many early childhood settings remained open, catering particularly to working mothers. Attendance at early childhood settings was often substantially reduced. Some of the televised education programmes were directed towards younger children to support those engaging from home. Specifically, programmes broadcast on Thursdays were aimed at children aged 0–5 years old, and Friday programmes were geared to children aged 5–6 years (Ministerio de Educacion de Cuba/Fondo de las Naciones Unidas para la Infancia, 2021). Services such as home-based care and home food deliveries were continued, albeit to a reduced extent in some areas (UNICEF, 2020c).

Where children were not able to attend early childhood settings, considerable changes in family life were noted. Many families had to find alternative childcare arrangements and/or reorganise family life in order for family members to keep working. In both instances, there were disruptions to the routines and supports for children and families and the potential for psychological stress. Parents noted the challenges associated with caring for children at home as well as providing educationally stimulating and supportive environments. Mothers, in particular, reported feeling overloaded. Despite this, there were also positive reports of parents and children spending more time together (Morey et al., 2020). The importance of schools and early childhood settings working with families to build trust, particularly around the safety of these settings for children has been recognised (UNICEF, 2020a).

No specific plans or policies to address the impact of COVID-19 or school closures on the transition to school have been identified in Cuba. However, to mark the return to school in September 2020, UNICEF initiated a project inviting children to share photos of their first day back at school (Garcia, 2020). Children from across Cuba shared their joy at returning to preschool and school, and even those who were not yet able to return to school shared images of learning from home and expressed their anticipation at meeting teachers and friends when this was possible. While not a specific programme to support transition, this project provided an avenue for children to share their perspectives and recognised the move back to school, as well as starting school, as times of significance.

As in other countries, the impact of school closures has been noted across several areas: the digital divide has highlighted inequities in digital connectivity and infrastructure; mental health concerns have risen; children's nutrition has been impacted; disparities related to social, economic, gender and disability provisions have been exacerbated and increased violence and abuse against children noted (Anderson & Delgado, 2021; UNICEF, 2020c; World Bank, 2021a).

Overview of Responses to COVID-19

While in each of the countries, there has been a range of educational strategies implemented in response to the pandemic, the relative invisibility of young children is striking. The lack of information about young children and their families makes it difficult to assess the impact of both the pandemic and strategies aimed to cushion its impact (Osorio & Cardenas, 2021). Children, as well as their families, have experienced social isolation and disruption to their daily lives and routines. Parents and other caregivers have been expected to take on the dual roles of caring and educating, often while trying to maintain their own employment. Most often mothers – and girls – have been tasked with managing these dual roles. Educational policies have often been developed quickly, with potentially unintended consequences. Often the implementation of these polices has highlighted inequalities – especially the digital divide. The delivery of educational input online also raises issues about the pedagogies adopted, with concerns that one-way transmission pedagogies have replaced interactive, play-based pedagogies. It will be important to monitor how this might be changed as schools and early childhood settings re-open.

Much focus has been directed towards school closures and efforts to re-open them. This is clearly important, particularly when food security is tied to school operation. Much less attention has been directed towards aspects of transition as educators, children and families manage the many changes encountered and seek to promote continuity.

Considerable attention has been paid to the academic consequences of school closures. In some countries, statements about school re-openings have been complemented by reference to the importance of addressing the socioemotional needs of children as they return to school. However, there appears to be scant attention to the wellbeing of young children as they are about to commence or continue their school journey. The levels and availability of support for families and educators during the transition also are unclear.

In more 'usual' times, transitions to school provide opportunities for relationship building between and among children, families, and educators. These relationships, in turn, provide security and support for those involved, contributing positively to their overall wellbeing and transition to school (Dockett & Perry, 2014; Zulfiqar et al., 2018). Responses to COVID-19 have curtailed many of these opportunities. As we move out of the pandemic – in whatever timeframe that involves – it will be critical to consider the wellbeing of children, their families, and educators, and to build the sorts of connections that convey a positive sense of value and belonging. Planning for transitions to school can be a central plank of these efforts.

Many countries in Latin America faced challenges in the development and implementation of policies and practices to support young children and families before the pandemic (Osorio & Cardenas, 2021). This included efforts to address transition to early childhood settings and school. Despite this, major inroads had been made through substantial efforts to improve the educational experiences of young children. The contributed chapters of this book have highlighted many of these. In the following discussion, we explore some of the recurrent themes from these chapters.

Transitions to School in Cuba, Brazil, Mexico, and Chile

There is a long history of early childhood education across Latin American countries. As in many other contexts, the nature and purpose of this focus has changed over time as understandings and expectations of young children and families as well as state-based commitments to the early years have changed. As one example, in recent decades much of the focus has moved from providing care for vulnerable child populations towards the pedagogical orientation of providing quality early childhood education and care experiences (Peralta & Hernandez, 2012). Changes have been noted in both research and practice across the early childhood field, all with the common aim of promoting positive early childhood education and care for young children. News of these changes often has not filtered into the broader national and international research and practice spheres; a situation Peralta and Hernandez (2012) explain by noting that the communities involved have tended to consider the changes as 'works in progress' and because, in various contexts, early childhood education has not attracted the same media attention as later years of education.

Early childhood education in Latin America has featured in a range of international publications (Araujo et al., 2013; Vegas & Santibáñez, 2010). However, this has not consistently been the case for research and practice around educational transitions involving young children and their families. Exceptions include *The Young Lives* study, exploring childhood transitions in Peru (Ames, 2009, 2011, 2013; Ames & Rojas, 2009; Ames et al., 2010); the studies of Neves and colleagues in Brazil (see, for example, Neves et al., 2017); the examination of transitions in Chile (Jadue-Roa, 2019; Jadue-Roa & Knust, 2019; Jadue-Roa et al., 2018; Pardo & Woodrow, 2014); and recent studies in Mexico (Urbina-Garcia, 2019, 2020). These studies, as well as those reported in each of the chapters, have progressed discussion of transitions from largely statistical indicators – such as the numbers of children starting school – to the processes, practices and policies that support transitions and the perspectives of those directly involved in transitions. The chapters within this book contribute further to this discussion.

Despite different approaches to, and reports of, transition across the four countries, there are also some recurrent themes across the chapters. These are seen in the characterisations of transition as processes of change, readiness for school, and movement between educational settings; tensions between perceived tenets of early childhood education and school education; efforts to listen to the perspectives of children at times of transition; and opportunities for early childhood and school educators and systems to work collaboratively to promote optimal transitions. In discussing these themes, we also offer the caveat that in representing country perspectives as unified and singular, we run the risk of simplifying often complex situations and silencing diverse voices. As a consequence, we urge readers to use the following discussion as a prompt for reflection on their own research, policy, and practice, rather than as a definitive account of the research, policy, and practice of others.

There are many ways to conceptualise transitions (see, for example, Dockett et al., 2017a, b; Dunlop, 2018; Jindal-Snape, 2010, 2016, 2018). Those featured in chapters of this book are the framing of transition as processes of change; transition as preparing children for school; and transition as movement.

Processes of change are highlighted by Cortazar, Poblete and Ahumada (Chap. 2) and Marega and Sforni (Chap. 6). The former draw on an ecological definition of transition emphasising processes of change and the relationship contexts that surround these. Noting potential tension between an externally imposed timeframe for transition and each individual's subjective experience, the latter chapter explains that

> from the subjective point of view, or rather, from the point of view of the person who experiences change, it is not something with a duration of one day or one month, but it involves a period before and after the fact in itself. Therefore, it is necessary to speak of a transition *process*. (Sforni, 2019, p. 285)

Most definitions of transition acknowledge the importance of change (Dockett et al., 2017a). While change is an integral stimulus for transition, it is the processes around that change that "generate new ways of being, operating and interacting to meet the changed demands of the new context" (Dockett et al., 2017b, p. 9). Changes occur not only in the spaces and places inhabited by children, but also in their roles, status, and identities as they engage with new people and new expectations. Change is also experienced by those around the child – as outlined in bio-ecological system approaches to transition (Bronfenbrenner & Morris, 2006; Dunlop, 2014; Perry et al., 2014) – including parents, other family members, and educators. This perspective is in line with the Multiple and Multi-dimensional Transitions theory (Jindal-Snape, 2016, 2018) which argues that children are likely to experience multiple concurrent transitions in several domains (e.g., psychological, academic) and contexts (e.g., home, preschool) over time. Further, children's transitions are likely to trigger transitions for significant others and vice versa.

However, transition does not only involve change. In most instances, elements of continuity can be discerned. Often continuity is provided by family and community, for example through continuity of relationships and support. Continuity can also be provided by curriculum or pedagogical alignment: the essence of continuity is building on what has gone before (Dockett & Einarsdóttir, 2017). In educational contexts, much attention has been paid to the discontinuities that occur between early childhood and primary education and to strategies that aim to address these (Boyle et al., 2018; Dockett & Perry, 2014). Often, discontinuities are regarded as problematic and to be avoided. However, it is also important to consider way in which discontinuities can provoke learning or change potentially negative situations (Dockett & Einarsdóttir, 2017).

The importance of collaboration among educators as a strategy to promote continuity is highlighted by Prado and Merli (Chap. 7). Despite official polices and documentation supporting this, the comments from teachers reported in the chapter indicate that such collaboration often does not happen. At the same time, they argue that professional dialogue has the potential to enhance the ways in which early childhood and school educators work together. Guglielmo, Jurdi, and Pereira (Chap. 9), in their detailed consideration of transitions within the Waldorf School system in Brazil, offer a similar position, identifying the potential of the transition space to promote opportunities for preschool and school educators to work together to promote positive educational outcomes, while also acknowledging that it is not always easy or comfortable to work in that space. Ciardella and Galain (Chap. 8) also call for greater debate about the potential continuities between the stages of early childhood and fundamental education, as a way of helping educators to plan for transitions. Further, Narea, Godoy, and Treviño (Chap. 3) ask us all to reflect on continuities and discontinuities as we ponder how to promote 'child-respectful' transitions.

Focus on children's academic and skill development feature in characterisations of transition as a process of 'getting ready for school' (Bingham & Whitebread, 2012; Pianta et al., 2007). Underpinning this is a focus on children's development and skills, particularly those required for functioning successfully in a school environment. For example, Garcia-Cabrero et al. (Chap. 4) describe a range of Mexican studies assessing the effectiveness of preschool programmes and intervention studies in helping children develop the skills they will need to succeed in school. They note clear discontinuities between preschool and school, with emphasis on play-based curricula in preschool and strong emphasis on academic development in schools.

Noting a similar difference between preschool and school in Cuba, Comans (Chap. 5) outlines a diagnostic process of assessing children's development and comparing this with the skills and knowledge they are expected to encounter in the first grade of school. While this strategy also emphasises the importance of children being ready for school, interactions between the early childhood educator and the first grade teacher, as they make this assessment, has the potential to promote collaboration and continuity.

Movement features in many definitions of transition – often referring to the physical movement made by children and families as they leave one setting and move to another (Dockett et al., 2017a). As indicated across the chapters, school settings are often quite different physically from early childhood settings; for example, classrooms and playgrounds often look, sound, feel, and even smell different. The pandemic changed these settings further as many learning experiences and interactions moved to virtual and/or socially distant spaces. As well, some spaces changed their functions – for example, as school and home spaces converged.

Each of the chapters describes vertical transitions – those that are expected to occur only once as children progress through the educational system (Pietarinen et al., 2010). For example, Cortazar et al. (Chap. 2) describe three transitions in Chile: as children move from home to nursery; from preschool to transition in early childhood education; and from the transition levels of primary school. These transitions are aligned with age, with children aged up to 3 years attending nursery, those aged 4–5 years attending transition, and children aged 6 years enrolled in primary school. Similar transitions are outlined by Comans (Chap. 5) as children in Cuba move from the individual and later group modes of home learning programmes within the family space, to kindergarten, preschool and then to the first grade of primary school.

Transitions aligned with age can be described as key life points that generate changes in the roles, status, and identities of individuals (Elder, 1998). As they are expected to occur only once, they can also constitute a rite of passage (van Gennep, 1960). For example, the first day of school is expected to occur only once. However, in the context of COVID-19, many children in each of the countries will have experienced their first days of school, followed by a period of school closure, a return to school – and another first day – perhaps another time of school closure and then another first day back at school. van Gennep's (1960) description of transition identifies it as a process involving three phases: the preliminal phase – where the individual separates from one status; the liminal phase – where the individual is between states; and the post-liminal phase – where the individual's new status is incorporated. Utilising this framework, it is quite possible that children making the vertical transition to school during COVID-19 experience a prolonged second phase of *betwixt and between* – not really sure if they are a school child and what that might mean for them. However, COVID-19 may also have provided opportunities for children to occupy liminal spaces proactively and take their time to adapt (Gordon et al., 2020).

Complementing vertical transitions are horizontal transitions – those made regularly between different settings, such as the daily movements made between home and school (Johansson, 2007; Vogler et al., 2008). These transitions connect different spheres of life. They are not linked to age in the same way as vertical transitions, as individuals make these movements on a regular basis. In the same way that vertical transitions have been impacted by the pandemic, children's movements between home and other spheres of life, such as school, will have been restricted. Around the world, disruptions to these horizontal transitions have been associated with increased levels of abuse and neglect, as well as reduced access to support (Thomas et al., 2020; UNICEF, 2021a; Usher et al., 2020) and food insecurity (Gaitán-Rossi et al., 2021). In addition, the regular monitoring and support usually provided by teachers has been removed during school closures. Alongside these negative changes, are also reports of the potentially positive impact of families spending time together and the use of technology to maintain contact with extended family and friends (Morey et al., 2020).

In each of the four countries, governments have instituted policies aimed at promoting early childhood education. This has been accompanied by increased government expenditure (Arrabal, 2019). In Cuba, Mexico, Brazil and Chile, early childhood education has been designated as the first level of the national education system. Despite preschool education being compulsory across Mexico, Brazil and Chile, and the expansion of provision, there remain high levels of variability in access and attendance (Arrabal, 2019). Cuba reports 99.5% of children under six as participating in early learning programs delivered either in settings or in homes (UNICEF, 2016).

The transitions to school discussed across the chapters are linked to age. The age at which children start school is defined with each country's legal framework. For example, the Brazilian constitution (Brasil, 1988) recognised early childhood education as a right for all. From 2005, legal changes lowered the age of compulsory school attendance from 7 to 6 years. As a consequence, elementary education was expanded from 8 to 9 years, and the period of early childhood education was reduced by 1 year. Opening up school education to young children can be considered a move to support equity, promoting access for all children to the education that has the potential to have a positive impact on their educational and life outcomes.

Promoting equity is one of three often cited reasons for supporting early childhood education worldwide. The other two reasons relate to economic benefits, with investment in early childhood education positioned as providing a positive return; and the impetus provided for increased female employment when early childhood services are available (Pardo & Woodrow, 2014). However, Marega and Sforni (Chap. 6) remind us that is not only access to education that is important, but also the nature of the education that is provided. Indeed, Pardo and Woodrow (2014) argue that the three reasons noted above are at odds with one of the core tenets of early childhood education – the intrinsic value in such education for children right now ('being'), rather than only as a future investment or as a contributor to the 'adult in the making' ('becoming').

The debate about notions of 'being' and 'becoming' is a worldwide phenomenon, with perceptions of children as social actors actively constructing and living their own childhoods opposed to views of children in terms of what they might become (Huang, 2019; Qvortrup, 2004; Uprichard, 2008). The conceptualisation of childhood influences not only how children are perceived but also the ways in which education is structured and delivered. Typically, the notion of childhood as a time of 'being' recognises children as integral members of society right now, actively constructing understandings and ways of being. The educational focus that follows from this view promotes social interactions, exploration, and child-initiated play. In contrast, the view of children as 'becomings' positions childhood as a time of preparation for adulthood and, through this, citizenship. In an educational sense, regarding children as 'becomings' emphasises the role of adults as holders of knowledge to be shared with children. While both positions are extremes and there is much to be gained from regarding children as both 'being' and 'becoming' (Uprichard, 2008), the conceptual framework surrounding children and childhood influences the provision and purpose of early childhood education. In this context, Ciardella and Galian (Chap. 8) urge us all to consider childhood as an important phase of life and not to focus only on children's 'lack of finishing'.

We see this in trends towards the schoolification – or schoolarisation – of early childhood education as part of moves to improve the educational outcomes at the primary and secondary levels (Arrabal, 2019). Schoolification (Moss, 2013) or schoolarisation (Ackesjö & Persson, 2019) positions early childhood education as a space for making children ready for school largely through the adoption of the content and methods of the primary school while, at the same time, being distanced from the wholistic, child-centred, play-based focus of early childhood education (OECD, 2006).

For example, preschool programmes in Brazil and transition programs in Chile for children aged 4–5 years are offered in the public school system. While there are policy guidelines about the inclusion of younger children into the public school system, several of the chapters in this book suggest that there is often considerable slippage between what is written in official documents and what happens in practice (see also Campos, 2018; Pardo & Opazo, 2019). For example, Marega and Sforni (Chap. 6) note concerns that locating young children in primary schools exposes them to formal and routine teaching situations, rather than the play-based expectations of early childhood education. Prado and Merli (Chap. 7) indicate that the introduction of the younger age group into school settings was not accompanied by additional professional learning opportunities for elementary teachers and as a consequence, the curriculum and pedagogy of elementary school filtered down to the preschool years. Narea et al. (Chap. 3) conclude that, despite resistance from early childhood educators and exhortations in government policy, there is a clear trend towards schoolification in Chile. Their proposed alternative perspective – that schools should be ready for children – draws on the framework outlined by Moss (2008, 2013) and advocates for the incorporation of elements of early childhood education within school settings. Several of the studies reported by Garcia-Cabrero et al. (Chap. 4) and Comans (Chap. 5) also note the emphasis on ensuring that children are prepared to enter primary school, rather than schools being prepared for children.

One of the consequences of schoolification is a narrowing of the curriculum to focus on literacy and numeracy, often at the expense of play and developmentally based curriculum. Gugliemo, Jurdi and Pereira (Chap. 9) confront this in their contrast of age-based and developmentally-based decisions about children's preparedness for school. Marega and Sforni (Chap. 6) take this a step further in their argument that playing and studying are not necessarily separate processes, noting that both are central elements of young children's learning. Comans (Chap. 5) also links play and study activity, noting that play can provide a vehicle for preparing children for study. However, this conceptualisation does not necessarily match the experiences and expectations of children. Ciardella and Galian's (Chap. 8) interviews with children indicated that children in school settings (years 1 and 5) dismissed play as the actions of babies. Instead, they identified their learning as dependent on their teachers.

Listening to the perspectives of those experiencing the transition to school has the potential to inform our understandings as well as policy and practice. This approach is applicable for educators and families, and also for children (Dockett et al., 2019). When we make efforts to listen to children, we often find that their expectations are different from those of adults. The comments from children reported by Ciardella and Galian (Chap. 8) provide an example of this. In particular, they highlight adult efforts to make transitions as smooth as possible, and children's association of transition with 'growing up' and changing, with such changes evidenced by changed environments, expectations and experiences (Dockett & Einarsdóttir, 2017). Much can be learned from recognising children as active in constructing their own transitions and managing change (Jadue-Roa, 2019; Lago, 2019).

Finally, as we consider the similarities and differences across countries as they promote optimal transition to school for all, we cannot ignore the influence of global agendas and international comparisons. For example, three of the countries represented in the book are either member nations of the OECD (Chile, Mexico) or are potential membership nations (Brazil). Further, large international organisations such as UNICEF, UNESCO, the World Bank, WHO, and OMEP are active across all four countries. The sharing of information, approaches, and reports about early childhood education in general, and transitions in particular, feeds into international comparisons and debates about issues such as provision, policy, practice, access, and outcomes (OECD, 2017). While the international focus has the potential to celebrate diversity, prompt greater investment in early childhood education and promote international collaboration, it can also generate greater scrutiny and promote a narrowing of perspectives about what constitutes effective approaches (Campbell-Barr & Bogatić, 2017).

Looking to the Future

As indicated in each of the chapters, there is the potential for much ongoing transitions research. The nature, focus and context of this research will vary. Nevertheless, considering the research reported in the chapters and the potential impact of COVID-19, there seem to be several common avenues for future investigation. While these foci may be similar across many parts of the world, the importance of context cannot be overlooked. We therefore anticipate that transitions research from Latin American countries will contribute to ongoing international conversations and influence national policies, projects, and practice.

It is unclear what the wellbeing, health, and education impacts of COVID-19 will be in both the short and long term. It is reasonable to expect that economic impacts will be felt for decades to come. The chapters in this book have reiterated the importance of young children's experiences of childhood, particularly their right to play. Yet across 2020–2021, the nature of childhood and children's experiences have changed dramatically for many. In addition to facing challenges, many children, families, and educators have demonstrated considerable strength and resilience. How we recognise the efforts made to address challenges and build on these strengths could determine future research and policy agendas for educational transitions. For example:

- Has the value we place on educators, including early childhood educators, been enhanced during the pandemic? If so, is this reflected in the status and professionalism of the workforce, as well as wages and conditions?

- How do we acknowledge the work of early childhood educators as they have rapidly adapted pedagogies and practices to respond to children and families? What are the long-term impacts of these changes?
- What are effective strategies to promote collaboration among early childhood and school educators as they support children making the transition to, or transition back to, school? How can these strategies contribute to efforts to make schools ready for children, as well as children ready for school?
- The pandemic has highlighted the importance of teacher-child relationships and challenges – particularly during educational transitions – where these have not been established or maintained. What research, policy, and/or practices are devoted to building or re-building the relationships necessary to support children's positive engagement, or re-engagement, with school?
- Parents and other family members have been recognised as critical contributors to their children's education. As we move out of the pandemic, how does this recognition of the importance of family perspectives contribute to a new vision of education in general and transition to school in particular?
- How can we use the disruption caused by the pandemic to reconsider the nature and purpose of education, particularly early childhood and early school education? The past 18 months has demonstrated that teaching and learning is not confined to classrooms or face-to-face interactions. What can we learn from adaptations to the pandemic about what we most value about early childhood education and how we can change the ways schools and early childhood settings function to reflect what we value?
- How can we ensure that children's wellbeing – as well as the wellbeing of families, educators, and communities – is at the centre of efforts to connect and re-connect children with education?
- What do commitments to greater equity and access for all children and families look like in early childhood? How can the focus on transition to school contribute to these commitments?
- The pandemic has highlighted – and sometimes exacerbated – disparities in education such as the digital divide. How can a focus on early childhood education contribute to the amelioration of these disparities?
- During the pandemic, children have demonstrated strengths and resilience. Their generation will also be required to manage many of the longer-term impacts of the pandemic. Yet their voices are rarely heard in educational conversations or in exploration of research, policy, and practice. How do we engage respectfully and authentically with children about educational issues, such as transitions? How can we promote children's engagement in educational decision-making?

Many of these directions are reflected in the World Bank's (2021c) call for nations to seize the opportunity to reimagine education so that it is:

- Equitable – where schools and homes have the conditions and support for learning;
- Effective – where teachers and schools are equipped to support each student at the level she/he needs; and

- Resilient – with education services that are well-managed, safe and free of violence and ensure continuity in the learning process between the school, home and community.

We support such moves and believe that a focus on transitions research has much to contribute. Rather than seeking a return to the situation before the pandemic, we see opportunities for positive change. This is important, as in the words of UNICEF Executive Director, Henrietta Fore, "children will never accept a return to 'normal' after the pandemic because 'normal' was never good enough" (UNICEF, 2020d, p. 2).

Conclusion

Across each of the chapters and reflecting the context in the four countries, tensions are noted as national policies highlight the importance and value of early childhood education and care, while at the same time positioning it as the first phase of compulsory education. Increasingly, policy makers and researchers are looking to transitions research to inform practice and policy directions. In countries where this has not yet occurred, international policy forums have already flagged the need to advance the quality and access of early childhood education as an equity issue (OECD, 2018). We note the global pressures that connect early childhood education with both social and academic futures and the many challenges faced as the world grapples with the COVID-19 pandemic. However, we are also heartened by the efforts of researchers to understand educational transitions and to explore ways in which they might work together to promote optimal experiences for all.

Several reasons have underpinned our efforts to share the perspectives of transition across the four countries represented in this book. First and foremost has been to access and share valuable research that is often not accessible to the English-speaking world. We do this not as a means to make judgements or comparisons, but rather as a prompt for reflection on our own practices and to contribute to national and international conversations about research, policy, and practice around educational transitions for young children and their families. The reports from each country are not presented as models to be replicated: rather as prompts to reflect upon what we each take for granted and to problematise our own expectations. As a learning community, we have much to learn from listening to others. Building networks where diverse experiences are valued and respected, as well as analysed, can help provide a platform that supports educators and researchers as they continue their work and branch out in new and challenging directions. Our aim in editing this book has been to do just that.

References

Ackesjö, H., & Persson, S. (2019). The schoolarization of the preschool class – Policy discourses and educational restructuring in Sweden. *Nordic Journal of Studies in Educational Policy, 5*(2), 127–136. https://doi.org/10.1080/20020317.2019.1642082

Ames, P. (2009, December). Quality and equity in learnings: Start at the beginning? *Tarea, 17*, 20. http://tarea.org.pe/images/TAREA_73_ingles_17Patricia_Ames.pdf. Accessed 10 July 2021.

Ames, P. (2011). Language, culture and identity in the transition to primary school: Challenges to indigenous children's rights to education in Peru. *International Journal of Educational Development, 32*(3), 454–462. https://doi.org/10.1016/j.ijedudev.2011.11.006

Ames, P. (2013). Learning to be responsible: Young children's transitions outside school. *Learning, Culture and Social Interaction, 2*(3), 143–154. https://doi.org/10.1016/j.lcsi.2013.04.002

Ames, P., & Rojas, V. (2009). *Childhood, transitions and well-being in Peru: A literature review* (Young Lives Technical Note No. 16). http://repositorio.iep.org.pe/bitstream/handle/IEP/737/otrostitulos_amespatricia.pdf?sequence=2&isAllowed=y. Accessed 10 July 2021.

Ames, P., Rojas, V., & Portugal, T. (2010). *Continuity and respect for diversity: Strengthening early transitions in Peru*. Bernard van Leer Foundation. https://issuu.com/bernardvanleerfoundation/docs/continuity_and_respect_for_diversity_strengthening. Accessed 11 July 2021.

Anderson, B., & Delgado, A. (2021). *Report no. 33 on COVID-19: Education through televised classes in Cuba and community efforts in Puerto Rico*. https://fcilsis.wordpress.com/2021/02/03/report-no-33-on-covid-19-education-through-televised-classes-in-cuba-and-community-efforts-in-puerto-rico/. Accessed 6 July 2021.

Araujo, M. C., López Bóo, F., & Puyana, J. M. (2013). *Overview of early childhood development services in Latin American and the Caribbean*. Inter-American Development Bank. https://publications.iadb.org/publications/english/document/Overview-of-Early-Childhood-Development-Services-in-Latin-America-and-the-Caribbean.pdf. Accessed 12 July 2021.

Arrabal, A. A. (2019). Compulsory preschool in Latin America: Comparative evolution and future challenges. In D. Farland-Smith (Ed.), *Early childhood education*. Intechopen. https://doi.org/10.5772/intechopen.81779

Atiles, J. T., Almodóvar, M., Vargas, A. C., Dias, M. J. A., & Zúñiga León, I. M. (2021). International responses to COVID-19: Challenges faced by early childhood professionals. *European Early Childhood Education Research Journal, 29*(1), 66–78. https://doi.org/10.1080/1350293X.2021.1872674

Berger, R. (2021). Our kids are not broken. *The Atlantic*. https://www.theatlantic.com/ideas/archive/2021/03/how-to-get-our-kids-back-on-track/618269/. Accessed 15 July 2021.

Bingham, S., & Whitebread, D. (2012). *School readiness. A critical review of perspectives and evidence*. TACTYC. https://www.eymatters.co.uk/wp-content/uploads/2020/08/Bingham-and-Whitebread-2012.pdf. Accessed 3 July 2021.

Boyle, T., Petriwskyj, A., & Grieshaber, S. (2018). Reframing transitions to school as continuity practices: The role of practice architectures. *Australian Educational Researcher, 45*, 419–434. https://doi.org/10.1007/s13384-018-0272-0

Brasil. (1988). *Constituição da República Federativa do Brasil* [Constitution of the Federal Republic of Brazil]. Senado Federal.

Broadway, B., Méndez, S., & Moschion, J. (2020). *Behind closed doors: The surge in mental distress of parents*. Melbourne Institute. https://melbourneinstitute.unimelb.edu.au/__data/assets/pdf_file/0011/3456866/ri2020n21.pdf. Accessed 12 July 2021.

Bronfenbrenner, U., & Morris, P. (2006). The bioecological model of human development. In W. Damon & R. M. Lerner (Eds.), *Handbook of child psychology Vol. 1: Theoretical models of human development* (6th ed., pp. 793–828). Wiley.

Campbell-Barr, V., & Bogatić, K. (2017). Global to local perspectives of early childhood education and care. *Early Child Development and Care, 187*(10), 1461–1470. https://doi.org/10.1080/03004430.2017.1342436

Campos, M. M. (2018). Curriculum and assessment in Brazilian early childhood education. In M. Fleer & B. van Oers (Eds.), *International handbook of early childhood education* (pp. 1147–1171). Springer.

Campos, M. M., & Vieira, L. F. (2021). COVID-19 and early childhood in Brazil: Impacts on children's well-being, education and care. *European Early Childhood Education Research Journal, 29*(1), 125–140. https://doi.org/10.1080/1350293X.2021.1872671

CEDEP. (2020). *Consulta Nacional sobre la situación de la Primera Infancia por Crisis COVID-19* [National consultation on the situation of early childhood due to COVID-19 crisis]. https://redprimerainfancia.cl/home. Accessed 10 July 2021.

Centro UC. (2021). *Efectos de la pandemia en el aprendizaje de niños y niñas pre-escolares* [Effects of the pandemic on the learning of pre-school children]. www.encuestas.uc.cl. Accessed 21 July 2021.

Chen, L.-K., Dorn, E., Sarakatsannis, J., & Wiesinger, A. (2021). *Teacher survey: Learning loss is global – And significant*. McKinsey & Company. https://www.mckinsey.com/industries/public-and-social-sector/our-insights/teacher-survey-learning-loss-is-global-and-significant#. Accessed 20 July 2021.

Cowie, H., & Myers, C.-A. (2020). The impact of the COVID-19 pandemic on the mental health and well-being of children and young people. *Children & Society, 35*(1), 62–74. https://doi.org/10.1111/chso.12430

Dietz, G., & Cortés, L. S. M. (2021). Mexican intercultural education in times of COVID-19 pandemic. *Intercultural Education, 32*(1), 100–107. https://doi.org/10.1080/14675986.2020.1843895

Dockett, S., & Einarsdóttir, J. (2017). Continuity and change as children start school – The current state of play. In N. Ballam, B. Perry, & A. Garpelin (Eds.), *Pedagogies of educational research. European and antipodean research* (pp. 133–150). Springer.

Dockett, S., & Perry, B. (2014). *Continuity of learning: A resource to support effective transition to school and school age care*. Australian Government Department of Education. https://docs.education.gov.au/system/files/doc/other/pdf_with_bookmarking_-_continuity_of_learning_-_30_october_2014_1_0.pdf. Accessed 21 July 2021.

Dockett, S., Griebel, W., & Perry, B. (Eds.). (2017a). *Families and the transition to school*. Springer.

Dockett, S., Griebel, W., & Perry, B. (2017b). Transition to school: A family affair. In S. Dockett, W. Griebel, & B. Perry (Eds.), *Families and the transition to school* (pp. 1–18). Springer.

Dockett, S., Einarsdóttir, J., & Perry, B. (Eds.). (2019). *Listening to children's advice about starting school and school age care*. Routledge.

Dunlop, A.-W. (2014). Thinking about transitions: One framework or many? Populating the theoretical model over time. In B. Perry, S. Dockett, & A. Petriwskyj (Eds.), *Transitions to school – International research, policy and practice* (pp. 31–46). Springer.

Dunlop, A.-W. (2018). Transitions in early childhood education. *Oxford Bibliographies*. https://doi.org/10.1093/OBO/9780199756810-0204

Eadie, P., Levickis, P., Murray, L., Page, J., Elek, C., & Church, A. (2021). Early childhood educators' wellbeing during the COVID-19 pandemic. *Early Childhood Education Journal*. https://doi.org/10.1007/s10643-021-01203-3

Economic Commission for Latin America and the Caribbean (ECLAC)/United Nations Educational, Scientific and Cultural Organisation (UNESCO). (2020). *Education in the time of COVID-19*. https://www.cepal.org/en/publications/45905-education-time-covid-19. Accessed 18 July 2021.

Elder, G. H., Jr. (1998). The life course as developmental theory. *Child Development, 69*, 1–12.

Elige Educar. (2020). *Situación de docentes y educadores en contexto de pandemia* [Situation of teachers and educators in the context of a pandemic] https://eligeeducar.cl/content/uploads/2020/07/Resultados_EncuestaEEcovid_SitioWeb_mi.pdf. Accessed 22 July 2021.

Engzell, P., Frey, A., & Verhagen, M. (2021). Learning loss due to school closures during the COVID-19 pandemic. *Proceedings of the National Academy of Science of the United States of America, 118*(17). https://doi.org/10.1073/pnas.2022376118

Gaitán-Rossi, P., Vilar-Compte, M., Teruel, G., & Pérez-Escamilla, R. (2021). Food insecurity measurement and prevalence estimates during the COVID-19 pandemic in a repeated cross-sectional survey in Mexico. *Public Health Nutrition, 24*(3), 412–421. https://doi.org/10.1017/S1368980020004000

Garcia, M. (2020). *A return to dreams and learning.* https://www.unicef.org/lac/en/stories/return-dreams-and-learning. Accessed 19 July 2021.

Gestrado. (2020). *Trabalho docent em tempos de pandemia. Relatório técnico* [Teachers work in times of pandemic. Technical report]. https://anped.org.br/sites/default/files/images/cnte_relatorio_da_pesquisa_covid_gestrado_v02.pdf. Accessed 20 July 2021.

Gordon, L., Rees, C., & Jindal-Snape, D. (2020). Doctors' identity transitions: Choosing to occupy a state of 'betwixt and between'. *Medical Education, 54*(11), 1006–1018. https://doi.org/10.1111/medu.14219

Gore, J., Fray, L., Miller, D., Harris, J., & Taggart, W. (2020). *Evaluating the impact of Covid-19 on NSW schools.* University of Newcastle. https://www.newcastle.edu.au/data/assets/pdf_file/0008/704924/Evaluating-the-impact-of-COVID-19-on-NSW-schools.pdf. Accessed 20 July 2021.

Government of Mexico. (2020). *Aprende en Casa.* https://aprendeencasa.sep.gob.mx/. Accessed 20 July 2021.

Guerrero, M., Saez, D., & Rivoir, V. (2020). *Evaluating the impact of the pandemic on early childhood development in Latin America and the Caribbean.* https://www.thedialogue.org/analysis/evaluating-the-impact-of-the-pandemic-on-early-childhood-development-in-lac/. Accessed 3 July 2021.

Hoffman, J., & Miller, E. (2020). Addressing the consequences of school closure due to COVID-19 on children's physical and mental well-being. *World Medical and Health Policy, 12*(3), 300–310. https://doi.org/10.1002/wmh3.365

Huang, J. (2019). Being and becoming: The implications of different conceptualizations of children and childhood in education. *Canadian Journal for New Scholars in Education, 10*(1), 99–105. https://journalhosting.ucalgary.ca/index.php/cjnse/article/view/61733. Accessed 26 July 2021.

Human Rights Watch. (2021). *Brazil: Failure to respond to education emergency.* https://www.hrw.org/news/2021/06/11/brazil-failure-respond-education-emergency. Accessed 15 July 2021.

Idele, P. (2021). Children and youth mental health under COVID-19. *Children and COVID-19 Research Library Quarterly Digest, 1*, 1–2. https://www.unicef-irc.org/files/documents/d-4181-Children-and-COVID-19-Research-Library-Digest-Issue-1-July-2021.pdf. Accessed 20 July 2021.

Instituto Rui Barbosa. (2020). *A educação não pode esperar. Ações para minimizar os impactos negativos à educação em razão do enfrentamento ao novo coronavirus* [Education cannot wait. Actions to minimize the negative impacts on education due to the fight against the new coronavirus. https://www.portaliede.com.br/wp-content/uploads/2020/06/Estudo_A_Educa%C3%A7%C3%A3o_N%C3%A3o_Pode_Esperar.pdf. Accessed 20 July 2021.

Jadue Roa, D. S., Whitebread, D., & Guzmán, B. G. (2018). Methodological issues in representing children's perspectives in transition research. *European Early Childhood Education Research Journal, 26*(5), 760–779. https://doi.org/10.1080/1350293X.2018.1522764

Jadue-Roa, D. (2019). Children's agency in transition experiences: Understanding possibilities and challenges. In J. Murray, B. Swadener, & K. Smith (Eds.), *The Routledge international handbook of young children's rights* (pp. 535–551). Routledge.

Jadue-Roa, D., & Knust, M. (2019). Young children's right to play during their transition from early childhood education to primary school in Chile. In S. Dockett, J. Einarsdóttir, & B. Perry (Eds.), *Listening to children's advice about starting school and school age care* (pp. 26–41). Routledge.

Jindal-Snape, D. (Ed.). (2010). *Educational transitions: Moving stories from around the world.* Routledge.

Jindal-Snape, D. (2016). *A–Z of transitions.* Palgrave Macmillan.

Jindal-Snape, D. (2018). Transitions from early years to primary and primary to secondary schools in Scotland. In T. Bryce, W. Humes, D. Gillies, & A. Kennedy (Eds.), *Scottish education* (5th ed., pp. 281–291). Edinburgh University Press.

Johansson, I. (2007). Horizontal transitions: What can it mean for children in the early years? In A.-W. Dunlop & H. Fabian (Eds.), *Informing transitions in the early years. Research, policy and practice* (pp. 33–44). The Open University Press.

Johns Hopkins University. (2021). *Mortality rates*. https://coronavirus.jhu.edu/data/mortality. Accessed 20 July 2021.

Lago, L. (2019). Different transitions: Children's different experiences of the transition to school. In S. Dockett, J. Einarsdóttir, & B. Perry (Eds.), *Listening to children's advice about starting school and school age care* (pp. 55–68). Routledge.

Lourenço, A. E. P., Sperandio, N., Pontes, P. V., & Monteiro, L. S. (2021). School feeding and food and nutrition security in the context of the Covid-19 pandemic in the northern region of the state of Rio de Janeiro, Brazil. *Food Ethics, 6*(11). https://doi.org/10.1007/s41055-021-00092-x

Ministerio de Educacion de Cuba/Fondo de las Naciones Unidas para la Infancia. (2021). Education in time of COVID-19. *The Cuban Experience.* https://www.unicef.org/lac/media/21176/file. Accessed 2 July 2021.

Ministry of Education. (2020). *Mineduc support during the Covid-19 pandemic*. https://www.mineduc.cl/apoyos-del-mineduc-durante-la-pandemia-del-covid-19/. Accessed 20 July 2021.

Miranda, L. C. (2020). The Covid-19 pandemic and childhood in Latin America and the Caribbean. In *Bernard van Leer Foundation, Early childhood matters* (pp. 10–13). Author. https://early-childhoodmatters.online/2020/the-covid-19-pandemic-and-childhood-in-latin-america-and-the-caribbean/?ecm2020. Accessed 12 July 2021.

Mochida, S., Sanada, M., Shao, Q., Lee, J., Takaoka, J., Ando, S., & Sakakihara, Y. (2021). Factors modifying children's stress during the COVID-19 pandemic in Japan. *European Early Childhood Education Research Journal, 29*(1), 51–65. https://doi.org/10.1080/1350293X.2021.1872669

Morey, A. G., Cabrera, R. C., Cruz, J. A., & Quintana, D. P. (2020). *Physical distancing caused by COVID-19: Psychological effects on Cuban children and adolescents*. UNICEF. https://www.unicef.org/cuba/media/2241/file/COVID19_III%20Psychological%20effects_EN.pdf.pdf. Accessed 21 July 2021.

Moss, P. (2008). What future for the relationship between early childhood education and care and compulsory schooling? *Research in Comparative and International Education, 3*(3), 224–234. https://doi.org/10.2304/rcie.2008.3.3.224

Moss, P. (Ed.). (2013). *Early childhood and compulsory education: Reconceptualising the relationship*. Routledge.

Neves, V. F. A., Munford, D., Coutinho, F. A., & Souto, K. C. N. (2017). Childhood and schooling: Entrance of children in elementary school. *Educação & Realidade, 42*(1), 345–369. https://doi.org/10.1590/2175-623655336

Nova Escola. (2021). *Educação em Rede*. https://novaescola.org.br/subhome/173/educacao-em-rede. Accessed 20 July 2021.

Núcleo Ciência pela Infância (NCPI). (2020). *Impacts of the COVID-19 pandemic on early childhood development, São Paulo*. Working Paper, Special Edition. https://bit.ly/wp-covid-eng. Accessed 19 July 2021.

OMEP Executive Committee, World Organisation for Early Childhood Education. (2020). OMEP position paper: Early childhood education and care in the time of COVID-19. *International Journal of Early Childhood, 52*, 119–128. https://doi.org/10.1007/s13158-020-00273-5

Organisation for Economic Co-Operation and Development (OECD). (2006). *Starting strong II. Early childhood education and care*. https://www.rch.org.au/ccch/media/CPH_D4_L2_Starting_Strong_II_ECEC_OECD_Report.pdf. Accessed 1 July 2021.

Organisation for Economic Co-Operation and Development (OECD). (2017). *Starting strong V. Transitions from early childhood education and care to primary education*. OECD. https://www.oecd.org/publications/starting-strong-v-9789264276253-en.htm. Accessed 20 July 2021.

Organisation for Economic Co-Operation and Development (OECD). (2018). *Education policy outlook: Mexico*. https://www.oecd.org/education/Education-Policy-Outlook-Country-Profile-Mexico-2018.pdf. Accessed 20 July 2021.

Organisation for Economic Co-Operation and Development (OECD). (2020a). *The impact of COVID-19 on student equity and inclusion: Supporting vulnerable students during school closures and school re-openings*. https://read.oecd-ilibrary.org/view/?ref=434_434914-59wd7ekj29&title=The-impact-of-COVID-19-on-student-equity-and-inclusion. Accessed 21 July 2021.

Organisation for Economic Co-Operation and Development (OECD). (2020b). School education during Covid-19: Were teachers and students ready? *Country Note*, Mexico. https://www.oecd.org/education/Mexico-coronavirus-education-country-note.pdf. Accessed 21 July 2021.

Organisation for Economic Co-Operation and Development (OECD). (2020c). *COVID-19: Protecting people and societies*. https://www.oecd.org/coronavirus/policy-responses/covid-19-protecting-people-and-societies-e5c9de1a/. Accessed 20 July 2021.

Organisation for Economic Co-Operation and Development (OECD). (2021). *Education policy outlook: Brazil*. https://www.oecd-ilibrary.org/education/education-policy-outlook-in-brazil_e97e4f72-en. Accessed 20 July 2021.

Osorio, A. M., & Cardenas, E. (2021). *Public policy responses and challenges to ensuring early childhood well-being in times of Covid-19: A comparative analysis for Latin America*. https://unesdoc.unesco.org/ark:/48223/pf0000376927. Accessed 22 July 2021.

Pardo, M., & Opazo, M.-J. (2019). Resistiendo la escolarización desde el aula. Explorando la identidad profesional de las docentes de primera infancia en Chile [Resisting schoolification from the classroom. Exploring the professional identity of early childhood teachers in Chile]. *Culture and Education, 31*(1), 67–92. https://doi.org/10.1080/11356405.2018.1559490

Pardo, M., & Woodrow, C. (2014). Improving the quality of early childhood education in Chile: Tensions between public policy and teacher discourses over the schoolarisation of early childhood education. *International Journal of Early Childhood, 46*, 101–115. https://doi.org/10.1007/s13158-014-0102-0

Park, E., Logan, H., Zhang, L., Kamigaichi, N., & Kulapichitr, U. (2020). Responses to coronavirus pandemic in early childhood services across five countries in the Asia-Pacific region: OMEP Policy Forum. *International Journal of Early Childhood, 52*, 249–266. https://doi.org/10.1007/s13158-020-00278-0

Pascal, C., & Bertram, T. (2021). What do young children have to say? Recognising their voices, wisdom, agency and need for companionship during the COVID pandemic. *European Early Childhood Education Research Journal, 29*(1), 21–34. https://doi.org/10.1080/1350293X.2021.1872676

Peralta, V., & Hernandez, L. (2012). Introducción [Introduction]. In V. Peralta & L. Hernandez (Eds.), *Metas educativas 2021. Antología de experiencias de la educación inicial iberoamericana* [Educational goals 2021. Anthropology of Ibero-American initial education experiences] (pp. 6–7). OEI/UNICEF/BBVA.

Perry, B., Dockett, S., & Petriwskyj, A. (Eds.). (2014). *Transitions to school – International research, policy and practice*. Springer.

Pianta, R., Cox, M., & Snow, K. (Eds.). (2007). *School readiness and the transition to kindergarten in the era of accountability*. Brookes.

Pietarinen, J., Soini, T., & Pyhältö, K. (2010). Learning and well-being in transitions. In D. Jindal-Snape (Ed.), *Educational transitions: Moving stories from around the world* (pp. 143–158). Routledge.

Pramling Samuelsson, I., Wagner, J. T., & Eriksen Ødegaard, E. (2020). The coronavirus pandemic and lessons learned in preschools in Norway, Sweden and the United States: OMEP Policy Forum. *International Journal of Early Childhood, 52*, 129–144. https://doi.org/10.1007/s13158-020-00267-3

Qvortrup, J. (2004). Editorial: The waiting child. *Childhood, 11*, 267–273.

Secretaria de Educación Publica. (2020). *Regreso a clases en la nueva normalidad. Cuidad de Mexico a 29 de mayo del 2020. Aprenda en Casa* [Return to classes in the new normal. Learning from Home]. https://aulas.see.gob.mx/wp-content/uploads/2020/06/regre-cla.pdf. Accessed 20 July 2021.

Sforni, M. S. de F. (2019). Transições no processo de escolarização: da educação infantil ao ensino fundamental e dos anos iniciais aos anos finais do ensino fundamental [Transition in the schooling process: From early childhood education to elementary school and from the early years to the final years of elementary school]. In Maringá, *Currículo da Educação Municipal de Maringá*. Maringá: Educação Infantil e Anos Iniciais do Ensino Fundamental.

Spiteri, J. (2021). Quality early childhood education for all and the Covid-19 crisis: A viewpoint. *Prospects*. https://doi.org/10.1007/s11125-020-09528-4

Thomas, E., Anurudran, A., Robb, K., Burke, T. F. (2020). Spotlight on child abuse and neglect response in the time of COVID-19. The Lancet, 5, e371. https://www.thelancet.com/action/showPdf?pii=S2468-2667%2820%2930143-2. Accessed 26 July 2021.

Times Educational Supplement. (2021, March 21). *Is it helpful to talk about 'lost learning'?* https://www.tes.com/magazine/article/it-helpful-talk-about-lost-learning. Accessed 29 July 2021.

Un Buen Comienzo. (2020). *Encuesta a equipos educativos de Un Buen Comienzo en el contexto de la pandemia* [Survey of educational teams from A Good Start in the context of the pandemic]. Fundacion Educacional Oportunidad. https://fundacionoportunidad.cl/documentacion/encuesta-a-equipos-educativos-de-un-buen-comienzo-en-el-contexto-de-la-pandemia/. Accessed 10 July 2021.

UNDIME Brasil. (2021). *Redes municipais de educação apontam internet e infraestrutura como maiores dificuldades enfrentadas em 2020, mostra pesquisa da Undime* [Municipal education networks point to internet and infrastructure as the greatest difficulties faced in 2020, shows UNDIME research]. https://undime.org.br/noticia/10-03-2021-13-17-redes-municipais-de-educacao-apontam-internet-e-infraestrutura-como-maiores-dificuldades-enfrentadas-em-2020-mostra-pesquisa-da-undime. Accessed 20 July 2021.

UNESCO. (2021). *National education responses to COVID-19: The situation of Latin America and the Caribbean*. https://unesdoc.unesco.org/ark:/48223/pf0000377074_eng?posInSet=1&queryId=ed793659-47f9-4a87-af13-36902b712d28. Accessed 19 July 2021.

UNICEF. (2016). *Early childhood development in Cuba*. https://www.unicef.org/cuba/media/591/file/early-childhood-development-cuba-2016.pdf. Accessed 18 July 2021.

UNICEF. (2020a). *LACRO COVID-19 education response: Update 20 COs achievements, challenges & next steps*. https://www.unicef.org/lac/en/media/20231/file. Accessed 10 July 2021.

UNICEF. (2020b). *Protecting children from violence in the time of COVID-19: Disruption in prevention and response services*. https://www.unicef.org/media/74146/file/Protecting-children-from-violence-in-the-time-of-covid-19.pdf. Accessed 18 July 2021.

UNICEF. (2020c). *Country office annual report 2020. Cuba*. https://www.unicef.org/media/100606/file/Cuba-2020-COAR.pdf. Accessed 19 July 2021.

UNICEF. (2020d). *Averting a lost COVID generation. A six-point plan to respond, recover and reimagine a post-pandemic world for every child*. https://www.unicef.org/reports/averting-lost-generation-covid19-world-childrens-day-2020-brief. Accessed 17 July 2021.

UNICEF. (2021a). *LSCRO COVID-19 education response: Update 24: Status of school's reopening*. https://www.unicef.org/lac/en/media/22416/file. Accessed 19 July 2021.

UNICEF. (2021b). *Across virtually every key measure of childhood, progress has gone backwards, UNICEF says as pandemic declaration hits one-year mark*. https://www.unicef.org/press-releases/across-virtually-every-key-measure-childhood-progress-has-gone-backward-unicef-says. Accessed 19 July 2021.

Uprichard, E. (2008). Children as 'being and becomings': Children, childhood and temporality. *Children and Society, 22*, 303–313. https://doi.org/10.1111/j.1099-0860.2007.00110.x

Urbina-Garcia, A. (2019). Preschool transition in Mexico: Exploring teachers' perceptions and practices. *Teaching and Teacher Education, 85*, 226–234. https://doi.org/10.1016/j.tate.2019.06.012

Urbina-Garcia, A. (2020). An intervention programme to facilitate the preschool transition in Mexico. *Frontiers in Education, 5*. https://doi.org/10.3389/feduc.2020.00095

Usher, K., Bhullar, N., Durkin, J., Gyamfi, N., & Jackson, D. (2020). Family violence and COVID-19: Increased vulnerability and reduced options for support. *International Journal of Mental Health Nursing*. https://doi.org/10.1111/inm.12735

van Gennep, A. (1960). *The rites of passage* (B. V. Minka & G. L. Caffee, Trans.). Routledge and Kegan Paul.

Vegas, E., & Santibáñez, L. (2010). *The promise of early childhood development in Latin America and the Caribbean*. The International Bank for Reconstruction and Development/The World Bank. https://publications.iadb.org/publications/english/document/The-Promise-of-Early-Childhood-Development-in-Latin-America-and-the-Caribbean.pdf. Accessed 19 July 2021.

Vogler, P., Crivello, G., & Woodhead, M. (2008). *Early childhood transitions research: A review of concepts, theory, and practice* (Working Paper 48). Bernard van Leer Foundation. http://oro.open.ac.uk/16989/1/. Accessed 19 July 2021

World Bank. (2021a). *Acting now to protect the human capital of our children: The costs of and response to COVID-19 pandemic's impact on the education sector in Latin America and Caribbean.* https://openknowledge.worldbank.org/handle/10986/35276?locale-attribute=en. Accessed 19 July 2021.

World Bank. (2021b). *Mission: Recovering education in 2021.* https://www.worldbank.org/en/topic/education/brief/mission-recovering-education-in-2021. Accessed 19 July 2021.

World Bank. (2021c). *Urgent, effective action required to quell the impact of COVID-19 on education worldwide.* https://www.worldbank.org/en/news/immersive-story/2021/01/22/urgent-effective-action-required-to-quell-the-impact-of-covid-19-on-education-worldwide. Accessed 19 July 2021.

World Health Organisation (WHO). (2020). *WHO Director-General's opening remarks at the media briefing on COVID-19 – 11 March 2020.* https://www.who.int/director-general/speeches/detail/who-director-general-s-opening-remarks-at-the-media-briefing-on-covid-19%2D%2D-11-march-2020. Accessed 19 July 2021.

World Health Organisation (WHO). (2021). *Cuba.* https://covid19.who.int/region/amro/country/cu. Accessed 19 July 2021.

Zulfiqar, N., LoCasale-Crouch, J., Sweeney, B., DeCoster, J., Rudasill, K. M., McGinnis, C., Acar, I., & Miller, K. (2018). Transition practices and children's development during kindergarten: The role of close teacher-child relationships. In A. Mashburn, J. LoCasale-Crouch, & K. C. Pears (Eds.), *Kindergarten transition and readiness* (pp. 265–281). Springer.

Sue Dockett is Emeritus Professor, Charles Sturt University, Australia, and Director, Peridot Education Pty Ltd. While recently retired from university life, Sue remains an active researcher in the field of early childhood education. Sue has been a long-time advocate for the importance of recognizing and responding to young children's perspectives. She maintains this position in her current work with children, families, and educators in explorations of transitions to school, children's play, and learning. Sue has published extensively both nationally and internationally in these areas. She is a co-chair of the Special Interest Group on Transitions at the European Early Childhood Education Research Association.

Bob Perry has recently retired after 45 years of university teaching and research. He is Emeritus Professor at Charles Sturt University, Australia, and Director, Peridot Education Pty Ltd. In conjunction with Sue Dockett, he continues research, consultancy, and publication in early childhood mathematics education; educational transitions, with particular emphasis on transition to primary school; research with children; and evaluation of educational programs. Bob continues to publish extensively both nationally and internationally in these areas. Currently, he is revising materials for a preschool mathematics intervention run by Australia's leading educational charity and, with Sue Dockett, has just published a book on the evaluation of educational transitions.